D1080156

Soups & Starters

ROBERT CARRIER'S KITCHEN

Soups & Starters

Marshall Cavendish   London Sydney & New York

Contents

Soups

Basic stocks   *8*

Simple stock-based soups   *12*

Knife & fork soups   *18*

Purée soups   *26*

Cream soups   *32*

Consommés   *40*

Starters

Simple starters   *48*

Finger food & dips   *56*

Seafood starters   *62*

Egg & cheese starters   *72*

Vegetable starters   *80*

Substantial starters   *90*

Savoury mousses   *98*

Pâtés & terrines   *104*

Index   *111*

Editor   Grizelda Wiles
Editorial Staff   Carey Denton
    Felicity Jackson
    Carol Steiger
Designer   Ross George
Series Editor   Pepita Aris
Production Executive   Robert Paulley
Production Controller   Steve Roberts

Photography
Bryce Attwell: 15, 23, 27, 85
Tom Belshaw: 69
Paul Bussell: 26, 34, 50, 57, 74
Alan Duns: 93
Laurie Evans: 64, 104
Robert Golden: 98
Melvin Grey: 48
James Jackson: 20, 58, 106, 108
Jhon Kevern: 36
Chris Knaggs: 19, 28, 40, 42, 65
David Levin: 90
Peter Myers: 14, 22, 33, 43, 66, 73, 83, 84, 107
Roger Phillips: 52, 53
Paul Webster: 78, 81
Paul Williams: 8, 10, 59, 100, 101
Cover picture: **Theo Bergstrom**

Weights and measures
Both metric and imperial measurements are given. As these are not exact equivalents, please work from one set of figures or the other. Use graded measuring spoons levelled across.

Time symbols
The time needed to prepare the dish is given on each recipe. The symbols are as follows:

     simple to prepare and cook

     straightforward but requires more skill or attention

     time-consuming to prepare or requires extra skill

🕐   must be started 1 day or more ahead

On the cover: Mussel soup, page 24, and Stuffed tomatoes, page 88

This edition published 1984
© Marshall Cavendish Limited 1984

Printed in Spain by
Artes Graficas Toledo, S.A.
D.L. T.O:–763–1984

Typeset by Performance Typesetting, Milton Keynes

Published by Marshall Cavendish House
58 Old Compton Street
London W1V 5PA
ISBN 0 86307 264 X (series)
ISBN 0 86307 267 4 (this volume)

All rights reserved. No part of this book may be reproduced or utilized in any form or by any means electronic or mechanical, including photocopying, recording, or by information storage and retrieval system, without permission from the copyright holders. Some of the material in this title has previously appeared in the publication **Robert Carrier's Kitchen.**

Have you ever been in that all-too-usual situation where the guests are all invited and the main course and dessert decided upon but you just can't think of the right first course to fit the occasion? Well, put your worries aside. *Soups and Starters* is packed with recipes and information to titillate your palate and your imagination.

Soups can be economical or luxurious, but either way they make a delicious start to a meal. A classic Minestrone or French onion soup, flavoured with blue cheese for a tangy difference, are both inexpensive family favourites. Or, for something a little more unusual but still easy to make, try Greek egg and lemon soup.

A cold Avocado soup or a Prawn bisque, made quickly and easily in the blender, will add an air of sophistication to your dinner table. Thickened with cream for a really rich flavour, garnished simply but effectively, either soup is a colourful and delicious introduction to a special meal. But not all creamy soups are for special occasions. Cream of tomato is probably the best known and best loved of all family soups.

Accompanied with crusty French or wholemeal bread, many of the soups in this book can be served as light lunches or family suppers, but the chapter on Knife and fork soups has tasty recipes for soups that are complete meals in themselves. Many are old favourites, such as Oxtail soup and Old-fashioned lamb broth, but how about trying Smoked haddock chowder or *Garbure*, a thick satisfying vegetable soup from the south-west of France.

The real job of a first course is to set the scene for the rest of the meal and to whet, not blunt, the appetites of your guests for what is to follow. French cooks have a real flair for presenting a selection of very simple salads, meticulously prepared and served in a well-flavoured vinaigrette or mayonnaise dressing. Try my recipe for Japanese radish and watercress salad, composed of simple ingredients which, together, make a most attractive dish. With a little flair and imagination, you will soon discover how easy it can be to create your own selection of hors d'oeuvres.

If you think the rest of your meal is going to be a bit light, compensate with a more substantial starter. Take a leaf out of the Italian's book and try opening the meal with pasta. Or try Herb and spinach crêpes which can be prepared well ahead of time. Barbecue spareribs will start the party in casual American style.

Pâtés and terrines are always popular with guests, and with the cook as well, as many of them actually benefit from being made two or three days in advance. Impress your guests with my Terrine of rabbit and walnuts – as well as tasting delicious, its layers of minced and whole meat and nuts look really impressive when the terrine is sliced.

With the knowledge and expertise you will gain from this information-packed volume you will be ready to tackle any dinner party with confidence.

Happy cooking and bon appétit!

Robert Carrier

Soups

BASIC STOCKS

Good, home-made stocks are cookery basics; without them there would be few soups or savoury sauces. Stocks are made from everyday ingredients and are surprisingly simple – and satisfying – to make.

People who are interested in cooking cannot consider themselves good cooks until they have learned to prepare basic stocks. Yet mastering the art of extracting all the goodness from meat or fish bones, scraps of meat, a few vegetables and a sprinkling of herbs is not at all difficult: after the initial preparation of ingredients (sometimes involving roasting the bones and vegetables for about 45 minutes) everything is simply put together in a pan and left to simmer, very gently, for several hours.

A large cooking pot is absolutely essential. It should have a heavy base and be about 5 L /9 pt in capacity. The size is important because you must start with a good quantity of water so that, after 3–4 hours cooking, there is still some stock left in the pot. There must be room enough in the pot to include the bones, meat and vegetables, plus enough water to cover them initially. The pot must not, however, be filled to the brim or the liquid will splash over the edges. And there must be room for manoeuvring a spoon when skimming.

Basic ingredients

It is important to remember that your stock can only be as good as the ingredients you put into it, so don't be tempted to treat it as a way of using up absolutely past-it ingredients. However, you may vary the ingredients according to what is available, using the following information as a guide.

Bones: beef, veal and poultry bones can be used for a basic meat stock, or fish bones for fish stock. The more meat there is on the bones the better the stock will be, and it is best if the bones have marrow in them.

In addition to giving flavour to the stock, bones contain a certain amount of gelatine, which gives the finished stock body, and a light set when it is cold. Raw veal bones, especially the knuckle, and calf's and chicken's feet contain the most gelatine.

A small amount of pork bone can be used, although too much will give the stock a sweet taste. Lamb and ham bones should not be used for a basic meat stock as their flavour is too strong, but they can be used on their own or with vegetables to make lamb or ham stock. Large bones should be chopped into big chunks. Ask your butcher to chop the bones for you, if you are buying them raw.

Meat: any scraps of meat add good flavour to a stock, provided they are not fatty. Add to the stock-pot with the water.

Vegetables: carrots, onions, celery and leeks are the vegetables most useful for stocks. A little parsnip may be added, but not potato as it is too starchy and will make the stock cloudy. Turnips, cauliflower and leafy vegetables are too strong in flavour, but over-ripe tomatoes make an excellent addition to a stock.

Herbs and spices are added for flavour, bay leaves, thyme and parsley being the most common additions. You can use the stripped parsley stalks and reserve the sprigs for garnishing. Peppercorns are commonly added to stocks but use very little salt; remember the volume of liquid will be considerably reduced. Salt can be added when the stock is used.

Making vegetable stock

You can make a very passable stock without bones, using vegetables as the main ingredient. Finely chop carrots, celery, leek and onion, and sauté them gently in a little butter and oil until lightly coloured. Then cover the pan tightly and sweat the vegetables over a low heat for 10–15 minutes. The flavour of the stock can be strengthened by sautéing a little diced fat salt pork or mild, unsmoked bacon in the oil before adding the vegetables. Add water – 1L /2 pt for every 500 g /1 lb vegetables, a stock cube, a bouquet garni and a squashy tomato or two, if available, then simmer gently for 1 hour before straining. Although this is not the most subtle of stocks, it makes a perfectly acceptable basis for any kind of vegetable soup.

Making meat and poultry stock

Browning: if you are making a brown stock, the bones and vegetables are first roasted for a while, so that they add a rich colour to the stock. The roasted ingredients are then put into the stock-pot. The roasting tin is deglazed by adding water to it and stirring over the heat to dislodge all the sediment and bits stuck to the sides and base, and this is added to the stock-pot too.

Simmering: for white stocks put the meat or poultry bones directly into the stock-pot with the vegetables. Pour in enough water to cover the ingredients by at least 25 mm /1 in. Bring almost to the boil, uncovered. The stock should only just barely bubble as it simmers. Never allow the liquid to boil, or the scum will be drawn into the stock and will make it cloudy.

Skimming: heat and salt draw a substance out of the meat and bones, which collects as a scum on the surface of the liquid. The easiest way to remove this is with a slotted spoon. Do not try to remove the white foam until it has collected into a definite scum, or it will drain through the slits of the spoon back into the stock.

Skim the scum at regular intervals, until the surface is absolutely clear. Add peppercorns and herbs after you have finished skimming so you don't remove them with the scum. You will find that veal bones produce the most scum, chicken the least.

Reducing: lengthy simmering is essential for good stock. The liquid should simmer so gently that it barely bubbles. Partially cover the pan of simmering stock but allow the steam to escape – covering the pan completely could turn the stock sour. During this time the flavours pass from the ingredients to the liquid, but the quantity of liquid itself is reduced by half to concentrate the flavour. Three or four hours simmering are necessary for a good meat stock.

Straining: first strain the stock through a colander to remove all the large pieces of bone, meat and vegetable. Then strain the stock through a fine sieve or a colander lined with muslin into a large bowl, or into a non-metal container if it is to be stored. Never leave the stock to stand for any length of time with the bones and vegetables still in it, or the stock will turn sour.

Degreasing: if you do not intend to use the stock immediately, the fat presents no problem: simply leave the stock to get cold and the fat will rise to the surface and congeal in a layer, which can be lifted off just before the stock is used. This layer of fat actually helps to preserve the stock by providing it with an effective seal, so it should be left unpierced if you intend to store the stock for some time.

If you are going to use the stock immediately, leave it to settle for 5 minutes, then skim off the fat with a spoon or a ladle. Remove any remaining globules of fat by

drawing small pieces of absorbent paper across the surface.

If the stock is particularly greasy and you do not have time to leave it to get cold so the fat sets on the top, use a large bulb baster, consisting of a heatproof white nylon tube and a rubber squeezing bulb. Strain some of the stock into a clear jug or bowl and leave it to settle for 5 minutes. Plunge the tube down to the bottom of the stock, draw out the clear stock and transfer it to another container. Continue in the same way until you have removed all the fatless stock. Remember to hold the tube vertical all the time to avoid any spurting out.

Making fish stock

A fish stock (*fumet* in French) will probably only need to be skimmed once to make the surface clear. It should be simmered, uncovered, for about 30 minutes.

Storing stock

Never store stock without first straining out the bones and vegetables. Left in, they will quickly cause the stock to turn sour.

Strain the stock into a non-metal container, cover it tightly, and label it. Keep the stock in the refrigerator, for no more than 4 days for meat stock, 2 or 3 days for vegetable stock and 24 hours for fish stock.

Stock can be frozen; to save space first boil the strained and degreased stock to reduce it by half, then freeze it in 150 ml / 5 fl oz measures, to be defrosted and diluted before use. Meat and poultry stocks can be frozen for 2 months, fish and vegetable stocks for 1 month.

Using stock cubes

Stock cubes are indispensable in the modern kitchen but they must be used with discrimination. They are excellent for quick sauces and as a base for soups, especially cream and puréed soups which depend on other ingredients for their main flavour. I use half a chicken stock cube to reinforce existing flavours – for example in fish stock or to add flavour to a bechamel sauce.

For clear broths, chicken stock cubes are better than beef, and their flavour can be improved by briefly simmering the dissolved cubes with a few chopped vegetables. Stocks made with cubes are unsuitable for any recipe in which they will be simmered and reduced, however, because they are heightened with monosodium glutamate and salt. These become too strong once reduced, and will overpower other flavours.

Left to right: Basic white stock, Brown beef stock and Basic chicken stock

Brown beef stock

Use fresh beef as well as bones to give this stock a rich, 'beefy' flavour.

1 hour,
then 2½–3 hours cooking

Makes 1.7 L /3pt
1 kg /2 lb veal knuckle bone, chopped into large chunks
500 g /1 lb beef knuckle bone, chopped into large chunks
3 Spanish onions
4 large carrots, roughly chopped
2 celery stalks, roughly chopped
2 leeks, thickly sliced
25–50 g /1–2 oz good beef dripping or butter
2 chicken feet, well scrubbed (optional)
1.4 kg /3 lb boned shin of beef, cut into 12 pieces
a few mushroom stalks or trimmings
3 over-ripe tomatoes
salt
3 sprigs of parsley
sprig of fresh thyme or a pinch of dried thyme
bay leaf
1 clove
9 black peppercorns

1 Heat the oven to 240C /475F /gas 9.
2 Rinse the bones and place in a large roasting tin. Roughly chop 2 onions and place them around the bones with the carrots, celery and leeks. Dot with dripping or butter. Roast for 40–45 minutes, turning occasionally, until richly browned.
3 Cut the remaining onion in half, then sear the cut sides by placing the onion halves, cut sides down, straight on a hot, ungreased frying-pan, until golden brown.
4 Place the contents of the roasting tin in a very large pot and pour over 3 L /5½ pt cold water. Add the seared onion halves, chicken feet, if using, shin of beef, mushroom stalks or trimmings and tomatoes.
5 Add 300 ml /10 fl oz cold water to the roasting tin, place it directly over the heat and bring to the boil, scraping the base and sides of the tin with a wooden spoon. Add this to the stock-pot.
6 Place the stock-pot over a low heat and bring to the boil. Reduce the heat so that the water barely bubbles. Allow the foam to settle into a scum on the surface, then skim it off with a slotted spoon. Add a sprinkling of salt to the pan to draw more scum out of the meat and bones; allow it to settle on the surface, then skim again. Continue to skim the surface from time to time until it is absolutely clear, then add the parsley, thyme, bay leaf, clove and peppercorns.
7 Partially cover the pan and simmer the stock very gently for 2½–3 hours, until it has reduced to about 1.7 L /3 pt.
8 Strain the stock through a colander, then strain it through a fine sieve into a large bowl (use a non-metal one if you intend to store the stock). Either leave the stock to get cold and remove the layer of set fat before using, or leave to cool for 5 minutes, then skim the fat from the top.

9

Light beef stock

Use this stock for subtly flavoured soups when beef stock is called for.

1 hour,
then 2½–3 hours cooking

Makes 1.7 L /3 pt
*1.5 kg /3 lb shin or neck of beef (meat and
    bone), meat removed from the bone, bone
    chopped*
*500 g /1 lb shin of veal (meat and bone),
    meat removed from bone, bone chopped*
3 Spanish onions
3 large carrots, roughly chopped
3–4 celery stalks, thickly sliced
2 leeks, thickly sliced
50 g /2 oz good beef dripping
100 g /4 oz lean ham
a few mushroom stalks or trimmings
2–3 over-ripe tomatoes
salt
3 sprigs of parsley
*sprig of fresh thyme or a pinch of dried
    thyme*
bay leaf
1 clove
9 black peppercorns

1 Heat the oven to 240C /475F /gas 9.
2 Rinse the beef and veal bones and place in a large roasting tin. Roughly chop 2 of the onions and place them around the bones with the carrots, celery and leeks. Dot with the dripping. Roast for 40–45 minutes, turning occasionally, until richly browned.
3 Cut the remaining onion in half, then sear the cut sides by placing the onion halves, cut sides down, straight on a hot, ungreased frying-pan, until golden brown.
4 Remove the excess fat from the meat.
5 Place the contents of the roasting tin in a very large pot and pour in 3 L /5¼ pt cold water. Add the seared onion halves, pieces of meat, ham, mushroom stalks or trimmings and tomatoes.
6 Add 300 ml /10 fl oz cold water to the roasting tin, place it over the heat and bring to the boil, scraping the base and sides of the tin with a wooden spoon. Add this to the stock-pot.
7 Place the stock-pot over a low heat and bring to the boil. Reduce the heat so that the water barely bubbles. Allow the foam to rise and settle into a scum on the surface, then skim it off with a slotted spoon. Add a sprinkling of salt to the pan to draw more scum out of the meat and bones; allow it to settle on the surface, then skim again. Continue to skim the surface from time to time until the stock is absolutely clear, then add the remaining ingredients.
8 Partially cover the pan and simmer the stock very gently for 2½–3 hours, until it has reduced to about 1.7 L /3 pt.
9 Strain the stock through a colander, then strain it again through a fine sieve into a large bowl (use a non-metal one if you intend to store the stock). Either leave the stock to get cold and remove the layer of set fat just before using, or leave the stock to cool for 5 minutes, then skim the fat from the top with a slotted spoon.

Basic white stock

30 minutes,
then 2½–3 hours cooking

Makes 1.7 L /3 pt
*1.5 kg /3 lb veal knuckle bone, chopped into
    large chunks*
2 chicken feet (optional)
1 chicken carcass (optional)
salt
3 large carrots, roughly chopped
3 Spanish onions, roughly chopped
3 celery stalks, roughly chopped
1 leek, thickly sliced
3 over-ripe tomatoes
3 sprigs of parsley
*sprig of fresh thyme or a pinch of dried
    thyme*
bay leaf
2 cloves
8 white peppercorns

1 Put the pieces of veal bone, chicken feet and carcass, if using, in a very large pot and pour in 3.5 L /6 pt water. Bring slowly to the boil over a very low heat.
2 Reduce the heat so that the water barely bubbles. Wait until a thick layer of scum has formed on the surface, then skim off carefully with a slotted spoon. Add a sprinkling of salt to draw more scum out of the bones, allow it to settle on the surface, then skim again. Continue to skim from time to time until the surface is absolutely clear, then add the chopped carrots, onions, celery stalks, leek, tomatoes, herbs, cloves and peppercorns.
3 Partially cover the pan and simmer the stock very gently for 2½–3 hours, until it has reduced to about 1.7 L /3 pt. Skim again if necessary.
4 Strain the stock through a colander to remove all the bones and vegetables, then strain it through a fine sieve into a large bowl (use a non-metal one if you intend to

Ingredients for stocks

store it). Either leave the stock to get cold and remove the layer of set fat just before using, or leave the stock to cool for 5 minutes and skim the fat from the top.

● White stock, which has a more delicate flavour than light or brown beef stock or bone stock, makes a perfect base for cream soups.

Basic chicken stock

Not only does this recipe provide you with a good stock, but a cooked chicken too! Chicken stock is one of the most frequently used of all stocks. Try to keep some always on hand.

3–4 hours

Makes 1.7 L /3 pt
1.8 kg /4 lb boiling fowl with its feet
salt
6 peppercorns
2 leeks, thickly sliced
2 large carrots, roughly chopped
1 Spanish onion, halved and stuck with 2 cloves
2 celery stalks, roughly chopped
bouquet garni
1 garlic clove

1 Place the boiling fowl (and the feet) in a very large pot and pour in 3.4 L /6 pt cold water. Add a sprinkling of salt and bring slowly to the boil.
2 Reduce the heat so that the water barely bubbles, then skim the surface with a slotted spoon. Add the peppercorns. Partially cover the pan and simmer gently for 1 hour, skimming again if necessary.
3 Add the leeks, carrots, onion stuck with cloves, celery, bouquet garni and garlic and simmer for 30 minutes, or until the chicken is meltingly tender.
4 Remove the chicken, chicken feet and vegetables from the stock and reserve the chicken to use in another recipe.
5 Continue to simmer the stock for 1–2 hours, until it has reduced to 1.7 L /3 pt.
6 Strain the stock through a fine sieve into a large bowl (use a non-metal one if you intend to store the stock). Leave the stock to get cold and remove the layer of set fat just before using or cool for 5 minutes, then skim the fat from the top.

Basic bone stock

Although less rich than a classic beef stock, a bone stock makes a very good base for soups and sauces, and is excellent for moistening casseroles. It is a fairly cheap stock to make as it uses no meat, and will be especially good if you manage to get some nice, meaty bones, including a marrow bone or two.

1 hour,
then 2½–3 hours cooking

Makes 1.7 L / 3 pt
1–1.5 kg /2–3 lb beef bones, chopped into large chunks
1 chicken carcass (optional)
2 Spanish onions, roughly chopped
2 celery stalks, roughly chopped
2 leeks, thickly sliced
2 carrots, roughly chopped
25–50 g /1–2 oz good beef dripping or butter
a few mushroom stalks or trimmings
2–3 over-ripe tomatoes (optional)
salt
3 sprigs of parsley
sprig of fresh thyme or a pinch of dried thyme
bay leaf
1 clove
9 black peppercorns

1 Heat the oven to 240C /475F /gas 9.
2 Rinse the bones and place them in a roasting tin with the chicken carcass, if using, and the onions, celery, leeks and carrots. Dot with the dripping or butter. Roast in the oven for 40–45 minutes, turning occasionally, until the bones and vegetables are richly browned.
3 Place the contents of the roasting tin in a very large pot and pour in 3 L /5½ pt cold water. Add the mushroom stalks and the tomatoes.
4 Add 300 ml /10 fl oz cold water to the roasting tin, place it directly over the heat and bring to the boil, scraping with a wooden spoon to dislodge any crusty bits. Add this to the stock-pot.
5 Place the stock-pot over a low heat and bring to the boil. Reduce the heat so that the water barely bubbles. Allow the foam to settle into a thick scum on the surface, then skim it off with a slotted spoon. Add a sprinkling of salt to draw more scum out of the bones; allow it to settle on the surface and skim again. Continue to skim the surface until it is absolutely clear, then add the herbs, clove and peppercorns.
6 Partially cover the pan and simmer the stock very gently for 2½–3 hours, until it has reduced to about 1.7 L /3 pt.
7 Strain the stock through a colander to remove the bones and vegetables, then strain it through a fine sieve into a bowl (use a non-metal one if you intend to store it). Leave the stock to get cold and remove the layer of fat just before using or cool for 5 minutes, then skim off the fat.

Basic fish stock

45 minutes

Makes 600 ml /1 pt
1.1 kg /2½ lb fish bones and trimmings (but not black skin)
salt
1 Spanish onion, roughly chopped
1 carrot, roughly chopped
1 celery stalk, roughly chopped
2–3 sprigs of parsley
sprig of fresh thyme or a pinch of dried thyme
bay leaf
about 25 g /1 oz mushroom stalks and trimmings
12 white peppercorns
½ chicken stock cube
thinly pared zest of ½ lemon
juice of ½ lemon

1 Rinse the fish bones and trimmings thoroughly under cold running water. Roughly chop the bones and trimmings and put them in a large pot with 700 ml /1½ pt cold water and a little salt.
2 Place the pan over a low heat and bring to the boil. Allow the scum to rise and then settle on the surface of the liquid, then skim it off with a slotted spoon.
3 Add the remaining ingredients except the lemon juice to the pan and simmer gently, uncovered, for about 30 minutes. Strain the stock through a muslin-lined sieve into a bowl (use a non-metal one if you intend to store the stock), then add the lemon juice.

SIMPLE STOCK-BASED SOUPS

A hot, hearty soup makes a perfect starter or midday snack – easy to make, and capable of great variety, these stock-based soups are also economical.

A good, home-made soup makes an excellent starter to a meal. It is the hallmark of a cook who values good ingredients and likes to serve them in a straightforward way.

The success of simple stock-based soups depends on well-flavoured stock, preferably home-made, as its main ingredient. Extra flavour can then be added with ingredients like cheese, vegetables and pulses. The choice is limitless, as leftover cooked food as well as fresh ingredients can be used. Many cooks agree that the best soups are those just thrown together from leftovers, never to be repeated: pleasing yourself is the only rule. A welcome clearance of leftovers is usually the start, and ingredients from cans, packets, bottles and the contents of the freezer are all suitable – but be careful not to overdo it!

Starting with a good stock, add any of the following for extra flavour:
● Two tablespoons of rice or any small pasta shapes will add body to soup. Try semolina, or sago for a different texture.
● To add a touch of luxury to white soup, stir in a little single cream.

● For padding out soup, add concentrated canned or packet soups.
● To increase the flavour, blend in a stock cube. Or stir in some sherry, wine, dry Marsala, or dry white vermouth.

Cooking time
The cooking time is determined by the time it takes to cook the hardest ingredient. Add the ingredients to the pan in the right order and at suitable intervals so that everything is ready at the same time. Ingredients like pulses, which require the longest cooking time, should be added right at the start. Add root vegetables, followed by softer vegetables, pasta or rice and, finally, any cooked ingredients.

Freezing
Most soups freeze well, but use herbs and spices sparingly and avoid adding garlic, cream, eggs or milk before freezing; add them when reheating.

French onion soup with blue cheese

French onion soup with blue cheese

🍴 1½ hours

Serves 6
75 g /3 oz butter
45 ml /3 tbls olive oil
2.5 ml /½ tsp caster sugar
550g /1¼ lb onions, sliced thinly into rings
1.5 L /2½ pt beef stock, home-made or from a cube
75 g /3 oz blue cheese
60 ml /4 tbls brandy
75 ml /5 tbls coarsely chopped walnuts
salt and freshly ground black pepper
6 slices of French bread, each 3 cm /1¼ in thick
butter for spreading
90 ml /6 tbls grated Gruyère cheese

1 In a large saucepan, heat 40 g /1½ oz butter with the olive oil and caster sugar. Add the onion rings and cook over a moderately low heat for 15–20 minutes, stirring frequently, until the onions are golden brown.
2 Gradually stir in the beef stock and bring to the boil. Lower the heat, cover the pan and simmer gently for about 1 hour. The soup should have reduced to about 1 L /2 pt. Meanwhile, heat the grill to high.
3 In a bowl, combine the blue cheese, remaining butter and 30 ml /2 tbls of hot stock from the soup. Mash with a fork to a smooth paste.
4 Stir the blue cheese paste, brandy and chopped walnuts into the soup until they are well blended. Season with salt and pepper.
5 Toast the slices of French bread and spread them on 1 side with butter. Put a round of toasted French bread into each of 6 flameproof soup bowls. Ladle the soup into the bowls. Sprinkle 15 ml /1 tbls grated Gruyère cheese on each toast round. Place the soup bowls under the heated grill for 3–4 minutes, until the cheese is golden brown. Serve immediately.

Greek egg and lemon soup

🍴 30 minutes

Serves 6
1.4 L /2½ pt chicken stock, home-made or from a cube
1 chicken leg or breast
3 eggs
30–60 ml /2–4 tbls lemon juice
finely grated zest of ½ lemon
90–120 ml /6–8 tbls cooked long-grain rice
salt and freshly ground black pepper
30–45 ml /2–3 tbls finely chopped fresh parsley

1 Bring the chicken stock to the boil in a pan and poach the chicken joint for 15–20 minutes.
2 Remove the chicken from the stock and leave until it is cool enough to handle. Strain the stock through a fine sieve into a clean pan. Skin and bone the chicken. Cut the flesh into very thin slivers.
3 In a mixing bowl, whisk the eggs lightly with the lemon juice to taste and the grated lemon zest. Beating vigorously with the whisk, add a ladleful of the stock to the egg mixture.
4 Bring the remaining stock to the boil. Remove from the heat, then add the cooked rice and slivered chicken. Stir in the egg mixture. Season with salt and pepper. Return to a very low heat and cook for 3–4 minutes, stirring constantly, or until the soup is hot and creamy. Do not allow the soup to boil again.
5 Stir in the finely chopped parsley and serve immediately.

Polish barley and mushroom soup

 overnight soaking, then about 55 minutes

Serves 6-8
15 g /½ oz butter
1 Spanish onion, halved and thinly sliced
100 g /4 oz button mushrooms, chopped
100 g /4 oz pearl barley, soaked overnight
1.1 L /2 pt beef stock, home-made or from a cube
1 large or 2 small carrots, diced
salt
freshly ground black pepper
225 g /8 oz potatoes, diced
150 ml /5 fl oz thick cream
150 ml /5 fl oz milk

1 In a large saucepan, heat the butter and sauté the thinly sliced onion and chopped mushrooms for 7-10 minutes, or until soft and golden, stirring occasionally with a wooden spoon.
2 Drain the pearl barley thoroughly and add to the pan with the beef stock, diced carrots and salt and freshly ground black pepper to taste.
3 Bring to the boil. Cover the pan and simmer gently for 30 minutes, stirring occasionally with the wooden spoon.
4 Add the diced potatoes and simmer for 10 minutes longer, or until the potatoes are cooked but not disintegrating, and the other vegetables are tender.
5 Stir in the thick cream and milk. Bring to boiling point, then correct the seasoning and pour the soup into a heated soup tureen or individual bowls. Serve immediately.

Minestrone

This is just one of the many varieties of this famous Italian soup.

 overnight soaking, then 1½ hours

Serves 6–8
250 g /8 oz dried kidney or haricot beans, soaked overnight in cold water
100 g /4 oz salt pork
25–40 g /1–1½ oz butter
2 garlic cloves, finely chopped
1 Spanish onion, cut into quarters or eighths
2.3–2.8 L /4–5 pt beef stock, home-made or from a cube
4 baby carrots, thinly sliced
4 celery stalks, thinly sliced
½ small cabbage, thinly sliced and cut into 5 cm /2 in lengths
4 curly endive leaves, cut into 5 cm /2 in strips
4–6 tomatoes, blanched, skinned, seeded and coarsely chopped
250 g /8 oz French beans, cut into 5 cm /2 in lengths
100 g /4 oz frozen peas
100–175 g /4–6 oz short-cut macaroni, or other small pasta shapes
salt
freshly ground black pepper
30 ml /2 tbls finely chopped fresh parsley
30 ml /2 tbls olive oil
60 ml /4 tbls freshly grated Parmesan cheese, to serve

Minestrone

1 Drain the soaked beans. Dice the salt pork, then melt the butter in a heavy-based saucepan or flameproof casserole and sauté the diced pork until it is brown. Add the garlic and onion and continue to sauté until the onion is golden.
2 Add 2.3 L /4 pt of the beef stock to the saucepan or casserole and bring to the boil. Add the drained beans, carrots and celery and boil for 10 minutes, then reduce the heat and simmer, uncovered, for 20 minutes.
3 Add the cabbage, endive, tomatoes and French beans to the pan. Bring back to the boil, then reduce the heat so that the water barely simmers, cover the pan and simmer very gently for 20 minutes.
4 Add the peas and macaroni (or other pasta shapes), bring back to simmering point and simmer gently for a further 20 minutes, until the pasta is cooked.
5 If you think there is not enough liquid in your soup, add some more stock. Season to taste with salt and freshly ground black pepper. Just before serving, stir in the finely chopped parsley and olive oil. Serve hot, sprinkled with grated Parmesan cheese.

Turnip soup

15 minutes

Serves 4
500 g /18 oz baby turnips, peeled
salt
850 ml /1½ pt hot chicken stock, preferably
    home-made
50 g /2 oz butter
2 garlic cloves, crushed
freshly ground black pepper
100 g /4 oz Gruyère cheese, grated
For the croûtons
4 slices of bread
50 g /2 oz butter for frying

1   Cut the turnips into small sticks, slightly
larger than matchsticks. Blanch them in
boiling salted water for 2 minutes. Drain
well.
2   Heat the butter in a heavy-bottomed
saucepan over medium-low heat until it
foams. Fry the garlic in the butter for 1
minute. Add the turnip sticks and cook for
about 4 minutes, turning them occasionally
until golden and tender.
3   To make the croûtons, remove the crusts
from the bread and cut the bread into cubes.
Melt the butter in a frying-pan over
medium-low heat and sauté the cubes until
brown on all sides, about 2 minutes. Drain
the cubes thoroughly on absorbent paper.
4   Divide the croûtons among 4 warmed
bowls. Season the hot stock with salt and
pepper and pour into the bowls. Spoon the
turnip sticks into the bowls and sprinkle
with the cheese. Serve the soup immediately.

Curry cream soup

35 minutes

Serves 6
1 small onion, chopped
300 g /11 oz mushrooms, coarsely chopped
75 g /3 oz butter
1 L /1¾ pt chicken stock, home-made or
    from a cube
25 g /1 oz flour
2.5 ml /½ tsp curry powder
salt
freshly ground black pepper
275 ml /10 fl oz thin cream
30 ml /2 tbls sherry or brandy (optional)
For the garnish
freshly chopped parsley

1   In a saucepan sauté the onion and
mushrooms in 50 g /2 oz butter for about 3
minutes or until soft. Pour in the chicken
stock. Cover and simmer for 15 minutes.
2   Meanwhile, melt the remaining 25 g /
1 oz butter in a small pan. Stir in the flour
and curry powder and cook for 1 minute.
Remove from the heat and add about 150 ml
/5 fl oz of the hot mushroom mixture to the
pan. Season with salt and pepper. Return to
the heat and stir until smooth.
3   Pour the contents of the small pan into
the larger pan of mushroom mixture and stir
to incorporate.
4   Stir in the cream and sherry or brandy,
if you are using it, and heat thoroughly
without bringing to the boil.
5   To serve, ladle the soup into warmed
individual bowls and garnish with parsley.

Turnip soup

Mixed vegetable borshch

**This is a substantial soup, full of chunky
vegetables.**

45 minutes

Serves 6
400 g /14 oz cooked beetroots, peeled
1 large onion
200 g /7 oz carrots
200 g /7 oz celery
1.2 L /2¼ pt ham stock, home-made or from
    a cube
15 ml /1 tbls soft brown sugar
30 ml /2 tbls red wine vinegar
1 garlic clove, crushed with a pinch of salt
freshly ground black pepper
For the garnish
150 ml /5 fl oz soured cream
250 g /9 oz potatoes, boiled and cut into
    5 mm /¼ in dice
30 ml /2 tbls freshly chopped parsley

1   Cut all the vegetables into small strips.
2   Bring the stock to the boil, put in the
vegetables, sugar, vinegar and garlic and
season with the pepper. Cover and simmer
for 20 minutes.
3   To serve, ladle the soup into heated
individual bowls. Top each one with a
spoonful of soured cream. Scatter the diced
potatoes on top and sprinkle over a little
chopped parsley.

Cold curried vegetable soup

⏲ 40 minutes,
  then 2 hours chilling

Serves 4
25 g /1 oz butter
15 ml /1 tbls mild curry powder
850 ml /1½ pt chicken stock, home-made or
  from a cube
10 ml /2 tsp brown sugar
175 g /6 oz green beans, topped, tailed and
  halved, or cut in thirds if very long
1 bunch spring onions, finely chopped
100 g /4 oz frozen peas
4 tomatoes, blanched, skinned, seeded and
  chopped
salt and freshly ground black pepper

1   Melt the butter in a medium-sized sauce-pan. When it is hot, add the curry powder and stir over a low heat for 3–4 minutes.
2   Blend in the chicken stock and brown sugar. Bring to the boil.
3   Add the prepared green beans and the finely chopped spring onions to the boiling curried liquid, bring back to the boil and cook for a further 4 minutes or until the beans are tender but not soft.
4   Reduce the heat, stir in the peas and the prepared tomatoes and simmer for 3 minutes. Season with salt and freshly ground black pepper to taste, if required. Carefully skim the surface to remove any fat. Cool the soup, then chill it for 2 hours.
5   Remove any remaining fat from the surface. Pour the chilled soup into a chilled tureen and serve immediately.

Unblended tomato soup

⏲ 35 minutes

Serves 4
800 g /1 lb 12 oz canned tomatoes
425 ml /15 fl oz vegetable or chicken stock,
  home-made or from a cube
25 g /1 oz butter
1 large onion, finely chopped
60 ml /4 tbls chopped mixed fresh herbs
salt and freshly ground black pepper
60 ml /4 tbls soured cream or natural
  yoghurt

1   Drain the tomatoes and add the juice to the stock, to make 600 ml /1 pt liquid.
2   Melt the butter in a saucepan over a low heat, stir in the onion and cook until it is soft. Add the tomatoes and herbs, cover and cook for 10 minutes.
3   Mash the tomatoes to a purée, using a potato masher, then pour in the stock. Season well with salt and freshly ground black pepper.
4   Bring the contents of the pan to the boil, cover and simmer for 15 minutes. Remove the pan from the heat.
5   Pour the soup into 4 individual soup bowls and swirl 15 ml /1 tbls soured cream or yoghurt on top of each serving.

● For a special touch, stir in 75 ml /3 fl oz dry sherry or Marsala after the pan is removed from the heat.
● For tomato and leek soup, use 2 medium-sized leeks instead of the onion.
● For tomato and lentil soup, stir in 100 g /4 oz split red lentils (no need to soak them first) when you add the tomatoes to the pan. Pour in the stock immediately, add a bay leaf and simmer for 45 minutes, or until the lentils have softened and disintegrated.

Cold curried vegetable soup

Soupe au pistou

Serves 6-8 as a starter, 4 as a main course
1.1 L /2 pt beef stock, home-made or from a cube
225 g /8 oz dried haricot beans, soaked overnight
225 g /8 oz green beans, cut into 5 mm /¼ in lengths
1 baby marrow or large courgette, sliced
2 medium-sized carrots, sliced
1 leek, sliced
1 potato, diced
salt and freshly ground black pepper
freshly grated Parmesan cheese, to serve
For the pistou sauce
4 large garlic cloves
4 sprigs fresh basil
75 ml /5 tbls olive oil
60 ml /4 tbls freshly grated Parmesan cheese

1   Bring the stock to the boil in a large saucepan. Drain the soaked haricot beans; add them to the pan and simmer, covered, for 1 hour, or until the beans are nearly tender.
2   Add the remaining prepared vegetables and season to taste with salt and freshly ground black pepper. Bring to the boil and simmer gently for about 15 minutes or until the vegetables are nearly tender, skimming any foam from the surface as necessary.
3   Meanwhile, prepare the pistou sauce: mash the garlic cloves to a paste with a pestle and mortar, or use a garlic press. Add the basil sprigs and continue to pound until reduced to a purée. Add the olive oil, a little at a time, beating constantly. Finally, stir in the grated Parmesan and pound until the sauce is smooth again.
4   Add the pistou to the soup, stir gently and simmer for a final 5 minutes. Serve hot, accompanied by a large bowl of grated Parmesan.

● This traditional Provençal soup owes much of its lovely strong flavour to the pistou sauce – a variation without pine nuts of the famous Genoese *pesto*.

 overnight soaking,
then 1½ hours

Oriental fish soup

Serves 4
350 g /12 oz haddock fillet
22.5 ml /1½ tbls cornflour
22.5 ml /1½ tbls dry sherry
45 ml /3 tbls soy sauce
a pinch of salt
1 Spanish onion, thinly sliced
850 ml /1½ pt fish stock, home-made or from a cube
22.5 ml /1½ tbls lemon juice
22.5 ml /1½ tbls finely chopped fresh parsley
15 ml /1 tbls finely chopped fresh coriander leaves

1   Using a sharp knife, skin the haddock, then cut it into 25 mm / 1 in squares.
2   In a medium-sized bowl, blend the cornflour with 25 ml /1 tbls water to a smooth paste. Stir in the sherry and half the soy sauce. Add the fish pieces and stir to coat.
3   In a saucepan, combine the salt, thinly sliced onion and fish stock. Bring to the boil, then reduce the heat and simmer for 10 minutes.
4   Add the fish and the sauce to the simmering liquid. Stir in the remaining soy sauce and the lemon juice. Simmer, uncovered, for 5 minutes or until the fish flakes easily with a fork.
5   Pour into 4 heated individual soup bowls and sprinkle with finely chopped parsely and coriander leaves. Serve immediately.

25 minutes

Danish cabbage soup

Serves 6
800 g /1¾ lb cabbage
50 g /2 oz butter
15 ml /1 tbls soft brown sugar
1 Spanish onion, thinly sliced
850 ml /1½ pt beef stock, home-made or from a cube
2.5 ml /½ tsp ground allspice
salt and freshly ground black pepper
150 ml /5 fl oz soured cream

1 Cut the cabbage into quarters and discard the outer leaves. Remove the core and slice the leaves thinly.
2 In a large heavy-based saucepan, melt the butter over a medium heat and stir in the soft brown sugar. Cook for 1–2 minutes, or until caramelized, stirring constantly with a wooden spoon.
3 Stir the sliced cabbage and onion into the caramelized sugar. Cook for about 4 minutes, or until the vegetables are simmering and well coated in caramelized sugar, stirring occasionally.
4 Pour in the beef stock and stir in the ground allspice. Season with salt and freshly ground black pepper to taste.
5 Cover and simmer gently for 35 minutes, or until the cabbage is tender, stirring occasionally.
6 Just before serving, stir in the soured cream. Heat through gently, without allowing the soup to boil. Correct the seasoning and serve immediately.

50 minutes

Vegetable soup

Serves 6
1.1 L /2 pt chicken stock, preferably home-made
100 g /4 oz French beans
4 courgettes
1 leek
150 g /5 oz cooked beetroot
salt and freshly ground black pepper

1 In a saucepan bring the chicken stock to the boil.
2 Meanwhile, top and tail the French beans; wipe the courgettes with a damp cloth and slice thinly. Remove the outer leaves from the leek and slice thinly; carefully wash the slices in cold water to remove all grit. Drain them well. Cut the beetroot into sticks about 5 mm /¼ in in diameter.
3 Add all the prepared vegetables to the boiling chicken stock. Simmer uncovered for 10 minutes or until the vegetables are tender. Season to taste with salt and freshly ground black pepper. Pour into hot soup plates and serve immediately.

25 minutes

KNIFE & FORK SOUPS

Try a chunky, hearty knife and fork soup for a complete meal-in-a-bowl. Traditional in origin, these soups range from British Oxtail and Cock-a-leekie to the chowders of North America.

Soup does not always have to be a classic, light first course delicately sipped before the roast is tackled. In this chapter there are a selection of soups which make more than adequate main course meals and should be eaten not only with a spoon but also with a knife and fork.

These are chunky dishes containing dried pulses and heaps of fresh vegetables, or hearty fish chowders which can be made with almost any fish you find available. Or try soups that also contain individual portions of meat or fish, either served in the soup or separately. *Bourride* is a classic dish served in this way. It is distinctive because of the *aïoli*, a garlic-flavoured mayonnaise,

which is used to thicken the soup and also accompanies the fish (see recipe).

All that is needed to turn these dishes into a substantial meal is a crisp green salad and some crusty French bread. Or you might prefer garlic or herb bread or a healthy granary loaf as an accompaniment; finish with a selection of cheeses or fresh fruit.

Despite the generous portions of meat and fish that are now served with these main course soups, they originated as a staple food of the peasants of Europe. The ingredients were more basic and they were especially popular because the soup could be left in the pot for some time, then put back over the fire and extra ingredients added to it as needed.

Some of these soups are based on stocks, others are broths. In the stock-based soups I have given the amount of stock needed, in which case you can use the stock recipes at the beginning of the volume, stock out of your freezer or even cubes. Some of the recipes have extra ingredients included in the basic stock, and instructions for making them are given in the recipe.

In the broths and chowders, the tasty liquid for the soup is made by simmering the meat or fish that is to be included in the dish with flavourings and water or milk. In this case the timing is important: it has to be long enough to get the goodness and flavour from the meat and tenderize it, but not so long that the meat becomes stringy. A broth is not strained – although the surface may be skimmed – the bones are simply removed before serving.

Always serve the soup in warmed soup bowls or ladle it into a warmed tureen. The soup itself should be piping hot.

Smoked haddock chowder

Dutch lentil soup

Serve this hearty soup with crusty bread for a cold-weather lunch.

🍴 1¼ hours

Serves 6
350 g /12 oz red lentils
*1.1 L /2 pt beef stock, home-made or from a
    cube*
175 g /6 oz bacon, in 1 piece
2 celery stalks, chopped
1 Spanish onion, chopped
2 garlic cloves, finely chopped
4 sprigs of parsley
1 bay leaf
1.5 ml /¼ tsp ground cumin
2.5 ml /½ tsp dried thyme
25 g /1 oz butter
100 g /4 oz ham, diced
100 g /4 oz garlic sausage, diced
salt and freshly ground black pepper
For the garnish
45 ml /3 tbls finely chopped fresh parsley
45 ml /3 tbls finely chopped gherkins
2 hard-boiled eggs, finely chopped
15 ml /1 tbls finely chopped raw onion

1   Place the lentils in the pan and add the beef stock, bacon, chopped vegetables and garlic. Bring to the boil, skim the surface, then add the parsley, bay leaf, cumin and thyme. Lower the heat, cover the pan and simmer for 30 minutes, or until the lentils are tender.
2   Remove the parsley, bay leaf and bacon from the pan, then rub the soup through a coarse sieve. Dice the bacon.
3   Melt the butter in a pan and sauté the diced bacon with the ham and garlic sausage until the bacon is golden. Stir into the soup, then reheat the soup and season it to taste with salt and pepper. Serve sprinkled with the finely chopped parsley, gherkins, hard-boiled egg and raw onion.

Old-fashioned lamb broth

🕐🍴 soaking barley overnight,
    then 3–3½ hours

Serves 4–6
*700 g /1½ lb scrag end neck of lamb, fat
    removed*
*15 ml /1 tbls pearl barley, soaked overnight,
    or 15 ml /1 tbls rice*
salt
white part of 2–3 small leeks
2 small carrots, sliced
1 small turnip, sliced
1 celery stalk, sliced
15 ml /1 tbls finely chopped fresh parsley
freshly ground black pepper

1   Place the lamb in a saucepan with 1.7 L /3 pt cold water and salt to taste. Cover and bring slowly to the boil. Skim well, then add the barley or rice and the vegetables.
2   Simmer the soup for 2–3 hours, or until

the meat has fallen off the bones and the vegetables are well cooked.
3   Discard the bones, leave the broth to cool for 5 minutes, then skim any fat. Add the parsley and pepper to taste.

Smoked haddock chowder

A chowder is a chunky fish and vegetable soup, often including salt pork or bacon. It is a speciality of the eastern coast of America, but particularly of New England. The name originated in Brittany where the soups were cooked in a pot called a *chaudière.*

🍴🍴 2 hours soaking,
    then 1 hour

Serves 6
750 g /1½ lb smoked haddock
425 ml /15 fl oz milk
350 g /12 oz potatoes
75 g /3 oz fat salt pork, or unsmoked bacon
40 g /1½ oz butter
30 ml /2 tbls flour
275 ml /10 fl oz thin cream
90 ml /6 tbls finely chopped onion
1½ celery stalks, chopped
salt and freshly ground black pepper
freshly grated nutmeg
15 ml /1 tbls finely chopped fresh parsley

1   Soak the smoked haddock in cold water for 2 hours before using.
2   Drain the haddock thoroughly and place

Dutch lentil soup

it in a large saucepan. Add the milk and 600 ml /1 pt water. Bring to the boil, then simmer for 1 minute. Remove from the heat. Cover the pan and leave to stand for 15 minutes. Drain the haddock, reserving 850 ml /1½ pt of the cooking liquid.
3   Cut the potatoes into 15 mm /½ in dice and rinse under cold water. Cut the fat salt pork, or unsmoked bacon, into slightly smaller dice.
4   In a large flameproof casserole, melt 25 g /1 oz butter. Blend in the flour with a wooden spoon and stir over a low heat for 2–3 minutes to make a pale roux. Gradually add the reserved haddock liquid, whisking continuously to prevent lumps forming, and bring the sauce to the boil. Stir in the thin cream.
5   Add the diced potatoes to the casserole and simmer gently for 10–15 minutes, until the potatoes are just tender.
6   Meanwhile heat the remaining 15 g /½ oz butter in a small frying-pan and sauté the salt pork, or unsmoked bacon, until golden. Add the finely chopped onion and chopped celery and continue to sauté for a further 5 minutes, until the onion and celery have softened.
7   Drain the haddock of any remaining liquid. Remove the skin and cut the fish into 25 mm /1 in pieces. Fold the haddock into the simmering soup together with the sautéed salt pork, or bacon, and vegetables. Season to taste with salt and freshly ground black pepper and freshly grated nutmeg and bring to the boil. Serve immediately, sprinkled with finely chopped parsley.

Mediterranean fish chowder

Reminiscent of the sun and sea of the Mediterranean coastline, this hearty soup combines the delicious fish and shellfish found in those waters with tomatoes, garlic, stock and wine.

❚❚ 1½ hours

Serves 8
1.4 kg /3 lb sea bream
375–500 g /¾–1 lb lemon sole
225 g /8 oz plaice fillets, skinned
225 g /8 oz whiting fillets, skinned
850 ml–1 L /1½–1¾ pt fish stock, home-made or from a cube
500 g /1 pt or 1 lb mussels, scrubbed clean and 'beards' removed
75 ml /3 fl oz dry white wine
bouquet garni
8 slices stale French bread, each 5–10 mm / ¼–½ in thick
1 garlic clove
90–120 ml /6–8 tbls olive oil
1 Spanish onion, thinly sliced
2 garlic cloves, crushed
225 g /8 oz canned peeled tomatoes, drained and juice reserved
30–60 ml /2–4 tbls tomato purée
30–60 ml /2–4 tbls coarsely chopped parsley
Tabasco sauce
100 g /4 oz boiled, peeled prawns, defrosted if frozen
salt and freshly ground black pepper

1 Skin and fillet the sea bream and the lemon sole, reserving heads and all trimmings including white skin. Add trimmings to the stock and simmer for 10 minutes.
2 Put the mussels in a saucepan with the wine and bouquet garni, cover and cook over high heat for 5–7 minutes, or until all the mussels have opened. Discard any that remain closed. Drain the mussels, wrap in a damp, clean tea-towel and store in the refrigerator until needed.
3 Toast the slices of stale French bread until they are crisp and golden on both sides. Cut the garlic clove in half and rub the hot toasted bread slices with the cut sides.
4 Heat the olive oil in a flameproof casserole and sauté the thinly sliced onion until it begins to change colour. Add the crushed garlic cloves and the juice from the canned tomatoes, then chop the tomatoes and add them to the pan. Add the tomato purée and the fish stock and continue to cook for 10 minutes, stirring frequently.
5 Cut the sea bream, lemon sole, plaice and whiting fillets into 25 mm /1 in squares. Add them to the pan with the coarsely chopped parsley and a dash of Tabasco to taste. Cook over a gentle heat for 5 minutes, or until the fish is just tender. Add the mussels in their shells and the prawns and heat through gently. Taste the soup and season with salt and pepper, to taste.
6 Place the toasted bread in the bottom of a heated soup tureen, ladle over the chowder and serve immediately.

Cock-a-leekie

This is a Scottish recipe. If you use an old-fashioned boiling fowl it will need to be cooked for much longer.

🕐❚ soaking overnight, then 1¾ hours

Serves 4
12 prunes, soaked overnight (optional)
75 g /3 oz pearl barley, soaked overnight
1.7 L /3 pt well-flavoured chicken stock, home-made or from a cube
1.4 kg /3 lb chicken
bouquet garni
5 ml /1 tsp dried thyme
500 g /1 lb leeks, washed and cut into 15 mm /½ in rings
salt and freshly ground black pepper
juice of 1 lemon

1 Drain the prunes, if using, and the pearl barley.
2 In a heavy, flameproof casserole large enough to take the chicken, combine the pearl barley and the chicken stock. Bring the stock to the boil, stirring occasionally. Cover

Oxtail soup and Garbure

and then simmer it gently for 50 minutes.
3 Put the chicken, breast side uppermost, into the stock with the bouquet garni and dried thyme. Cover and simmer gently for 20 minutes.
4 Add the leek rings and soaked prunes, if using, and season with salt and pepper, to taste. Cover and simmer for a further 20 minutes, stirring occasionally.
5 Turn the chicken breast side down to ensure it cooks evenly; cover and cook for a further 10 minutes or until tender. Remove the chicken with a carving fork to a wooden board.
6 Add the lemon juice to the liquid in the casserole and correct the seasoning. Leave at a simmer, uncovered, until ready for use.
7 Joint the chicken into 8 portions and place 2 portions into each warmed individual soup bowl. Ladle the soup over the chicken, evenly distributing vegetables and prunes, if used. Serve immediately.

● Even if you prefer not to serve the prunes, they add richness to the flavour of the broth during cooking and can be removed at the last moment.

Garbure

A *garbure* is a thick, satisfying vegetable soup, with cabbage the predominating flavour. It originated in the south-west of France (*garbure* is a Basque name) but is now eaten all over France. It is characterized by the slice of bread covered with a thick vegetable purée that is served in the soup.

overnight soaking,
then 3 hours

Serve 6
250 g /8 oz dried haricot beans, soaked
*   overnight*
1 Spanish onion stuck with 6—8 cloves
1 small carrot
bouquet garni
salt and freshly ground black pepper
75 g /3 oz butter
¼ medium-sized white cabbage, shredded
1 medium-sized turnip, thinly sliced
2 large carrots, thinly sliced
white part of 3 leeks, thinly sliced
3 celery stalks, thinly sliced
2 medium-sized potatoes, thinly sliced
1.7 L /3 pt chicken stock, home-made or
*   from a cube*
45 ml /3 tbls olive oil
2 crusty rolls, cut into 15 mm /½ in slices
40 g /1½ oz Gruyère cheese, grated
30 ml /2 tbls freshly chopped parsley

1   Drain and place the soaked beans in a saucepan with the onion stuck with cloves, small carrot, bouquet garni and enough water to cover. Season with freshly ground black pepper, to taste. Bring to the boil, then cover the pan, lower the heat and simmer gently for 2 hours, or until the beans are tender. Drain off the liquid and discard. Discard the onion, carrot and bouquet garni.
2   Meanwhile, melt 25 g /1 oz butter in a large saucepan. Add the shredded cabbage, thinly sliced turnip, carrots, leeks and celery and cook gently, stirring occasionally with a wooden spoon, for 15—20 minutes.
3   Add the cooked beans, the thinly sliced potatoes and the chicken stock to the pan and season with salt and pepper to taste. Cover and simmer for 20—30 minutes until all the vegetables are tender.
4   Heat the grill to high.
5   Meanwhile prepare the croûtes. Heat 40 g /1½ oz butter and the olive oil in a large frying-pan and fry the sliced rolls for 2 minutes on each side, turning with a fish slice until golden. Drain and keep warm.
6   With a slotted spoon, transfer a quarter of the vegetables from the soup to an electric blender, leave to cool a little, then purée until smooth. In a small saucepan, melt the remaining butter. Add the puréed vegetables and cook, stirring continuously, for 10 minutes until the purée thickens to the consistency of mashed potatoes.
7   To serve, spread the purée on the croûtes, doming it well. Sprinkle with grated Gruyère cheese and brown under the grill for 5 minutes. Ladle the soup into heated bowls and place the croûtes on top. Sprinkle with chopped parsley.

Oxtail soup

5½—6½ hours, overnight chilling, then 30 minutes

Serves 6
2 oxtails, separated at each joint
25 g /1 oz flour
salt and freshly ground black pepper
60—90 ml /4—6 tbls cognac
1 Spanish onion, coarsely chopped
4 carrots, quartered
5 ml /1 tsp dried thyme
60 ml /4 tbls finely chopped fresh parsley
2 bay leaves
425 ml /15 fl oz beef stock, home-made or
*   from a cube*
425 ml /15 fl oz red wine

1   Heat the oven to 250C /500F /gas 10.
2   Sprinkle the flour onto a large flat plate and season well with salt and freshly ground black pepper. Roll the oxtail segments in the seasoned flour and place them in a large roasting tin. Brown them in the oven for 15 minutes. Turn the segments over and continue cooking for a further 15 minutes. Remove the tin from the oven and carefully

pour off any fat. Transfer the oxtail segments and any sediment to a large flameproof casserole.
3   Reduce the heat to 170C /325F /gas 3. Heat the cognac in a ladle. Set it alight and pour it over the oxtail segments. Once the flames have died out, add the coarsely chopped onion, quartered carrots, dried thyme, 30 ml /2 tbls of the finely chopped parsley, the bay leaves, beef stock, red wine and 600 ml /1 pt water. Season with salt and freshly ground black pepper to taste and cook in the oven for 2½ hours.
4   Reduce the heat again to 110C /225F / gas ¼ and cook the soup for a further 2—3 hours or until the meat is tender. Remove from the oven and allow to cool, then refrigerate overnight.
5   To serve, remove the fat from the surface of the soup with a spoon. Bring the soup to the boil, then simmer for 15—20 minutes, until the oxtail segments are heated through thoroughly. Sprinkle with the remaining finely chopped parsley and serve.

● It is important to chill this soup so that you can remove the fat completely, otherwise it will be unpleasantly greasy. Reheat the meat thoroughly before serving.

21

Corsican tomato soup

On an island where beef is expensive, a little has to go a long way.

🔪🔪 1½ hours

Serves 4
250 g /8 oz shin of beef
25 g /1 oz butter
1 Spanish onion, finely chopped
1 garlic clove, finely chopped
500 g /1 lb tomatoes, skinned, seeded and coarsely chopped
1.1 L /2 pt beef stock, home-made or from a cube
1.5 ml /¼ tsp dried basil
salt and freshly ground black pepper
45 ml /3 tbls long-grain rice

1 With a sharp knife, cut the shin of beef into 15 mm /½ in cubes, discarding the gristle.
2 In a large saucepan, melt the butter and brown the beef cubes for 2–3 minutes on each side. Remove with a slotted spoon to a heated plate and keep warm.
3 Add the finely chopped onion to the saucepan and cook for 5 minutes until lightly coloured, stirring occasionally with a wooden spoon. Add the finely chopped garlic and coarsely chopped tomatoes and simmer gently, stirring continuously, for 7–10 minutes until the tomatoes are reduced to a purée.
4 Add the beef stock and dried basil to the pan and return the beef. Season with salt and freshly ground black pepper to taste. Bring to the boil, cover and simmer gently for 45 minutes.
5 Sprinkle the rice into the soup and cook

Corsican tomato soup

for a further 15 minutes, or until the rice is tender. Serve immediately.

● This soup depends for its flavour on the rich ripeness of the fleshy Italian-style tomatoes. If really tasty tomatoes are not in season, use canned tomatoes.

Waterzooi of chicken

Originating in the Flemish sector of Belgium, a *waterzooi* may be made with chicken or fish. Add more vegetables and potatoes when you cook the chicken for a chunkier version.

🔪🔪 2¼–2¾ hours

Serves 4
1.4 kg /3 lb chicken, cleaned, with giblets and feet reserved
chicken carcass, or a veal bone
2 celery stalks, chopped
1 Spanish onion, chopped
4 carrots, chopped
½ lemon, thinly sliced
4 sprigs of parsley
1.1 L /2 pt chicken stock, home-made or from a cube
salt and freshly ground black pepper
bouquet garni
½ bottle dry white wine
25 g /1 oz butter, softened
30 ml /2 tbls flour
150 ml /5 fl oz thick cream
30 ml /2 tbls freshly chopped parsley

1 Put the giblets and feet of the chicken with the carcass (or veal bone) in a large saucepan. Add the chopped celery, onion and carrots, thinly sliced lemon and parsley sprigs. Add the stock to the pan and season with freshly ground black pepper, to taste. Bring to the boil and simmer uncovered for 1–1½ hours.
2 Strain the stock into a clean pan, pressing the vegetables through a sieve to extract as much flavour as possible. Discard the vegetables, giblets and bones.
3 Cut the chicken into 4 portions and add them to the stock. Add the bouquet garni and dry white wine. Cover and simmer for 45 minutes or until the chicken is tender when pierced with a knife.
4 Remove the chicken portions with a slotted spoon. Put them on a heated dish and keep hot.
5 Mash the softened butter and the flour together to form a *beurre manié* and whisk it into the simmering soup in tiny pieces. Cook for 3–4 minutes longer, stirring, until the soup is smooth and thickened. Stir in the thick cream until blended. Do not allow the soup to boil, or it will curdle.
6 Return the chicken pieces to the pan, correct the seasoning with salt and freshly ground black pepper and heat through.
7 To serve, place the chicken portions in heated individual soup bowls. Pour the soup over the chicken, sprinkle with chopped parsley and serve.

La bourride provençale

This is the Provençal fisherman's stew, made with whichever meaty fish happens to be available. The essential flavouring ingredient is garlic; use a little or a lot according to your taste.

 45 minutes

Serves 6
1 kg /2 lb fish fillets (bass, haddock or grey mullet)
1 medium-sized onion, finely chopped
bouquet garni
salt and freshly ground black pepper
850 ml /1½ pt boiling water
6 rounds of bread
25 g /1 oz butter
30 ml /2 tbls olive oil
2 garlic cloves, crushed
For the aïoli
6 garlic cloves, finely chopped
4 egg yolks
salt and freshly ground black pepper
600 ml /1 pt olive oil
30 ml /2 tbls lemon juice

1 First make the aïoli: put the finely chopped garlic in a bowl with the egg yolks. Season with salt to taste, and whisk in the olive oil gradually as for mayonnaise. Add the lemon juice (the garlic flavour should be dominant) and pepper to taste.
2 Cut the fish into serving-size chunks and place in a large saucepan. Add the finely chopped onion and bouquet garni and season with salt and freshly ground black pepper. Pour in the boiling water and simmer gently for 10 minutes, or until the fish is tender.
3 Meanwhile cut the bread into 7.5 cm /3 in circles. Heat the butter and olive oil in a frying-pan. Add the crushed garlic cloves. Fry the bread circles for 2–3 minutes on each side in garlic butter until golden brown. Drain on absorbent paper and keep warm while you finish preparing the soup.
4 When the fish is cooked remove it from the saucepan with a slotted spoon. Drain it well and keep it warm on a heated serving platter.
5 Reserve a quarter of the aïoli and strain the fish bouillon over the rest of the aïoli, a little at a time, blending with a whisk. Return it to the pan and cook over a low heat for 10 minutes, stirring continuously, until the soup coats the back of a wooden spoon. Do not let the soup come to the boil or it will curdle.
6 To serve, place the fried croûtons in the bottom of a heated tureen and pour the soup over them. Serve the fish separately with a little of the remaining aïoli accompanying each portion.

● Many French soups are flavoured and thickened like this, with a separately made sauce such as aïoli or with a similar sweet red pepper version, known as *sauce rouille*, because of its rust colour.

Hotch potch

The traditional Scottish hotch potch was made with mutton, but today we prefer the less fatty lamb. Lightly cooked peas and lettuce add crunch to the soup.

45 minutes

Serves 6
1.1 L /2 pt white stock, home-made or chicken stock from a cube
6 lamb chops
6 carrots, diced
4 young turnips, diced
8 spring onions, sliced
salt and freshly ground black pepper
1 cauliflower, broken into florets
350 g /12 oz frozen peas
1 lettuce, shredded
15 ml /1 tbls finely chopped fresh parsley

Hotch potch

1 Bring the stock to the boil in a large saucepan.
2 Remove any excess fat from the lamb chops and add the chops to the pan. Simmer gently for 10 minutes.
3 Add the diced carrots and turnips and sliced spring onions to the pan. Season with salt and freshly ground black pepper, to taste, and simmer for a further 10 minutes. Skim the soup to remove any fat from the surface.
4 Add the cauliflower florets to the pan and simmer for a further 5 minutes. Add the frozen peas and shredded lettuce and simmer for 3–5 minutes more, until the vegetables are cooked but still crunchy. Correct the seasoning.
5 To serve, place the lamb chops in heated individual soup bowls. Spoon the soup and vegetables over the chops and sprinkle with finely chopped parsley.

Mussel soup

Serves 4

1 kg /2 pt or 2 lb mussels
1 Spanish onion, finely chopped
1 garlic clove, finely chopped
300 ml /10 fl oz dry white wine
65 g /2½ oz butter
45 ml /3 tbls flour
2.5 ml /½ tsp dry mustard
1.5 ml /¼ tsp ground turmeric
salt
freshly ground black pepper
30 ml /2 tbls olive oil
4 slices of white bread
30 ml /2 tbls coarsely chopped
   fresh parsley
60 ml /4 tbls thick cream
sprigs of flat-leaved parsley,
   to garnish

1   Scrub the mussels clean in several changes of fresh water and pull off the beards. Discard any mussels that are cracked or do not close tightly when tapped.
2   Place the finely chopped onion and garlic and the white wine in a small saucepan and simmer for 20 minutes or until the onion is soft.
3   Meanwhile, put the mussels in a large saucepan and add 850 ml /1½ pt water. Cover the pan tightly and cook over a high heat, shaking the pan, for about 5 minutes or until the shells open. Then lower the heat and simmer, covered, for a further 3 minutes.
4   Remove the mussels from the pan with a slotted spoon, discarding any which are still shut. Remove and discard the top shell from each mussel and keep the mussels warm. Strain the liquid through a muslin-lined sieve into a bowl and reserve.
5   In a large saucepan, melt 40 g /1½ oz butter and blend in the flour. Gradually add the strained mussel liquor and the wine and onion mixture, beating vigorously with a wire whisk to prevent lumps forming.
6   Stir in the dry mustard and ground turmeric, and season to taste with salt and freshly ground black pepper. Simmer gently for 2–3 minutes or until the soup has thickened.
7   Heat the remaining butter and the olive oil in a frying-pan. Cut heart shapes from each of the bread slices and fry them for 1–2 minutes on each side or until golden. Drain the croûtons on absorbent paper and keep warm.
8   Add the mussels on the half shell to the soup. Stir in the coarsely chopped parsley and thick cream, and reheat gently without boiling. Spoon the soup into individual heated soup bowls and garnish each portion with a croûton and a sprig of flat-leaved parsley.

 45 minutes

Cod chowder

Serves 4-6 as a starter, 2-3 as a main course

500 g /1 lb cod fillet
275 ml /10 fl oz milk
40 g /1½ oz butter
50 g /2 oz salt pork, diced
1 Spanish onion, sliced
4 celery stalks, finely chopped
15 ml /1 tbls flour
2 medium-sized potatoes, thickly sliced
bay leaf
salt and freshly ground white pepper
75 ml /3 fl oz thick cream
30 ml /2 tbls finely chopped fresh parsley
a pinch of paprika

1   Skin the cod, cut it into pieces if necessary, and place it in a medium-sized saucepan. Pour in the milk, cover and bring to a simmer. Simmer gently for 10 minutes or until the cod flakes easily with a fork.
2   Strain the milk into a measuring jug and make it up to 700 ml / 1¼ pt with water. Reserve the liquor. Flake the cod and remove any bones. Reserve.
3   In a saucepan, melt 25 g /1 oz butter. Add the diced salt pork and sauté for 5 minutes, or until golden brown, stirring occasionally with a wooden spoon. Remove with a slotted spoon and reserve.
4   Add the sliced onion and finely chopped celery to the fat in the pan and sauté over a moderate heat, stirring occasionally with the wooden spoon, for about 5 minutes, or until tender but still crisp. Remove from the heat and reserve.
5   Meanwhile, melt the remaining butter in a large saucepan and blend in the flour. Cook over a low heat, stirring, for 2–3 minutes to make a pale roux. Gradually pour in the reserved liquor and stir vigorously with a wire whisk to prevent lumps forming. Bring to the boil, still stirring, to thicken slightly.
6   Add the sliced potatoes and the sautéed onion and celery to the soup, with the bay leaf. Season to taste with salt and freshly ground white pepper, then simmer gently for 15–20 minutes, or until the potatoes are tender.
7   Stir in the flaked cod and the thick cream, correct the seasoning and heat through gently.
8   To serve, ladle the soup into individual heated soup bowls. Sprinkle with the diced pork, the parsley and a little paprika.

 45 minutes

Mediterranean stewed fish and soup

Serves 4 for 2 courses
700 g /1½ lb cod or haddock,
    filleted
6 medium-sized potatoes, very
    thinly sliced
bay leaf
1 onion, finely chopped
1 celery stalk, chopped
2 garlic cloves, crushed,
    plus 1 whole garlic clove
5 ml /1 tsp salt

freshly ground black pepper
5 ml /1 tsp chopped fennel leaves
5 ml /1 tsp freshly chopped
    parsley, plus extra to garnish
5 ml /1 tsp grated orange zest
75 ml /3 fl oz olive oil
boiling water
4 × 25 mm /1 in thick slices of
    toasted French bread
275 ml /10 fl oz aïoli (page 23)
4–5 sprigs of fennel, to garnish

1   Cut the fish into serving pieces and arrange in the bottom of a
large saucepan. Cover with the sliced potatoes.
2   Add the bay leaf, finely chopped onion, celery and crushed
garlic. Sprinkle with the salt, a generous amount of freshly ground
black pepper, the fennel, chopped parsley and grated orange zest.
Pour on the olive oil and add boiling water to cover. Simmer for
about 15–20 minutes or until the potatoes are tender.
3   Strain the cooking liquid into another saucepan and arrange the
fish and potatoes on a warmed serving dish. Keep warm.
4   Cut the whole garlic clove in half. Rub the rounds of toast well
with the cut side of 1 half and rub the insides of 4 soup bowls with
the other half.
5   Put the pan of reserved cooking liquid over moderate heat and
bring to the boil. Put the aïoli in a bowl and pour in a little of the
hot liquid, whisking. Pour this into the pan of cooking liquid.
Return the pan to the heat and simmer gently, stirring, until the
soup thickens slightly. Do not boil.
6   Either place the rounds of toast in the soup bowls and pour the
soup over or serve the toast separately for your guests to add to their
soup if they wish.
7   To serve the fish and potatoes, sprinkle them with chopped
parsley and garnish with sprigs of fennel.

● A traditional dish in the South of France, Mediterranean fish stew
makes both a fish soup and a substantial main course.

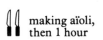
making aïoli,
then 1 hour

Creole crab gumbo

Serves 6
25 g /1 oz butter
30 ml /2 tbls olive oil
1 Spanish onion, chopped
1 small green pepper, chopped
30 ml /2 tbls flour
bouquet garni
1 garlic clove, finely chopped
strip of lemon zest
a dash of Tabasco sauce
400 g /14 oz canned peeled tomatoes
salt and freshly ground black pepper
350 g /12 oz canned crabmeat
12 large, boiled peeled prawns, defrosted if frozen
225 g /8 oz okra
300 ml /10 fl oz milk
150 ml /5 fl oz thick cream

1   In a saucepan heat the butter and olive oil. Add the chopped
onion and green pepper and sauté for 7–10 minutes or until tender
but not browned, stirring occasionally with a wooden spoon.
2   Blend in the flour and cook for a further 2 minutes, still stirring
occasionally. Add the bouquet garni, finely chopped garlic, strip of
lemon zest, Tabasco sauce and canned tomatoes. Season with salt
and freshly ground black pepper to taste and stir to blend. Cover
and simmer gently for 15 minutes. Stir in the crabmeat and prawns.
Cook for a further 5 minutes.
3   Meanwhile, bring a saucepan of salted water to the boil. Wipe
the okra with a damp cloth and trim off the stalk ends. Add to the
water and simmer for 5 minutes. Drain. Rinse under cold running
water and drain again.
4   Gradually stir the milk and cream into the tomato mixture and
finally add the drained okra. Correct the seasoning. Reheat the soup
gently, remove the bouquet garni and lemon zest and serve
immediately.

● A dish from Louisiana in the American South, *gumbo* is basically
an okra soup, made with generous portions of fish or meat.

45 minutes

PUREE SOUPS

Soups made from vegetables or fruit cooked until tender, then puréed with their cooking liquid, are full of flavour and goodness, yet are simplicity itself to make.

Purée soups are ideal for the novice cook, as they are easy and quick to make, yet very satisfying to eat.

You can make purée soups using either a single vegetable or fruit or a combination of both and, because the ingredients will be reduced to a pulp, you can use slightly over-ripe vegetables or fruit which might otherwise go to waste, such as the outer leaves of lettuce, slightly tough end-of-season peas, or mushroom stalks.

Making the soup

The first step in making a purée soup is to clean the ingredients and, if necessary, peel them – there is no need to peel ingredients that are to be sieved because the skins will be caught in the sieve. Roughly chop or slice the vegetables or fruit.

Sweating the ingredients in butter or olive oil will add flavour and texture to most purée soups: melt the fat in a heavy-based saucepan, add the vegetables or fruit and stir to coat them all over. Cover and cook gently over a low heat for a few minutes to soften them. Then add the liquid, seasonings and herbs and spices. Bring to simmering point, lower the heat and cook until the ingredients are tender, but do not overcook or, the flavour and colour will be lost.

There are three ways to make a purée: by using an electric blender, a vegetable mill or a sieve. A vegetable mill, though not as quick and easy as a blender, has the advantage of giving a range of textures – simply choose the fine, medium or coarse attachment. Pushing the ingredients through a sieve will give a fine purée and remove any stringy fibres or bits of skin. It is sometimes necessary to sieve the purée resulting from a blender or mill, for example when making a celery or fresh tomato purée.

After you have puréed the soup, return it to the rinsed and dried saucepan to reheat gently, if you are serving it hot, or leave it to cool. Adjust the seasoning before serving.

Garnishing the soup

Smooth purée soups are even more appetizing when topped with a complementary garnish – a swirl of cream or yoghurt, crispy croûtons (page 14) or fried bacon bits, thin slices of lemon or lime, chopped hard-boiled egg or fresh herbs, in sprigs or chopped.

Jerusalem artichoke and lemon soup

Jerusalem artichoke and lemon soup

🖌 1 hour

Serves 4
25 g /1 oz butter
500 g /1 lb Jerusalem artichokes, peeled and thinly sliced
2 medium-sized onions, thinly sliced
850 ml /1½ pt chicken stock, home-made or from a cube
2 thinly pared strips of lemon zest
bouquet garni
salt and freshly ground black pepper
10 ml /2 tsp lemon juice, or more
150 ml /5 fl oz yoghurt
thinly sliced lemon, to garnish
30 ml /2 tbls freshly chopped parsley, to garnish

1 Melt the butter in a saucepan over a low heat. Stir in the artichokes and onions. Cover and cook gently for 10 minutes.
2 Pour in the stock and bring it to the boil. Add the lemon zest and bouquet garni and season to taste with salt and pepper. Cover and simmer for 20 minutes.
3 Discard the zest and bouquet garni. Purée the soup in a blender or put it through a vegetable mill. Return to the rinsed-out pan. Add about 10 ml /2 tsp lemon juice and the yoghurt. Taste and add extra lemon juice if required.
4 Reheat gently, without boiling, and serve garnished with lemon and parsley.

Chilled Angostura soup

🖌 40 minutes, plus cooling and chilling

Serves 6
30 ml /2 tbls olive oil
2 medium-sized onions, finely chopped
2 garlic cloves, finely chopped
½ red pepper, finely chopped
½ green pepper, finely chopped
400 g /14 oz canned peeled tomatoes
600 ml /1 pt chicken stock, home-made or from a cube
20 ml /4 tsp Angostura bitters
salt and freshly ground black pepper
For the garnish
finely chopped fresh parsley
2 hard-boiled eggs, chopped
croûtons (page 14)

1 Heat the oil in a saucepan over moderate heat, add the onion and fry until soft but not coloured. Add the garlic and red and green peppers and cook for 5 minutes.
2 Blend the tomatoes and juice to a purée. Add to the pan with half the chicken stock and simmer, uncovered, for 15 minutes.
3 Remove the pan from the heat and blend half of this tomato and chicken mixture to a purée. Combine with the remaining tomato mixture, chicken stock, Angostura bitters

and salt and freshly ground black pepper to taste. Transfer the soup to a large bowl, let it cool and chill it.
4 Serve the soup well chilled, garnished with finely chopped parsley, chopped hard-boiled egg and croûtons.

Aubergine soup

⏲ 1 hour 10 minutes

Serves 4-6
15 ml /1 tbls olive oil
1 large onion, chopped
15 ml /1 tbls dry sherry
400 g /14 oz aubergines, chopped
250 g /9 oz potatoes, chopped
1 L /1¾ pt beef stock, home-made or from a cube
15 ml /1 tbls tomato purée
1 bay leaf
2.5 ml /½ tsp oregano
salt
freshly ground black pepper
30–45 ml /2–3 tbls milk
croûtons, to garnish (page 14)

1 Heat the oil in a large saucepan. Sauté the onion for 2–3 minutes, until just soft.

2 Add the sherry, aubergines, potatoes, beef stock, tomato purée, bay leaf, oregano, salt and pepper. Bring to the boil, then cover and simmer for 45 minutes.
3 Sieve or purée the soup, return it to the rinsed-out pan and reheat. Stir in the milk and, when hot, serve with the croûtons.

Cheddar cheese soup

⏲ cooking the rice, then 1 hour 20 minutes

Serves 4
1 L /1¾ pt chicken stock, home-made or from a cube
60 ml /4 tbls olive oil
1 Spanish onion, thinly sliced
4 small tomatoes, thinly sliced
1 bay leaf, crumbled
2.5 ml /½ tsp paprika
2.5 ml /½ tsp ground cinnamon
salt and freshly ground black pepper
90 ml /6 tbls cooked rice
175 g /6 oz strong Cheddar cheese, grated
juice of ½ lemon
15 ml /1 tbls finely snipped fresh chives, to garnish

Chilled Angostura soup

1 Bring the chicken stock to the boil in a saucepan.
2 Meanwhile, in a heavy-based saucepan, heat the olive oil over a low heat. Cook the thinly sliced onion for 10 minutes or until very soft, stirring occasionally with a wooden spoon. Add the thinly sliced tomatoes, crumbled bay leaf, paprika and cinnamon and cook for another minute.
3 Pour the boiling chicken stock over the tomato and onion mixture. Season with salt and freshly ground black pepper to taste, then cover and simmer for 1 hour.
4 Add the cooked rice to the soup, then purée it in a blender. Sieve the puréed soup and return it to the rinsed-out saucepan.
5 Heat the soup through, then add the grated Cheddar cheese and let it melt, stirring constantly. Add the lemon juice and adjust the seasoning. Serve the soup in heated soup bowls, garnished with the finely snipped chives.

● Any hard English cheese would make a good substitute for the Cheddar used in this recipe.
● Use crisp fried croûtons or crumbled bacon bits as garnishes for the soup, instead of, or as well as, the chives.

Carrot soup with yoghurt

🥄 45 minutes

Serves 4
25 g /1 oz butter
500 g /1 lb carrots, thinly sliced
1 large onion, finely chopped
5 ml /1 tsp ground coriander
1 L /1¾ pt chicken or light beef stock, home-
   made or from a cube
salt and freshly ground black pepper
bouquet garni
10 ml /2 tsp cornflour
150 ml /5 fl oz yoghurt
1 garlic clove, crushed with a pinch of salt
For the garnish
1 carrot, coarsely grated
sprigs of flat-leaved parsley

1   Melt the butter in a saucepan over a low
heat. Stir in the carrots, onion and
coriander. Cover and cook gently for 7
minutes.
2   Pour in the stock and bring to the boil.
Season and add the bouquet garni. Cover

Carrot soup with yoghurt

the ingredients and simmer for 20 minutes.
3   Meanwhile, blend the cornflour with the
yoghurt in a saucepan. Bring the mixture
slowly to the boil, stirring. Simmer for 2
minutes and remove from the heat.
4   Remove the bouquet garni. Purée the
carrots in a blender with the cooking liquid.
Stir in the garlic.
5   Stir the yoghurt into the soup and return
to the rinsed-out saucepan. Reheat gently
and serve in heated soup bowls, garnished
with grated carrot and sprigs of parsley.

Leek and asparagus soup

🥄 30 minutes

Serves 4
50 g /2 oz butter
500 g /1 lb leeks, finely chopped
300 ml /10 fl oz milk
bay leaf
850 ml /1½ pt chicken stock, home-made or
   from a cube
250 g /8 oz canned asparagus tips, drained
salt and freshly ground black pepper
freshly chopped chervil or parsley, to
   garnish

1   Melt the butter over moderate heat and
cook the leeks for 10 minutes or until soft.
2   Meanwhile, in a small pan, bring the
milk and bay leaf almost to boiling point
over low heat. Remove the bay leaf.
3   Add the stock, milk and asparagus to the
leeks, then leave to cool slightly.
4   Blend the soup to a purée, then return to
the rinsed-out pan and heat through. Adjust
the seasoning and serve, garnished with
freshly chopped chervil or parsley.

Potato and carrot soup

🥄 1 hour 20 minutes

Serves 4
250 g /8 oz floury potatoes, thickly sliced
2 large carrots, thickly sliced
1 celery stalk, thickly sliced
700 ml /1¼ pt beef stock, home-made or
   from a cube
15 g /½ oz butter
¼ Spanish onion, very finely chopped
a pinch of dried marjoram
salt and freshly ground black pepper
croûtons (page 14), to garnish
crisply fried crumbled bacon, to garnish

28

1 Put the potatoes, carrots and celery in a large pan, pour in the stock and bring to the boil. Partially cover the pan and simmer for 40–50 minutes, until the vegetables are almost disintegrating.
2 Purée the soup in an electric blender or put through a vegetable mill until smooth. Then rub through a fine sieve into a bowl.
3 Melt the butter in the rinsed-out pan and fry the finely chopped onion for 6–8 minutes, until it is richly coloured but not burned.
4 Return the purée to the pan and season with the marjoram, salt and freshly ground black pepper to taste. Simmer for 5–10 minutes, stirring occasionally.
5 Serve the soup hot in heated soup bowls, garnished with the croûtons and crisply fried crumbled bacon.

Red bean soup

 overnight soaking,
then 1½ hours

Serves 4–6
250 g /8 oz red kidney beans, soaked overnight
salt and freshly ground black pepper
60 ml /4 tbls olive oil
2 large garlic cloves, finely chopped
30 ml /2 tbls finely chopped fresh parsley

1 Drain the kidney beans and transfer to a heavy-based saucepan with 1.4 L /2½ pt cold water. Bring to the boil and boil vigorously for 10 minutes, then reduce the heat and simmer slowly for about 1 hour, or until tender.
2 Remove half the beans with a slotted spoon and transfer to a blender. Add a little of the bean liquid, if necessary, and purée until smooth. Alternatively, press the beans through a fine sieve.
3 Return the puréed beans to the saucepan with the rest of the beans and season to taste with salt and freshly ground black pepper. Keep hot.
4 In a small frying-pan, heat the olive oil. Sauté the chopped garlic in the hot oil until just golden. Stir the chopped parsley into the oil and garlic mixture and add to the soup. Serve very hot.

Celery and Stilton soup

1½ hours

Serves 4
50 g /2 oz butter
1 head of celery, chopped, with the leaves reserved
2 medium-sized onions, chopped
1 L /1¾ pt light vegetable or chicken stock, home-made or from a cube
salt and freshly ground black pepper
150 ml /5 fl oz milk
100 g /4 oz Stilton cheese
2 egg yolks, beaten
croûtons or celery leaves, to garnish

1 Melt the butter in a large, heavy-based saucepan. Add the chopped celery, the celery leaves and the onions. Cover and cook gently, stirring occasionally, for 10 minutes or until the vegetables are soft but not coloured.
2 Pour in the stock and season lightly. Bring to the boil, then simmer, uncovered, for about 30 minutes, until the vegetables are quite tender.
3 Allow the soup to cool slightly, then blend to a purée. Press through a sieve to remove any fibres and return to the rinsed-out pan. Add the milk and reheat gently, but do not allow to boil.
4 Meanwhile, remove and discard the cheese rind and mash the cheese to a soft paste, then blend into the beaten egg yolks, a little at a time.
5 Stir 30 ml /2 tbls of hot soup into the cheese and milk mixture. Add the mixture to the pan and cook gently, stirring constantly, until the soup has thickened. Do not allow to boil. Adjust the seasoning and serve in heated bowls, garnished with croûtons or celery leaves.

Curried apple soup

30 minutes,
plus cooling and chilling

Red bean soup

Serves 4
500 g /1 lb dessert apples
a few drops of lemon juice
15 g /½ oz butter
½ Spanish onion, finely chopped
15 ml /1 tbls mild curry powder
600 ml /1 pt hot chicken or vegetable stock, home-made or from a cube
5 cm /2 in piece of cinnamon stick
200 ml /7 fl oz cold milk
thin slices of lemon or lime, to garnish

1 Quarter, core, peel and chop the apples. As you prepare them, place them in a bowl of cold water containing the lemon juice.
2 Melt the butter in a heavy-based saucepan. Thoroughly drain the apples and add them to the pan with the onion. Cover and cook gently, stirring occasionally, until soft but not coloured.
3 Add the curry powder and cook over a medium heat, stirring, for 2–3 minutes. Pour in the hot stock and add the cinnamon stick. Bring to the boil, cover the pan, and simmer for 10 minutes, stirring.
4 Remove the cinnamon stick and purée the soup until smooth. Cool, then stir in the milk. Chill, covered, for at least 2 hours.
5 Just before serving, stir the soup well and garnish with lemon or lime slices.

Watercress soup

Serves 6
25 g /1 oz butter
1 medium-sized onion, finely chopped
2 bunches watercress
850 ml /1½ pt chicken stock, home-made or from a cube
salt and freshly ground black pepper
20 g /¾ oz butter
20 g /¾ oz flour
lemon slices, to garnish

1   Melt the butter in a large, heavy-based saucepan, add the finely chopped onion and cook over a moderate heat for 10 minutes or until soft.
2   Meanwhile, cut off and discard the bottom third of the watercress stalks. Finely chop the remaining leaves and stalks.
3   Add the finely chopped watercress to the onion, cover the pan and cook gently for 5 minutes, shaking the pan occasionally. Pour on the chicken stock, bring to the boil and simmer the soup for 10 minutes. Season with salt and freshly ground black pepper to taste.
4   Purée the soup in a blender. Return the soup to the rinsed-out pan and bring slowly to the boil. Mash the butter and flour together to make a *beurre manié* and add to the soup, a little at a time, whisking vigorously so that it does not form lumps.
5   Simmer the soup for 2–3 minutes, until it has thickened. Correct the seasoning and serve in heated bowls, garnished with lemon slices.

Fresh tomato soup

Serves 4
900 g /2 lb very ripe tomatoes
600 ml /1 pt beef stock, home-made or from a cube
salt and freshly ground black pepper
a generous pinch of sugar
5–10 ml /1–2 tsp tomato purée (optional)
50 g /2 oz cooked rice
fresh dill or parsley sprigs, to garnish

1   Cut the tomatoes in half and remove and discard the seeds and juice. Chop the flesh roughly.
2   Put the beef stock in a saucepan and add the chopped tomatoes. Simmer gently for 10 minutes.
3   Allow to cool slightly, then purée the mixture in a blender. Rub the purée through a fine sieve into the rinsed-out saucepan to remove the skins.
4   Bring the soup slowly to the boil. Season to taste with salt, freshly ground black pepper and a good pinch of sugar. If you feel the tomato flavour does not come through strongly enough, add a little tomato purée diluted with 15 ml /1 tbls of the soup.
5   Stir in the cooked rice, allow to heat through and serve in heated soup bowls, garnished with sprigs of dill or parsley.

● Make this dish when tomatoes are at their cheapest and most flavoursome.

1 hour

cooking the rice,
then 30 minutes

Lentil soup with lettuce

Serves 4
100 g /4 oz small green lentils
1 L /1¾ pt chicken stock, home-made or from a cube
1 Spanish onion, stuck with 1 clove
bouquet garni
1 lettuce
50 g /2 oz butter
salt and freshly ground black pepper

1   Rinse and drain the lentils, discarding pieces of grit and any discoloured lentils. Put the lentils in a medium-sized saucepan with the chicken stock, the onion stuck with a clove and the bouquet garni. Bring to the boil, then reduce the heat and simmer, partially covered, for 45 minutes–1 hour or until tender. Remove from the heat, discard the onion and bouquet garni and leave to cool a little.
2   Meanwhile, cut each lettuce leaf in half down the centre vein and shred all the leaves finely.
3   Melt 25 g /1 oz butter in a saucepan. Add the shredded lettuce, cover and sweat for 5 minutes, or until the lettuce has wilted and softened.
4   Pour the cooled soup into a blender and purée until smooth. Alternatively, push it through a fine sieve, using the back of a wooden spoon. Return the puréed soup to the rinsed-out pan.
5   Stir in the finely shredded wilted lettuce and the rest of the butter. Season with salt and freshly ground black pepper to taste. Reheat the soup gently and serve very hot.

🍴 1¼ hours

Country potato soup

Serves 6
500 g /1 lb floury potatoes, thinly sliced
1–2 celery stalks, chopped
600 ml /1 pt beef stock, home-made or from a cube (more if needed)
600 ml /1 pt milk
15 g /½ oz butter
2 large leeks, very finely chopped
15 ml /1 tbls flour
30–45 ml /2–3 tbls freshly chopped parsley
salt and freshly ground black pepper
croûtons (page 14) or crisply fried crumbled bacon, to garnish

1   Put the potatoes and celery in a large, heavy-based saucepan. Cover with 600 ml /1 pt stock and the milk and bring slowly to the boil. Cover partially to prevent the liquid reducing too much and simmer gently for 40–45 minutes, or until the vegetables are practically disintegrating.
2   When the soup is cooked, press the vegetables and stock through a fine sieve, puréeing in a blender first, if wished. Set aside.
3   Melt the butter in the rinsed-out pan, add the finely chopped leeks and cook slowly, covered, for 4–5 minutes, until lightly coloured.
4   Sprinkle with flour and continue to stir over a low heat for a further 2–3 minutes, until the roux becomes a nutty colour. Add the sieved soup gradually, stirring to prevent lumps from forming. Bring to the boil and dilute with more stock if necessary.
5   Add the parsley and season with salt and freshly ground black pepper to taste. Simmer for 5–10 minutes, then serve the soup in heated bowls, garnished with the croûtons or bacon.

🍴 1 hour 15 minutes

CREAM SOUPS

Hot, thick and rich for winter, or light, creamy and chilled for summer, cream soups can meet any occasion, however grand. And these especially delicious soups are easy to prepare.

A cream soup may be either a purée with thick cream and, perhaps, eggs or egg yolks added, or a thickened flavoured liquid. Both types most often have stock – usually chicken – as their basis, though milk or water may be used instead. These delicately flavoured soups are much improved by the use of home-made stocks.

Purée soups are very simple: the ingredients, which may include vegetables, meat, fish, poultry or game, are cooked and then puréed. To turn the soup into a cream soup, add thick cream or a mixture of egg yolks and cream.

Alternatively, soups can be thickened by a roux, by arrowroot, tapioca or sago, by ground nuts or simply by an egg and cream liaison.

A bisque originally signified a simple puréed soup made of pigeons or other game, but over the years it has come to mean one made from prawns or other crustaceans, or from molluscs such as oysters.

Adding eggs

When adding eggs to a soup, it is necessary to take great care that they do not curdle from too high a heat.

To enrich a soup with a whole egg, break the egg into a small bowl and beat it with a fork. Add a little of the hot stock, blend well, then stir the mixture back into the rest of the soup. If only an egg yolk is to be used, beat it with 15 ml / 1 tbls milk or water and add it in the same way as the whole egg.

To use an egg and cream liaison: first beat the eggs and cream together with a fork. Remove the saucepan of soup from the heat and allow it to cool a little before stirring the eggs and cream into it. Then return the saucepan to a gentle heat and reheat the soup, stirring continuously and being careful not to let it boil.

Using yoghurt

If you are a weight-watcher and do not want to use thick cream, you can still enjoy these soups. Simply replace the thick cream with natural yoghurt. But be sure that the soup doesn't boil, or it will curdle.

Crème fraîche

The French crème fraîche is cream that has been allowed to thicken and ferment slightly. It has a slightly tangy flavour, but is not sour. Crème fraîche is excellent in soups as its tangy taste gives a less rich effect than thick cream. Although you would have to go to France to find the real crème fraîche, you can make a very good substitute at home using the following instructions:

Mix two parts thick cream with one part soured cream and leave at room temperature for 5–6 hours, or until it has thickened. Stir, then cover and refrigerate. It will keep for up to one week.

Blender prawn bisque

This rather special-tasting soup is deceptively simple to cook.

🍴 15 minutes

Serves 4–6
225 g / 8 oz boiled, peeled prawns or
   shrimps, defrosted if frozen
90 ml / 6 tbls tomato purée
600 ml / 1 pt chicken stock, home-made or
   from a cube (more if needed)
½ Spanish onion, finely chopped
120 ml / 8 tbls thick cream
1.5 ml / ¼ tsp paprika
salt and freshly ground white pepper
15–30 ml / 1–2 tbls dry sherry
15 ml / 1 tbls finely chopped fresh parsley
15 ml / 1 tbls finely snipped fresh chives

1 Set aside half a dozen of the best prawns or shrimps for garnish and put the remainder in a blender with the tomato purée, chicken stock and finely chopped onion. Blend.
2 Pour the purée into a pan and stir over a low heat until just below boiling point.
3 Add the cream and paprika and season to taste with salt and freshly ground black pepper. Continue to cook over a low heat for 2–3 minutes longer, stirring constantly.
4 Add a little more stock if the soup seems too thick, and flavour with sherry.
5 Serve in heated soup bowls, garnished with the reserved prawns or shrimps and a sprinkling of finely chopped parsley and snipped chives.

Cream of tomato soup

🍴 1 hour

Serves 4
700 g / 1½ lb ripe tomatoes
25 g / 1 oz butter
1 Spanish onion, thinly sliced
1 carrot, thinly sliced
30 ml / 2 tbls flour
600 ml / 1 pt chicken stock, home-made or
   from a cube
bay leaf
15 ml / 1 tbls sugar
a pinch of freshly grated nutmeg
salt and freshly ground black pepper
150 ml / 5 fl oz thick cream or crème fraîche
5–10 ml / 1–2 tsp tomato purée (optional)
15 ml / 1 tbls finely snipped fresh chives

1 Halve the tomatoes horizontally and squeeze out the seeds into a nylon sieve set over a bowl. Using a wooden spoon, press the seeds against the sieve to extract all the juice. Coarsely chop the tomato flesh.
2 Melt the butter in a saucepan, add the thinly sliced onion and carrot and cook gently for 5–6 minutes, until soft. Stir in the flour and cook for a further 3–4 minutes. Add the coarsely chopped tomato flesh, the juice strained from the tomato seeds, chicken stock, bay leaf and sugar. Season to taste with nutmeg, salt and freshly ground black pepper. Bring to the boil, stirring continuously, then reduce the heat and simmer gently, uncovered, for 20–30 minutes.
3 Cool the soup slightly, then purée it in a blender. Rub the soup through a sieve into the rinsed-out saucepan and stir in the thick cream or crème fraîche.
4 Reheat the soup gently. Add the tomato purée, if necessary, to heighten the tomato flavour, and serve the soup, in heated bowls, sprinkled with the snipped chives.

Cold avocado soup

Don't make this soup more than an hour before you want to serve it, or you will risk discoloration and loss of flavour.

🍴 10 minutes,
   then maximum 1 hour chilling

Serves 4
2 large, ripe avocado pears (each 250 g / 8 oz)
600 ml / 1 pt chilled chicken stock, home-
   made or from a cube
15 ml / 1 tbls snipped fresh chives
5 ml / 1 tsp freshly chopped tarragon
150 ml / 5 fl oz thick cream
30–45 ml / 2–3 tbls lemon juice
6–8 drops Tabasco sauce
salt and freshly ground white pepper
finely snipped fresh chives, to garnish

1 Halve the avocados, remove the stones and keep them on 1 side. Using a stainless steel teaspoon, scoop the avocado flesh out of the skin, making sure that you remove all the dark green flesh right next to the skin. Chop the flesh coarsely.
2 Place the chopped avocado flesh in the goblet of a blender with the chilled chicken stock, chives and tarragon. Blend to a smooth purée. Transfer the soup to a large bowl, stir in the thick cream, lemon juice and Tabasco and season to taste with salt and freshly ground white pepper. Drop the avocado stones carefully into the bowl of soup and chill in the refrigerator for no more than 1 hour. The stones help the soup keep its colour.
3 Just before serving, remove the avocado stones from the soup. Pour into individual soup bowls and serve, garnished with the finely snipped chives.

● Be sure to use chilled chicken stock, as hot stock will cook the avocado and produce a slightly bitter-tasting soup.

Saffron soup with fresh herbs (page 36), Cold avocado soup and Cream of tomato soup

Cream of tomato and corn soup

🔪 50 minutes

Serves 6
1 Spanish onion, finely chopped
50 g / 2 oz butter
30 ml / 2 tbls flour
bay leaf
425 ml / 15 fl oz chicken stock, home-made or
    from a cube
800 g / 1 lb 12 oz canned peeled tomatoes
15 ml / 1 tbls sugar
freshly grated nutmeg
salt and freshly ground black pepper
350 ml / 12 oz canned sweetcorn, drained
2 medium-sized egg yolks, beaten
150 ml / 5 fl oz thick cream
10–15 ml / 2–3 tsp freshly chopped chives
10–15 ml / 2–3 tsp freshly chopped parsley

1 In a large saucepan, sauté the onion in butter until transparent. Add the flour and bay leaf and cook, stirring constantly, for 2 minutes. Add the chicken stock and tomatoes and season with sugar, nutmeg, salt and pepper to taste. Simmer for 20 minutes.
2 Reserve 90 ml / 6 tbls of the sweetcorn kernels, add the remainder to the pan and cook for 10 minutes more. Remove the bay leaf, then purée the soup in a blender.
3 Just before serving, add the reserved sweetcorn to the blended soup. Bring the soup slowly to the boil, remove it from the heat, allow it to cool for a few minutes. Blend the egg yolks with 75 ml / 3 fl oz thick cream and 30 ml / 2 tbls of the hot soup. Add to the soup and heat through for a few minutes until slightly thickened. Correct the seasoning and serve in heated bowls, garnished with a swirl of the remaining thick cream and the chopped chives and parsley.

Potato and watercress soup

🔪 1 hour

Serves 4
250 g / 8 oz potatoes, thinly sliced
1 large leek, sliced
1 bunch watercress
600 ml / 1 pt chicken stock, home-made or
    from a cube
1 ham bone (optional)
salt and freshly ground black pepper
200 ml / 7 fl oz thick cream or crème fraîche
sprigs of watercress, to garnish

1 Put the sliced potatoes and the sliced leek in a saucepan. Cut off and discard the bottom third of the watercress stalks. Chop the leaves and stalks and add to the pan.
2 Add the chicken stock and the ham bone, if using. Bring to the boil, season with salt and freshly ground black pepper to taste, cover and simmer gently for 25 minutes or until the vegetables are tender. Leave to cool.

Cream of tomato and corn soup

3 Purée the soup, then pass it through a fine sieve into the rinsed-out saucepan.
4 Reheat gently, then stir in the thick cream or crème fraîche. Heat through over a low heat and correct the seasoning.
5 Pour into a heated soup tureen or individual bowls, garnish and serve.

Fresh mushroom soup

🔪 20–30 minutes,
   plus chilling if serving cold

Serves 4
250 g / 8 oz mushrooms, finely chopped
50 g / 2 oz butter
30 ml / 2 tbls flour
425 ml / 15 fl oz chicken stock, home-made
    or from a cube
150 ml / 5 fl oz milk
30 ml / 2 tbls finely chopped fresh parsley
juice of ½ lemon
150 ml / 5 fl oz thick cream
salt and freshly ground black pepper

1 Blend the mushrooms to a smooth purée. Melt the butter, add the flour and cook gently for 3–4 minutes. Stir in the chicken stock, a little at a time. Bring to the boil, stirring.
2 Add the milk, puréed mushrooms, parsley and lemon juice and cook for 5 minutes. Stir in the cream and season with salt and pepper. Reheat to serve hot, or cool to serve cold.

Pea and cucumber soup

🔪🔪 1 hour

Serves 4–6
250 g / 8 oz frozen peas
1 large potato, sliced
½ Spanish onion, sliced
1 L / 1¾ pt chicken stock, home-made or from
    a cube
50 g / 2 oz butter
1 cucumber, peeled and seeded
2 medium-sized egg yolks
150 ml / 5 fl oz thick cream
salt and freshly ground black pepper
watercress leaves, to garnish

1 Cut off the stem ends of the Brussels sprouts. If the sprouts are young, remove any wilted or damaged outside leaves; if they are older, remove the tough outside leaves entirely. With a sharp knife, cut a cross in the base of each sprout. Soak the sprouts in cold water with a little salt for 15 minutes.
2 Meanwhile, bring the chicken stock to the boil in a large saucepan. Drain the Brussels sprouts and add them, along with the thinly sliced celery and onion. Return to the boil, then lower the heat and simmer for 15–20 minutes, until the vegetables are very soft.
3 Blend the soup to a purée in a blender or rub it through a fine sieve, then season with a pinch of ground cloves and salt and freshly ground black pepper to taste. Thin the soup to the desired consistency with thick cream.
4 If you are serving the soup hot, pour it into the rinsed-out pan and reheat it very gently, stirring all the time, without letting it boil. Pour into heated bowls and garnish each serving with a paper-thin slice of lemon.
5 If you are serving the soup cold, leave it to cool, then chill it in the refrigerator until required. Pour into bowls and garnish with finely snipped fresh chives or young, green spring onion tops.

Curried pineapple soup

🍴 30 minutes,
plus cooling and chilling

Serves 6
25 g / 1 oz butter
30 ml / 2 tbls finely chopped onion
5–10 ml / 1–2 tsp curry powder
15 ml / 1 tbls flour
850 ml / 1½ pt chicken stock, home-made or
from a cube
4 egg yolks
450 g / 1 lb peeled fresh pineapple or drained
canned pineapple, diced
300 ml / 10 fl oz thick cream
salt and freshly ground white pepper
15 ml / 1 tbls finely chopped fresh parsley, to
garnish

1 Melt the butter in a large, heavy-based saucepan. Sauté the finely chopped onion over moderate heat, stirring occasionally, until transparent.
2 Stir the curry powder and flour into the onion. Cook, stirring constantly, for 1–2 minutes. Gradually stir in the chicken stock and bring to the boil, stirring. Remove from the heat.
3 Lightly beat the egg yolks with 60 ml / 4 tbls water, then blend in some of the hot soup mixture. Stir the egg mixture into the soup. Return to the heat and cook gently, stirring with a wooden spoon, until slightly thickened, about 7–8 minutes.
4 Strain the soup through a sieve into a bowl and allow it to cool. Cover and chill in the refrigerator for at least 2 hours.
5 To serve, stir the diced pineapple and the thick cream into the soup until well blended. Add salt and freshly ground white pepper to taste. Spoon into bowls, sprinkle with the chopped parsley and serve.

Place the frozen peas and sliced potato and onion in a large, heavy saucepan. Add 300 ml /10 fl oz of the chicken stock and 25 g /1 oz butter. Simmer for about 20 minutes, until the vegetables are tender. Allow to cool slightly.
Pour the contents of the pan into a blender. Add 125 ml /4 fl oz water and blend until smooth. Press the purée through a sieve, and reserve.
Cut the cucumber into matchstick-sized pieces and simmer in the remaining butter for 5–10 minutes or until tender stirring occasionally to prevent them colouring. Remove the pan from the heat.
Beat the egg yolks lightly. Add the thick cream and the pea purée, and beat until well blended.
Heat the remaining chicken stock. Stir in the puréed mixture and cook over a low heat, stirring constantly, until the soup is smooth and thick. Remove the pan from the heat before the soup comes to the boil to prevent the egg yolks curdling.
Season to taste with salt and freshly ground black pepper. Add the cucumber sticks and watercress leaves to the soup and serve immediately in a heated soup tureen or individual bowls.

Cream of Brussels sprouts soup

Deliciously creamy and smooth, this soup of puréed Brussels sprouts is equally good served hot with paper-thin slices of lemon or cold sprinkled with snipped chives or spring onion tops.

🍴 45 minutes,
plus chilling if serving cold

Serves 4
500 g / 1 lb Brussels sprouts
salt
850 ml / 1½ pt chicken stock, preferably
home-made
1 celery stalk, thinly sliced
1 small onion, thinly sliced
a generous pinch of ground cloves
freshly ground black pepper
about 300 ml / 10 fl oz thick cream
For the garnish (if served hot)
4 paper-thin slices of lemon
For the garnish (if served cold)
15 ml / 1 tbls finely snipped fresh chives or the
tops of young spring onions

Saffron soup with fresh herbs

This truly elegant golden soup takes only a short time to make.

🖌 45 minutes

Serves 4–6
250 g / 8 oz onions, coarsely chopped
250 g / 8 oz potatoes, coarsely chopped
1.1 L / 2 pt milk
1 chicken stock cube, crumbled
1.5–2.5 ml / ¼–½ tsp powdered saffron
salt and freshly ground black pepper
600 ml / 1 pt thick cream
For the garnish
15–30 ml / 1–2 tbls finely chopped fresh
  parsley, chives or tarragon
4–6 very thin lemon slices
30–45 ml / 2–3 tbls salted whipped cream

1 Put the coarsely chopped onions and potatoes in a large pan with the milk and crumbled chicken stock cube. Simmer gently, uncovered, until the potatoes are soft.
2 Leave the mixture to cool a little, then purée it in a blender. Rub the mixture through a sieve into a large bowl, then return it to the rinsed-out pan. Stir in the powdered saffron and season to taste with salt and freshly ground black pepper. Add the thick cream and heat through gently.
3 Pour the soup into heated bowls and sprinkle with finely chopped parsley, chives or tarragon. Garnish each serving with a lemon slice topped with a little salted whipped cream.

Broccoli cream soup

Make this soup with either fresh or frozen broccoli, and serve it hot or cold.

🖌 30 minutes,
   plus chilling if serving cold

Serves 6
850 ml / 1½ pt chicken stock, home-made or
  from a cube
550 g / 1¼ lb fresh or frozen broccoli, sliced
  (defrosted if frozen)
1 stalk celery, thinly sliced
1 small onion, thinly sliced
a generous pinch of ground cloves
salt
freshly ground black pepper
about 300 ml / 10 fl oz thick cream
For the garnish (if served hot)
6 lemon slices
45 ml / 3 tbls salted whipped cream
For the garnish (if served cold)
finely snipped fresh chives or the tops of
  young spring onions

1 Put the chicken stock in a large saucepan and bring to the boil. Add the sliced broccoli and the celery and onion. Bring back to the boil and simmer for 15–20 minutes, or until the vegetables are very soft.
2 Purée all the vegetables and the stock

Pear vichyssoise Rainbow Room

in a blender or rub through a fine sieve.
3 Season to taste with ground cloves, salt and freshly ground black pepper, and thin down to the desired consistency with thick cream.
4 If you are serving the soup hot, reheat it very gently without allowing it to boil, stirring constantly. Pour into a heated soup tureen or serving bowls and garnish with slices of lemon mounded high with a topping of salted whipped cream.
5 If you are serving the soup cold, allow it to cool, then chill well in the refrigerator. Pour into individual serving bowls and sprinkle each one with the finely snipped chives or young spring onion tops.

Pear vichyssoise Rainbow Room

This superb chilled soup comes from the famous Rainbow Room restaurant at the top of the Rockefeller Center in New York City.

🖌 50 minutes,
   plus cooling and chilling

Serves 4
2 ripe pears, peeled, cored and diced
5 ml / 1 tsp lemon juice
25 g / 1 oz butter
white part of 1 leek, thinly sliced
¼ Spanish onion, thinly sliced
175 g / 6 oz potatoes, sliced
600 ml / 1 pt chicken stock, home-made or
  from a cube
425 ml / 15 fl oz thick cream
a pinch of freshly grated nutmeg
salt and freshly ground black pepper
4 small sprigs of watercress, to garnish

1 Place the diced pears in a bowl with the lemon juice and cold water to cover.
2 Melt the butter in a large saucepan and sauté the sliced leek and onion for 3 minute or until soft but not at all coloured. Add the potato, half of the pears (drained) and the chicken stock and simmer, uncovered, for 30 minutes.
3 Cool the soup slightly, then purée in a blender. Pour it into a large bowl and cool.
4 Stir the thick cream into the soup and season it to taste with nutmeg, salt and pepper. Chill.
5 Serve the soup well chilled, garnishing each serving with some of the remaining diced drained pear, a grating of nutmeg and a sprig of watercress.

Chilled salmon cream soup

🍴 25 minutes,
plus cooling and chilling

Serves 4
25 g / 1 oz butter
1 small garlic clove, finely chopped
1 Spanish onion, sliced
1 green pepper, chopped
250 g / 8 oz fresh salmon in 1 piece, skinned
150 ml / 5 fl oz strong chicken stock, home-made or from a cube
275 ml / 10 fl oz milk
1.5 ml / ¼ tsp Tabasco sauce
salt and freshly ground black pepper
150 ml / 5 fl oz thick cream
60 ml / 4 tbls finely chopped fresh dill
30 ml / 2 tbls dry sherry
For the garnish
5 ml / 1 tsp horseradish sauce
60 ml / 4 tbls salted whipped cream

1 Melt the butter in a saucepan and sauté the chopped garlic, sliced onion and chopped green pepper until the onion is transparent.
2 Add the salmon, chicken stock, milk, Tabasco, salt and freshly ground black pepper to taste. Bring to simmering point, then simmer gently for 10 minutes.
3 Cool the soup slightly, then blend to a purée. Transfer to a large bowl and leave until cold.
4 Stir the thick cream and chopped dill into the cold soup, then cover and chill well in the refrigerator.
5 When you are ready to serve the soup, stir in the sherry and pour the soup into individual serving bowls. Fold the horseradish sauce into the salted whipped cream, then garnish each serving with a spoonful of the flavoured cream.

Almond soup

🍴 40 minutes

Serves 4
25 g / 1 oz butter
1 medium-sized onion, finely chopped
1 garlic clove, finely chopped
1 bay leaf
850 ml / 1½ pt chicken stock, home-made or from a cube
175 g / 6 oz almonds, blanched and chopped
1 egg yolk
150 ml / 5 fl oz thick cream
salt and freshly ground white pepper
15 ml / 1 tbls finely chopped fresh parsley

1 In a heavy-based saucepan, melt the butter. Add the finely chopped onion and cook over a moderate heat for 7–10 minutes or until softened, stirring occasionally.
2 Stir in the finely chopped garlic and add the bay leaf, chicken stock and chopped almonds. Bring to the boil, then reduce the heat, cover and simmer gently for 20 minutes. Remove and discard the bay leaf. Leave to cool slightly.

3 Blend the slightly cooled soup to a purée, then return to the rinsed-out saucepan through a fine sieve.
4 In a bowl, blend the egg yolk and thick cream together, add a little of the hot soup, then return to the pan. Reheat gently without boiling. Season with a little salt and white pepper to taste.
5 Pour into a heated soup tureen. Garnish with finely chopped parsley and serve.

Senegalese soup

🍴 30 minutes,
plus cooling and chilling

Serves 4–6
15 g / ½ oz butter
15 ml / 1 tbls very finely chopped onion
2.5–5 ml / ½–1 tsp curry powder
850 ml / 1½ pt well-flavoured chicken stock, preferably home-made
100 g / 4 oz cooked chicken breast meat, cut into thin strips
4 egg yolks
300 ml / 10 fl oz thick cream
salt and freshly ground white pepper
15–30 ml / 1–2 tbls freshly chopped parsley

1 Heat the butter in a large saucepan. Add the finely chopped onion and cook gently, stirring occasionally, until it is very soft but not brown. Add the curry powder to taste and cook, stirring constantly, for 3–4 minutes.
2 Add the chicken stock and bring to the boil, stirring, then add the thin strips of chicken. Remove from the heat and allow to cool a little.
3 Beat the egg yolks and half of the thick cream in a small bowl until well blended. Add a little of the hot soup and return to the pan. Reheat gently without boiling, stirring with the wooden spoon. When the soup has thickened slightly, add salt and freshly ground white pepper to taste and leave to cool.
4 When the soup is completely cold, whip the remaining thick cream. Stir most of the whipped cream into the soup, reserving a little for the garnish. Chill the soup and the reserved whipped cream in the refrigerator for about 2 hours.
5 To serve, pour the soup into individual bowls and top each with a spoonful of whipped cream and then with some freshly chopped parsley.

Senegalese soup

Peanut soup

Serves 4–6
15 g / ½ oz butter
1 small onion, finely chopped
5 ml / 1 tsp curry powder
850 ml / 1½ pt chicken stock, home-made or from a cube
100–150 g / 4–5 oz smooth peanut butter
4 egg yolks
300 ml / 10 fl oz thick cream
salt and freshly ground black pepper
15–30 ml / 1–2 tbls freshly snipped chives

1   Heat the butter in a large saucepan. Add the onion, cover and cook gently until soft and transparent, about 10 minutes. Add the curry powder and cook, stirring, for 2–3 minutes.
2   Add the chicken stock and peanut butter and bring to the boil. Whisk well, then allow to cool a little.
3   Beat the egg yolks and thick cream with a fork until well blended, add a little of the hot soup, then return to the saucepan.
4   Reheat over a very low heat, stirring constantly, until the soup has thickened. Correct seasoning; the soup may already be salty enough, as both chicken stock and peanuts contain salt.
5   Sprinkle the soup with freshly snipped chives and serve at once.

 30 minutes

Green summer soup

Serves 4
850 ml / 1½ pt chicken stock, home-made or from a cube
120 ml / 8 tbls finely chopped fresh parsley
90 ml / 6 tbls finely chopped watercress
300 ml / 10 fl oz thick cream
2 egg yolks, beaten
lemon juice
salt
a pinch of cayenne pepper

1   In a large saucepan bring the chicken stock, finely chopped parsley and watercress to the boil. Reduce the heat and simmer gently for 15 minutes.
2   Allow the soup to cool slightly, then transfer it to a blender. Blend until the herbs have completely disintegrated and the soup is smooth and green.
3   In a small bowl, stir together the thick cream and beaten egg yolks with a little of the hot soup. Add them to the soup and blend again until smooth.
4   Reheat the soup over a low heat, stirring constantly, until slightly thickened. Do not allow the soup to boil, or it will curdle.
5   Remove the soup from the heat, add a squeeze of lemon juice and season with salt and cayenne pepper to taste. Cool the soup, then chill in the refrigerator. Serve the soup very cold.

40 minutes,
plus cooling and chilling

Fish and saffron soup

Serves 4

250 g /8 oz onions, sliced	**For the green butter**
250 g /8 oz potatoes, sliced	15–30 ml /1–2 tbls finely
450 ml /15 fl oz milk	chopped fresh parsley
1 chicken stock cube,	50 g /2 oz butter, softened
crumbled	lemon juice
350 g /12 oz halibut, turbot,	freshly ground black pepper
flounder or sole, filleted,	**For the garnish**
skinned and cut into 4 pieces	4 thin slices of lemon
salt	30 ml /2 tbls salted whipped
600 ml /1 pt thick cream	cream
2.5 ml /½ tsp powdered saffron	15 ml /1 tbls finely chopped
a pinch of turmeric (optional)	fresh herbs
freshly ground black pepper	heart-shaped croûtons

1   Place the sliced onions, potatoes, milk and chicken stock cube in a saucepan, bring to the boil, then cook gently for about 15 minutes, until the vegetables are soft.
2   Meanwhile, make the green butter. Pound the finely chopped parsley in a mortar and work in the softened butter. Season to taste with lemon juice and freshly ground black pepper. Chill until needed.
3   Allow the soup to cool slightly, then blend the mixture to a purée and strain through a fine sieve.
4   Place the fish in a pan and cover with salted water. Poach for 5 minutes or until just tender. Drain and remove any bones from the fish. Keep warm.
5   Place the soup over a low heat, add the cream and saffron (and a little turmeric for added colour, if liked), and bring to the boil. Simmer for 5 minutes, stirring, then add the pieces of fish. Season and heat through gently.
6   Spread the croutons with the chilled green butter. Serve the soup hot in heated soup bowls, with a piece of fish in each bowl. Garnish with a slice of lemon topped with a little salted whipped cream and a dusting of finely chopped herbs, and serve with the croûtons and green butter.

1 hour

Blender spinach soup

Serves 4

50 g /2 oz butter
1 kg /2 lb fresh spinach, chopped
275 ml /10 fl oz thick cream
275 ml /10 fl oz chicken stock, home-made or from a cube
salt and freshly ground black pepper

1   Melt the butter in a medium-sized, heavy-based saucepan over a low heat. Add the chopped spinach and cook gently, stirring constantly, until tender. Remove the pan from the heat and allow to cool slightly.
2   Blend the spinach to a purée in an electric blender. Return the purée to the rinsed-out saucepan and stir in 225 ml /8 fl oz of the cream and the chicken stock. Season with salt and freshly ground black pepper to taste.
3   Reheat the soup over a low heat, stirring constantly with a wooden spoon. Ladle into heated soup bowls, swirl a little of the reserved cream in each bowl, and serve immediately.

● Frozen spinach can be used instead of fresh for this delightfully easy soup; use only 500 g /1 lb and do not defrost before cooking.

30 minutes

CONSOMMES

Few things can rival a carefully clarified consommé as an elegant first course. Refine home-made stocks to make them sparkling clear, then flavour and garnish the clarified stock to make sophisticated soups.

Clarification is the term used in cooking to describe the refining of a home-made stock, to remove small floating particles and to turn the cloudy liquid into a clear, sparkling one. The stock is simmered with flavouring and colouring additions (onion and leek, carrot or celery and a little minced raw beef or fish) and also with crushed egg shells and frothed egg whites. The gradual coagulation of the egg whites throughout the soup gathers up all the bits into a 'head', and this is discarded.

Once the stock has been clarified, it becomes consommé. This elegant, sophisticated soup can be served as it is, usually garnished with vegetable shapes. Or it can be used, with the addition of gelatine, to make aspic jelly.

Clarifying stock

To clarify stock you will need a 3.4 L /6 pt heavy-bottomed saucepan (enamelled or stainless steel is best), a balloon whisk or wooden spoon, a large sieve or colander, a piece of muslin or a clean tea-towel and a large bowl.

To prepare the pan and cloth, three-quarters fill the 3.4 L /6 pt saucepan with cold water and bring it to the boil. Line a large sieve or colander with the clean tea-towel or piece of muslin and pour the boiling water through it to remove any possible taste of detergent. Wring out the cloth and wipe out the pan. Both are now scrupulously clean and ready to use for simmering the stock, vegetables and meat, before straining them to make the consommé, as shown in the step-by-step pictures below.

Finishing consommé

If you are going to use the consommé immediately, remove any fat by drawing strips of absorbent paper across the surface. Alternatively, cool and chill the consommé, then remove the coagulated fat from the surface. Meat or chicken consommé can be stored for up to a week, fish consommé for only a day or two. All consommés that have been stored should be reboiled before serving, so remember to allow enough time for the consommé to cool again if you wish to serve it cold.

Variations on consommé

● Consommé à l'orange: garnish each bowl of consommé with 2.5–5 ml /½–1 tsp finely shredded watercress leaves and half a slice of unpeeled orange, cut into 3 wedges.
● Tarragon consommé: add 3 sprigs of fresh tarragon to 1.1 L /2 pt cold consommé, bring slowly to the boil, then cover the pan and leave to infuse in a warm place (over the pilot light or in a low oven) for 20 minutes. Strain the consommé through a muslin-lined sieve. Garnish each portion with 2 or 3 blanched tarragon leaves or a sprinkling of chopped fresh tarragon.
● Madeira or sherry consommé: flavour 1.1 L /2 pt beef consommé with 15 ml /1 tbls dry Madeira or dry sherry before serving.
● Consommé with pasta: pasta shapes, of which there are an infinite variety in different sizes, can all be used to garnish a consommé. Add 50 g /2 oz pasta shapes to 1.1 L /2 pt boiling consommé and simmer for 15–18 minutes. Serve immediately.

Consommé orientale (page 43)

How to clarify stock

Combine the finely chopped vegetables and minced meat or fish in the cleaned saucepan. Whisk the 2–3 egg whites to a froth and add, with the crushed shells, to the vegetable mixture.

Remove all the fat from the surface of the stock (if it is cold, it will be set like a lid). Pour the stock into a second large pan, without disturbing any sediment at the bottom of the stock. Bring to the boil.

Pour the boiling stock onto the egg whi mixture in the saucepan, a little at a tim whisking with a balloon whisk or beatin constantly with a wooden spoon so that t egg whites do not cook.

Your sparkling, clear consommé will make a delicious soup as it is, served hot or cold. With the addition of flavourings and carefully prepared garnishes, it is transformed into an elegant first course.

You can serve most of the consommés in this chapter cold as well as hot; only Saffron seafood consommé, Soup with eggs Pavianstyle and Watercress consommé with lemon dumplings cannot be served cold.

If you want to serve a consommé cold, first allow it to cool, then chill it lightly in the refrigerator. Keep an eye on the consommé, and if it shows signs of setting remove it from the refrigerator and leave it to stand at room temperature.

Beef consommé

🕐 🍴 making the stock, then 1½ hours

Makes 1.1 L/2 pt, serves 6
350 g/12 oz lean minced beef
2 leeks, trimmed and fairly finely chopped
2 celery stalks, fairly finely chopped
½ Spanish onion, fairly finely chopped
2 soft, over-ripe tomatoes, chopped (optional)
whites and crushed shells of 2 eggs
1.7 L/3 pt cold, home-made beef stock (see page 10), skimmed of all fat

1 In a large, heavy-bottomed saucepan, combine the lean minced beef, fairly finely chopped leeks, celery, onion and soft tomatoes, if using. Whisk the egg whites until frothy and add to the pan with the crushed shells. Mix well.
2 Place the stock in a separate pan and bring to the boil. Pour it, a little at a time, onto the egg white mixture, whisking constantly. Bring the mixture to the boil, whisking all the time. As soon as the mixture comes to the boil, stop whisking. Turn the heat right

ring the mixture slowly to the boil, whisking the time. As soon as it comes to the boil, op whisking. Reduce the heat, then allow e thick scum to rise to the surface of the ock.

Simmer very gently, uncovered, for 1 hour (or just 5 minutes for fish stock). Do not stir. Remove from the heat, then gently draw back the scum from one quarter of the surface to reveal the clear stock below.

Line a sieve with scalded muslin and stand it over a bowl. Ladle the clarified stock into the sieve (being careful not to disturb the scum). Use a bulb baster if you prefer. The liquid in the bowl is now consommé.

down, then allow the thick pad of foam to rise to the surface. Simmer very gently, uncovered, for 1 hour. Do not stir.

3   Line a large sieve or colander with muslin and stand it over a bowl. Using a slotted spoon, gently draw the scum back from about one quarter of the clarified stock. Lower a ladle through this gap and, disturbing the scum as little as possible, ladle the clarified stock into the muslin-lined sieve or colander. (Alternatively, draw off the stock with a bulb baster, then pass the clear stock through the muslin.)

4   If you do not intend to use the consommé immediately, leave it to cool, then chill it in the refrigerator. Carefully lift off any congealed fat from the surface of the cold consommé, then transfer the consommé to storage jars, cover and chill until needed. It will keep for up to a week, but must be reboiled before use, even if you intend to serve it cold.

5   If you wish to use the consommé as soon as you have made it, skim the fat by drawing strips of absorbent paper over the surface, or by drawing off the fatless consommé with a bulb baster.

6   Either serve the consommé as it is, piping hot or lightly chilled, or, alternatively, use the beef consommé as a base to make one of the more complex consommés on the following pages.

Chicken consommé

making stock,
then 1½ hours

Makes 1.1 L /2 pt, serves 6
350 g /12 oz pie veal, minced
2 leeks, trimmed and fairly finely chopped
2 celery stalks, fairly finely chopped
2 carrots, fairly finely chopped
½ Spanish onion, fairly finely chopped
whites and crushed shells of 2 eggs
1.7 L /3 pt cold, home-made chicken stock
    (page 11), skimmed of all fat

1   In a large, heavy-bottomed saucepan combine the minced veal, fairly finely chopped leeks, celery, carrots and onion. Whisk the egg whites until frothy and add to the pan of meat and vegetables with the crushed shells. Mix well.

2   Place the stock in a separate pan and bring to the boil. Pour it, a little at a time, onto the egg white mixture, whisking constantly. Bring the mixture to the boil, whisking all the time. As soon as the mixture comes to the boil, stop whisking. Turn the heat right down, then allow the thick pad of foam to rise to the surface. Simmer very gently, uncovered, for 1 hour. Do not stir.

3   Line a large sieve or colander with muslin and stand it over a bowl. Using a slotted spoon, gently draw the scum back from about one quarter of the clarified stock. Lower a ladle through this gap and, disturbing the scum as little as possible, ladle the clarified stock into the muslin-lined sieve or colander. (Alternatively, draw off the clear stock with a bulb baster, plunging it to the bottom each time, then pass the clear stock through the muslin.)

42

4   If you do not intend to use the consommé immediately, leave it to cool, then chill it in the refrigerator. Carefully lift off any congealed fat from the surface of the cold consommé, then transfer the consommé to storage jars, cover and chill until needed. It will keep for up to a week, but must be reboiled before use, even if you intend to serve it cold.

5   If you wish to use the consommé as soon as you have made it, skim off the fat by drawing strips of absorbent paper across the surface, or by drawing off the fatless consommé with a bulb baster.

6   Serve the chicken consommé as it is, piping hot or lightly chilled. Alternatively, you can use it as a base to make one of the more complex consommés on the following pages.

Fish consommé

making stock,
then 40 minutes

Makes 850 ml /1½ pt, serves 4
125 g /4 oz lemon sole, filleted and
    minced
½ Spanish onion, finely chopped
1 carrot, finely chopped
white part of 1 leek, finely chopped
3 parsley stalks
3–4 mushroom stalks, finely chopped
10 white peppercorns
bay leaf
a pinch of dried thyme
1.5 ml /¼ tsp tomato purée
juice of 1 lemon
3 egg whites, whisked to a froth
1.5 ml /¼ tsp salt
1.1 L /2 pt cold fish stock (page 11)

1   In a large, heavy-bottomed saucepan place the minced lemon sole, finely chopped Spanish onion, carrot and leek, the parsley and mushroom stalks, peppercorns, bay leaf dried thyme, tomato purée, lemon juice whisked egg whites and salt.

2   Place the stock in a separate pan and bring to the boil. Pour it, a little at a time onto the egg white mixture, whisking constantly. Bring the mixture to the boil, whisking continuously. As soon as the mixture comes to the boil, stop whisking. Turn the heat right down, then allow the thick pad of foam to rise to the surface. Simmer the stock uncovered, for 5 minutes.

3   Remove the pan from the heat, cover with a lid and leave to infuse for 10 minutes.

4   Line a large sieve or a colander with a piece of clean muslin and stand it over a bowl. Using a slotted spoon, gently draw the scum back from about one quarter of the clarified stock. Lower a ladle through this gap and disturbing the scum as little as possible, ladle the clarified stock into the muslin-lined sieve or colander and leave to drain. (Alternatively, draw off the clear stock with a bulb baster, then pass the clear stock through the muslin-lined sieve.)

5   If you do not intend to use the consommé immediately, leave it to cool, then transfer it to storage jars, cover and chill for no more than 2 days. Bring the consommé to the boil before using it.

● Fish stock is more difficult to clarify than meat stock, owing to its high protein content If you find that your consommé is not absolutely clear after this operation, strain it into a clean pan and start the clarification process over again.

Consommé creole

Saffron seafood consommé

Consommé creole

This delicious, light consommé can be served either hot or cold.

🔪🔪 making consommé,
then 30 minutes

Serves 6
1.1 L /2 pt chicken consommé (see recipe)
For the garnish
75 g /3 oz long-grain rice
1 green pepper
4–5 medium-sized tomatoes, blanched,
   skinned, halved and seeded

1   Rinse the long-grain rice in a sieve under cold running water until the water runs clear. Shake out as much water as possible and dab the rice completely dry with a clean cloth or absorbent paper.
2   Place the chicken consommé in a large saucepan and bring to the boil. Add the rice, bring back to the boil, stir twice, then cover and simmer very gently for 15 minutes. (Be careful that you do not overcook the rice.)
3   Meanwhile prepare the garnish. Using a sharp knife, cut 2 squares from the pepper, each 20 mm /¾ in across, and then cut them to make 9 smaller squares from each one. Then cut 18 squares, each 10 mm /½ in across, from the tomatoes.
4   Add the squares of green pepper and peeled tomato and continue to simmer for 3–5 minutes, until the rice is just cooked and the diced peppers and tomatoes are tender.
5   Either serve the consommé immediately in heated individual bowls, or leave it to cool, then chill it slightly in the refrigerator before serving in chilled bowls.

Consommé with vegetable julienne

🔪🔪 making consommé,
then 25 minutes

Serves 6
green part of 1 medium-sized leek
2 medium-sized carrots
1 turnip, or a chunk of swede
15 g /½ oz butter,
   plus extra for greasing
1.1 L /2 pt beef consommé (see recipe)
butter, for greasing

1   Prepare the garnish: cut all the vegetables into sticks, about 4 mm /1½ in long and as thin as matchsticks.
2   Place the vegetable sticks in a pan with the 15 g /½ oz butter and 150 ml /5 fl oz of the beef consommé. Cover the surface with a piece of buttered greaseproof paper, bring to the boil and simmer gently for about 5 minutes, until the vegetables are tender but still crisp.
3   Add the remaining consommé to the pan and bring to the boil. Ladle into heated individual bowls and serve immediately, or cool and chill slightly before serving in chilled bowls.

● For Consommé brunoise, cut the vegetables into 3 mm /⅛ in dice and cook them in the butter and stock for 5 minutes until tender but still crisp.

Consommé orientale

🔪🔪 making consommé,
then 20–30 minutes

Serves 6
1.1 L /2 pt beef consommé (see recipe)
For the garnish
50 g /2 oz carrot, sliced and cut into small
   shapes
50 g /2 oz turnip, sliced and cut into small
   shapes
salt
25 g /1 oz long-grain rice
a pinch of saffron powder
50 g /2 oz cooked beetroot, sliced and cut into
   small shapes

1   Cook the carrot and turnip shapes in boiling salted water until tender but still crisp. Drain and rinse under cold water.
2   Cook the rice in boiling salted water with a pinch of saffron. Drain well.
3   Place the consommé in a large pan with the carrot and turnip shapes and the saffron rice, and bring to boiling point. Remove the pan from the heat so it does not boil.
4   Serve the consommé hot or cold, adding the cooked beetroot shapes just before serving. (Do not add them before the last moment, or they will colour the consommé.)

● The classic shape for the vegetables in a Consommé orientale is tiny crescents, but you can cut them into other pretty shapes.

Saffron seafood consommé

🔪🔪 making consommé,
then 30 minutes

Serves 4
4 tightly closed mussels, washed and scraped
2.5 ml /½ tsp powdered saffron
60 ml /4 tbls dry white wine
1 sole fillet, cut into 4 thin strips
4 oysters
8 boiled, peeled prawns, defrosted
   if frozen
850 ml /1½ pt fish consommé (see recipe)
30 ml /2 tbls finely snipped fresh chives or
   finely chopped fresh tarragon

1   Put 10 mm /½ in water in a saucepan, add the mussels, cover and cook over a medium heat, shaking regularly, until the mussels open (2–3 minutes). Remove the mussels from their shells.
2   Place the saffron in a small pan with the dry white wine and bring to a gentle simmer, stirring. Poach the strips of sole in this mixture for 1–2 minutes, until they are opaque. Remove with a slotted spoon, reserving the saffron-wine mixture.
3   Open the oysters, pour off the liquid and poach the oysters in the saffron-wine mixture until they begin to curl at the edges. Remove them from the liquid with a slotted spoon and trim off the curled edges. Add the prawns to the saffron-wine mixture and heat through. Remove with a slotted spoon.
4   Place a mussel, a strip of sole, an oyster and 2 prawns in each of 4 heated soup bowls. Add the consommé to the saffron-wine mixture and bring to the boil. Pour the consommé over the fish and sprinkle with chives or tarragon. Serve immediately.

43

Consommé niçoise

Serves 6
500 g /1 lb ripe tomatoes, blanched, skinned, seeded and roughly
*   chopped*
2 celery stalks, roughly chopped
1.1 L /2 pt chicken consommé (see recipe)
salt and freshly ground black pepper
For the garnish
250 g /8 oz firm tomatoes
200 g /7 oz canned pimentos
50 g /2 oz French beans, cooked and diced
50 g /2 oz potatoes, cooked and diced
15–30 ml /1–2 tbls finely chopped fresh chervil or parsley

1   Put the roughly chopped tomatoes and celery into a large
saucepan with the chicken consommé. Bring to the boil, then reduce
the heat and simmer for 30 minutes.
2   Meanwhile, make the garnish. Blanch, skin and seed the
tomatoes. Cut the flesh into 3 mm /⅛ in dice. Drain the pimentos
and cut them into 3 mm /⅛ in dice.
3   Strain the consommé through a muslin-lined sieve into a clean
pan. Add the diced tomatoes and pimentos, and the cooked diced
French beans and potatoes. Season to taste with salt and freshly
ground black pepper. Bring the consommé to boiling point and
immediately remove it from the heat.
4   Ladle the consommé into individual heated soup bowls. Sprinkle
with finely chopped chervil or parsley and serve immediately.

● In this recipe, tomatoes and celery are cooked with the consommé
and then strained; this is to intensify the flavour of the finished
consommé.
● This consommé is also delicious chilled slightly before serving.
Sprinkle with the herbs at the last minute.

 making consommé,
then 1 hour

Mushroom and watercress consommé

Serves 4
30 ml /2 tbls dried mushrooms
½ bunch of watercress
250 g /8 oz button mushrooms
1.1 L /2 pt chicken or beef consommé (see recipes)
salt and freshly ground black pepper
lemon juice (optional)

1   Soak the dried mushrooms in hot water for at least 2 hours.
Wash the watercress, discarding any damaged or discoloured leaves.
Separate the leaves from the stems.
2   Reserve 2–4 whole button mushrooms for garnish and chop the
remainder finely. Combine the chopped mushrooms in a saucepan
with the chicken or beef consommé.
3   Drain the liquid from the dried mushrooms into a small bowl,
then squeeze the dried mushrooms over the bowl to extract their
juice. Discard the dried mushrooms.
4   Add the dried mushroom juice and watercress stems to the
consommé. Bring to the boil, lower the heat and simmer for 10
minutes. Correct the seasoning, adding a little salt and freshly
ground black pepper, and lemon juice, if wished, to taste.
5   Strain the consommé into soup bowls and garnish each serving
with a few slices of fresh, raw mushroom and watercress leaves.

 making consommé, 2 hours soaking,
then 25 minutes

Soup with eggs Pavian-style

Serves 6
6 rounds French bread
40–50 g /1½–2 oz butter
45 ml /3 tbls freshly grated Parmesan cheese
6 very fresh eggs (see below)
1.1 L /2 pts hot beef consommé (see recipe)

1 Fry the rounds of French bread in butter until golden on both sides.
2 Lay a round of bread at the bottom of each of 6 soup bowls. Sprinkle each round with 7.5 ml /½ tbls freshly grated Parmesan cheese.
3 Break an egg into each bowl to one side of (not over) the bread, taking great care not to break the yolk.
4 Bring the consommé to the boil and, without removing the pan from the heat, carefully ladle boiling consommé into each bowl. Serve immediately.

● This famous Italian soup, *zuppa alla pavese*, comes from Pavia in north-west Italy; it is an Italian classic and very simple to make. You must use very fresh eggs, otherwise the white will run all over the bottom of the bowl and turn into a nasty froth when it comes into contact with the boiling consommé.

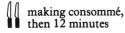
making consommé, then 12 minutes

Watercress consommé with lemon dumplings

Serves 6

For the dumplings
50 g /2 oz stale, coarse breadcrumbs
1.5 ml /¼ tsp grated lemon zest
a large pinch of dried thyme
5 ml /1 tsp freshly chopped parsley
25 g /1 oz softened butter
1 medium-sized egg yolk
salt
freshly ground black pepper
freshly grated nutmeg

For the consommé
4 sprigs of watercress
2 medium-sized carrots
2–4 celery stalks
3–4 green leaves of leek
850 ml /1½ pt beef consommé (see recipe)
45–60 ml /3–4 tbls dry Madeira
10 ml /2 tsp finely chopped fresh parsley

1 Place the ingredients for the dumplings in a large mixing bowl and knead together to form a smooth paste. Roll the dumpling mixture into a sausage shape and chill for 30 minutes.
2 Meanwhile, prepare the vegetables for the consommé – remove the watercress leaves from the stems and reserve. Thinly slice the carrots and celery stalks and finely dice the leek leaves.
3 Divide the chilled dumpling mixture into 36 portions and roll each one into a neat ball.
4 Poach the dumplings in a large pan of simmering, salted water for 15–20 minutes, or until they bob to the surface. Drain and reserve.
5 To make the consommé, simmer the thinly sliced carrots and celery and diced leek leaves with the watercress stems in one third of the beef consommé for 8–10 minutes, or until the vegetables are cooked through.
6 Remove the watercress stems and add the remaining beef consommé to the pan. Stir in the watercress leaves and Madeira to taste. Heat through.
7 Serve the consommé in warmed bowls, garnished with the dumplings and finely chopped parsley.

● If the carrot and celery are thick, halve or quarter them lengthways before slicing.

making consommé, 10 minutes, plus 30 minutes chilling, then 45 minutes

Gazpacho

Serves 4
6 large ripe tomatoes, blanched and skinned
½ Spanish onion, thinly sliced
1 green pepper, seeded and thinly sliced
½ cucumber, peeled and thinly sliced
1 clove garlic, finely chopped
salt and freshly ground black pepper
dash of Tabasco sauce
90 ml /6 tbls olive oil
45 ml /3 tbls wine vinegar
150–300 ml /5–10 fl oz chicken consommé, chilled (see recipe)
15 ml /1 tbls finely chopped fresh parsley or chives
For the garlic croûtons
1 garlic clove
4 rounds of French bread
25–40 g /1–1½ oz butter

1   Quarter and seed the tomatoes, dice the flesh coarsely and combine in a bowl with the thinly sliced onion, green pepper and cucumber and finely chopped garlic. Season to taste with salt and freshly ground black pepper and a dash of Tabasco sauce.
2   Add the olive oil and wine vinegar, stir to blend and leave to marinate for at least 30 minutes in the refrigerator.
3   Meanwhile, prepare the garlic croûtons. Cut the garlic clove in half and rub each round of bread on both sides with the cut side of the garlic clove. Reserve the garlic clove. Heat the butter in a frying-pan and sauté the bread on both sides until golden. Remove from the pan and rub both sides of the croûtons again with the reserved cut garlic clove.
4   Just before serving, lift off any cold, congealed fat from the surface of the chilled chicken consommé. Add the consommé and the chopped parsley or chives to the vegetables in the marinade. Stir to blend, adjust the seasoning and pour into a large tureen. Serve with the garlic croûtons.

making consommé,
then 50 minutes including marinating

Consommé Celestine

Serves 8
1.1 L /2 pt beef or chicken consommé (see recipe)
60 ml /4 tbls freshly grated Parmesan cheese
For the pancake garnish
25 g /1 oz flour
pinch of salt
½ large egg, lightly beaten
75 ml /3 fl oz milk
2.5 ml /½ tsp olive oil
5 ml /1 tsp finely chopped fresh parsley
2.5 ml /½ tsp finely snipped fresh chives
a large pinch of finely chopped fresh tarragon
oil for greasing

1   Make the pancake batter. Sift the flour and salt into a bowl. Make a well in the centre. Add the lightly beaten egg and gradually pour in the milk, stirring from the centre with a wooden spoon to incorporate the flour smoothly. When the batter is free of lumps, stir in the olive oil and the finely chopped herbs. Cover and leave to rest for at least 1 hour before making the pancakes.
2   Heat the consommé just before making the pancakes and keep it warm.
3   Heat an 18 cm /7 in frying-pan until a few drops of water sprinkled on the surface sizzle away almost immediately. Once the pan is hot, grease it with a wad of absorbent paper soaked in oil. Spoon about 30 ml /2 tbls batter into the pan and swirl it around so that the batter completely covers the base.
4   Cook over a moderate heat until the pancake is opaque and dry on top, with air bubbles starting to form under the surface. Turn it over with a palette knife and cook on the other side. Remove it from the pan. Sprinkle it with 15 ml /1 tbls freshly grated Parmesan cheese and roll up tightly. Keep it warm while you make the remaining 3 pancakes.
5   When you have finished cooking the pancakes and are ready to serve, slice each pancake thinly and place half a pancake in each soup bowl. Pour the hot consommé over the pancakes and serve immediately.

making the consommé,
then 2 hours including resting batter

Starters

SIMPLE STARTERS

A glamorous starter can set the scene for an impressive meal, whetting the appetites of your guests and keeping them in a state of delicious anticipation for the food that is to follow.

Simple, quick starters that need no special effort are the best ones to experiment with first. They are the ideal, no-fuss start to a meal as you can do all the work in advance, and, because they are light and attractive to serve, they will do their proper job – to tempt the appetite before the main courses are served, rather than blunt it.

The majority of the ideas given in this chapter require little more than basic cooking processes and use easily available salad and store cupboard ingredients. But they do demonstrate one of the cardinal rules of cooking – careful attention to detail. There is a world of difference between clumsily hacked herbs and those that have been finely chopped; between vegetables sliced thinly and evenly with a sharp knife and thick chunks mutilated by a blunt blade; or between a simple salad dressing carefully prepared with good olive oil and wine-flavoured vinegar or fresh lemon juice and some seasoned witches' brew that smothers flavours when it is meant to enhance them.

Elegant hors d'oeuvre ideas

In Paris or any other French city, one of the first things you notice when you enter a small restaurant or bistro is a selection of little rectangular dishes filled with a variety of simple salads – thin slices of ripe, red tomatoes brushed with a little olive oil and wine vinegar and sprinkled with finely chopped parsley, spring onion tops or chives; finely shredded carrot dressed with a pinch of sugar and a little lemon juice or a delicate balance of vinegar and olive oil; a salad of cooked green beans in a tarragon-flavoured dressing; and some halved hard-boiled eggs delicately bathed in golden, freshly-made mayonnaise. These simple basics are usually accompanied by a dish of crisp, white radishes and one of sardines in oil, as well as freshly-baked French bread.

You can serve your own selection of hors d'oeuvres as a starter: arrange an assortment of small dishes of crisp, uncooked vegetables in a well-flavoured dressing.

Clockwise: cut the top from a fresh chilli, slice down in strips and fold them back for a flower. Cut a lily petal from a pepper and use a cocktail stick to attach a spring onion for a stem and a piece of turnip for the centre. Cut a spring onion down in strips and soak in cold water to open. Snip carrot or turnip slices for flowers. To make an accordian, make cuts almost through a radish and soak in iced water to open. For a chrysanthemum, cut through a button onion many times and soak in iced water until it opens. Cut a pimento flower with a tiny biscuit cutter, sculpt a flower from a carrot or cut a wheel. Make a tomato rose by winding up thinly pared tomato skin.

Bring out the flavour of a dish of chilled, sliced tomatoes with spring onion segments, serve dishes of radishes and olives, and add a salad of crisp, peeled, sliced cucumber, dressed with lemon juice, thick cream and herbs. Dress up the selection with a dish of Italian sausage, Parma ham or hard-boiled eggs masked with home-made mayonnaise.

Quick vegetable ideas

Radishes: wash and trim tops and tails. Serve with a sprinkling of coarse sea salt, olive oil and lemon juice.

Olives are improved by marinating in several spoonfuls of olive oil, a crumbled bay leaf and a sprinkling of rosemary. Leave for several days, turning regularly. The olives will plump up and acquire a luxurious flavour.

Canned vegetables are invaluable for mixed starters. Drain and rinse them and marinate for 1 hour in a well-seasoned vinaigrette. Add a little finely chopped onion and fresh herbs or chopped capers to serve.

Try some of the following ideas: artichoke hearts cut into thin strips and tossed with mayonnaise or vinaigrette; tiny new potatoes with soured cream dressing, topped with crumbled grilled bacon; red kidney beans or chick peas tossed in vinaigrette flavoured with chopped parsley; thin strips of red pimento tossed in vinaigrette dressing with finely chopped parsley, anchovies and garlic; tiny pickled beets served sliced with a soured cream dressing.

Quick ideas with seafood

Canned anchovy fillets: drain and serve them in individual dishes, topped with thin strips of canned pimento or bottled capers. Dress them up with a little fresh olive oil and a squeeze of lemon juice to bring out the flavour. Use them to decorate and give a unique, salty flavour to other hors d'oeuvres: make thin strips by cutting the fillets lengthways and arrange them over a fresh tomato salad; sprinkle chopped anchovies on a haricot bean salad, a potato salad or a hard-boiled egg mayonnaise. Use finely chopped anchovies in a vinaigrette.

Canned crab: toss pieces of crab with diced tomato, avocado and hard-boiled egg in a well-flavoured vinaigrette dressing. Try mixing crab with a little chopped onion and green pepper in home-made mayonnaise.

Canned sardines: serve the sardines on fingers of buttered toast, garnished with

How to slice, dice and chop

Chopping onions: top, use coarsely chopped onions for a raw garnish: cut into thin slices and dice. Left, medium chopped onion; right, finely chopped onion.

Slice vegetables thinly with a small, sharp knife. Cut celery and carrots across the grain. Bottom, cut vegetables on the bias for slices that are bigger but are no thicker.

For vegetable matchsticks or julienne strips, cut 5 cm /2 in lengths and square up ends. Slice lengthways thinly, then cut again into strips keeping the width the same.

---

sieved hard-boiled egg yolk, or a little finely chopped parsley and a squeeze of lemon juice or, more simply, as they are, as part of an hors d'oeuvre selection. I like to mash sardines, too, with a little lemon juice, curry powder, finely chopped onion and mayonnaise or butter to serve as a pâté.

Canned tuna fish can be served in its own oil, or mix it with pimento strips or green beans. Mash it with lemon juice, finely chopped onion and mayonnaise to make a pâté or spread.

Smoked trout is one of my favourite starters. Skin the trout (one small one per person or a large one, filleted, for two) and serve with brown bread and lemon wedges.

Smoked salmon heads the list of 'special occasion appetizers'. Temptingly fragrant, it is best served slightly chilled in paper-thin slices on a lightly oiled platter. Accompany it with thin slices of buttered brown bread, lemon wedges and freshly milled black pepper to bring out the smoky flavour.

Mayonnaise and vinaigrette

Many recipes for starters use either mayonnaise or a vinaigrette dressing.

Mayonnaise is a powerful and useful accompaniment to cold beef, veal, chicken, lobster, crab and salmon. It can be served mixed with pieces of lobster, chicken, ham, turkey or assorted vegetables. It takes kindly to the addition of fresh herbs, mustard, freshly grated horseradish, tomato purée, saffron, capers or finely chopped gherkins or cucumber. It is the perfect accompaniment to hard-boiled eggs and a 'must' with chilled prawns. With the addition of dry white wine, vinegar, lemon juice or milk, mayonnaise is perfect for potato salad, and, with liquid aspic added, it becomes a coating for cold chicken or duck.

Vinaigrette dressing is simple to prepare (see recipe) and once you have perfected your blend of oils and vinegars, you have the basis for a fine vinaigrette and many delicious variations.

Mayonnaise

🔪 20 minutes

Makes about 275 ml /10 fl oz
2 medium-sized egg yolks
2.5 ml /½ tsp Dijon mustard
salt and freshly ground black pepper
10–15 ml /2–3 tsp lemon juice
275 ml /10 fl oz olive oil

1 Place the egg yolks in a small mixing bowl or pudding bowl with the mustard and salt and freshly ground black pepper to taste. Wring out a cloth in very cold water and twist it around the bottom of the bowl to keep it steady and cool.
2 Use a rotary whisk (or a wire whisk or fork) to beat the yolk mixture to a smooth paste. Add a little lemon juice.
3 Add about 50 ml /2 fl oz of the olive oil, drop by drop, beating continuously. Add a little more lemon juice, then some more oil, beating all the time.
4 Continue adding the oil in a thin stream, beating continuously, until the mayonnaise is really thick. Season to taste with salt, pepper and lemon juice, if necessary.

Simple mayonnaise variations
● For horseradish mayonnaise, add the juice of ½ small lemon and salt to taste to 275 ml /10 fl oz plain mayonnaise. Just before serving, stir in 30 ml /2 tbls freshly grated horseradish. This sauce is delicious with hard-boiled egg salads or seafood.
● Russian mayonnaise dressing is pale pink in colour and perfect with eggs, cooked vegetable salads and seafood. To 275 ml /10 fl oz plain mayonnaise, add 30 ml /2 tbls tomato ketchup, · a dash of Tabasco or Worcestershire sauce and 5 ml /1 tsp each freshly chopped chives and canned pimento.
● For cucumber mayonnaise, to serve with watercress or fish (especially salmon), add a

7.5 cm /3 in length of cucumber, finely chopped, and 15 ml /1 tbls finely chopped parsley to 275 ml /10 fl oz plain mayonnaise.
● Mustard mayonnaise can be served with eggs or potato salad. Simply flavour your mayonnaise with additional Dijon or dry mustard.
● Adding saffron to mayonnaise gives it a very special, delicate flavour. It is superb with steamed turbot or gull or duck eggs.
● For aïoli, a mayonnaise from Provence flavoured with garlic, use 4 large garlic cloves, salt, 225–275 ml /8–10 fl oz olive oil, 2 beaten egg yolks, pepper and lemon juice. Crush the garlic to a smooth paste with a little salt, add 15 ml /1 tbls oil and blend well. Mix the eggs with the garlic paste, then add the remaining oil as for mayonnaise. Season with salt, pepper and lemon juice.

Quick blender mayonnaise

🔪 2 minutes

Makes about 275 ml /10 fl oz
2 medium-sized egg yolks
15 ml /1 tbls wine vinegar or lemon juice
2.5 ml /½ tsp dry mustard
2.5 ml /½ tsp salt
a pinch of freshly ground black pepper
275 ml /10 fl oz olive oil

1 Place the egg yolks in an electric blender with the wine vinegar or lemon juice, mustard, salt, freshly ground black pepper and 30 ml /2 tbls cold water. Cover and blend at maximum speed for 5 seconds, or until well mixed.
2 Remove the centre of the lid of the blender and, with the motor turned to maximum, add the oil in a thin, steady trickle. Taste and adjust the seasoning, if necessary, and use as required.

Basic vinaigrette

The right proportions of vinegar or lemon juice to oil provide the basis of a French dressing.

🔪 5 minutes

Makes about 150 ml /5 fl oz
30 ml /2 tbls wine vinegar or lemon juice
coarse salt
freshly ground black pepper
dry or French mustard (optional)
90–120 ml /6–8 tbls olive oil

1   In a bowl, stir the vinegar or lemon juice with a generous pinch of coarse salt and freshly ground black pepper to taste. Add a little mustard, if desired.
2   Beat in the olive oil with a fork until the dressing thickens and emulsifies.

Variations on vinaigrette
● For herb dressing, to serve with tomato or celery salads or artichoke hearts, flavour the basic vinaigrette with 1 garlic clove, finely chopped, and 5 ml /1 tsp each finely chopped fresh parsley (or chervil), marjoram, basil and chives.
● For tarragon dressing, to serve with cucumber, lettuce or avocado salads, flavour the basic vinaigrette with 5–10 ml /1–2 tsp chopped fresh tarragon leaves.
● For curry dressing, to serve with chicory, endive or pear salads, flavour the basic vinaigrette with 2.5 ml /½ tsp curry powder, and 5 ml /1 tsp very finely chopped shallot.
● For soy dressing, to serve with Chinese leaves, grated carrots or radishes, flavour the basic vinaigrette with 2.5 ml /½ tsp sugar, 15 ml /1 tbls soy sauce and a pinch of monosodium glutamate.
● For mint dressing, to serve with carrot or cauliflower salad or melon, flavour the basic vinaigrette with 30 ml /2 tbls finely chopped fresh mint, 15 ml /1 tbls finely chopped fresh parsley and 2.5 ml /½ tsp Dijon mustard.

● For a thicker dressing, drop an ice cube into it and stir for a minute or two. Remove the ice cube and serve.

Tomato salad

🔪 5 minutes

Serves 4
4–6 ripe tomatoes
90–120 ml /6–8 tbls olive oil
30–45 ml /2–3 tbls wine vinegar
salt and freshly ground black pepper
30–45 ml /2–3 tbls finely chopped parsley
1–2 garlic cloves, finely chopped

1   Wipe the tomatoes clean and slice them across into even slices. Place them in an hors d'oeuvre dish.
2   Mix the olive oil, wine vinegar and salt and freshly ground black pepper to taste. Pour this dressing over the salad.
3   Sprinkle the salad with finely chopped parsley and garlic to taste.

Raw beetroot salad

🔪 15 minutes

Serves 2–4
2 medium-sized or 1 large raw beetroot
  (about 350 g /12 oz)
1 tart apple (about 175 g /6 oz)
30–45 ml /2–3 tbls lemon juice
30–45 ml /2–3 tbls thick cream
a pinch of sugar
salt and freshly ground black pepper
15 ml /1 tbls finely chopped fresh parsley

1   Scrub the beetroots under cold running water. Drop them into a pan of boiling water for 2 minutes, then drain and peel.
2   Coarsely grate the raw beetroots and the unpeeled apple. Place them in a serving dish with lemon juice to taste, thick cream and sugar. Toss well and season to taste with salt and freshly ground black pepper.
3   Sprinkle the salad with the finely chopped parsley. Chill until ready to serve.

Green bean salad

Cook the beans until they are just tender but still distinctly crisp to the bite.

🔪 15 minutes,
   plus cooling

Serves 4–6
450–700 g /1–1½ lb fresh young green beans
salt
90–120 ml /6–8 tbls olive oil
30–45 ml /2–3 tbls tarragon vinegar
freshly ground black pepper
30–45 ml /2–3 tbls very finely chopped
  onion
30–45 ml /2–3 tbls very finely chopped
  fresh parsley
½ garlic clove, very finely chopped

1   Top and tail the young green beans. Bring a pan of salted water to a brisk boil. Drop in the beans (immersion of green vegetables in boiling water helps to 'set'

Clockwise from the front: Green bean salad, Raw beetroot salad, Cooked lentil salad, Grated carrot salad, Saffron rice salad and Tomato salad

their brilliant colour); bring to the boil again and simmer until just tender: 3–8 minutes, depending on their age.
2   Meanwhile, place the olive oil in a small bowl with the tarragon vinegar and salt and freshly ground black pepper to taste. Beat the mixture with a fork until it forms an emulsion. Stir in the very finely chopped onion, parsley and garlic.
3   As soon as the beans are cooked, drain them thoroughly in a colander and put them in a serving dish.
4   Pour the dressing over the steaming beans. Toss thoroughly and taste for seasoning, adding more salt and freshly ground black pepper if necessary. Serve cold.

3 Remove the garlic clove and bay leaf from the lentils, and add the wine vinegar and salt and freshly ground black pepper.
4 Prepare the dressing. Place the finely chopped onion in a bowl with the chopped parsley, mustard and salt and freshly ground black pepper to taste. Mix well, then pour in the olive oil, little by little, beating the mixture continuously, until it thickens. Flavour to taste with lemon juice.
5 Pour the dressing over the lentils and mix thoroughly. Garnish with anchovy fillets, tomato wedges and black olives.

Grated carrot salad

15 minutes

Serves 4–6
450 g /1 lb young carrots, scraped
60 ml /4 tbls olive oil
20 ml /4 tsp lemon juice
salt and freshly ground black pepper
a pinch of caster sugar
lettuce leaves, to garnish

1 Coarsely grate the carrots. Place them in a bowl with the olive oil and lemon juice and toss well. Season to taste with salt and freshly ground black pepper, add the caster sugar and toss again.
2 Pile the mixture on a serving dish lined with lettuce and chill until ready to serve.

Saffron rice salad

40 minutes,
plus chilling

Serves 4–6
350 g /12 oz haddock, cooked and flaked
a good pinch of powdered saffron
90 ml /6 tbls dry white wine
850 ml /1½ pts hot chicken stock, home-made or from a cube
350 g /12 oz long-grain rice
salt and freshly ground black pepper
90–120 ml /6–8 tbls olive oil
40 ml /2½ tbls white wine vinegar
60 ml /4 tbls finely chopped fresh parsley
1–2 garlic cloves, finely chopped
1.5 ml /¼ tsp dry mustard
For the garnish
4 tomatoes, cut in wedges
ripe olives

1 Mix the saffron with the white wine. Place it in a large saucepan with the hot chicken stock, rice and salt and freshly ground black pepper to taste.
2 Cover the saucepan and simmer until the rice is tender and has absorbed all the liquid. (About 20–30 minutes.) Cool.
3 Make a dressing with the olive oil, white wine vinegar, finely chopped parsley, garlic and dry mustard. Toss the cooked saffron rice and flaked cooked haddock in a bowl with the dressing and season generously with salt and black pepper, adding more olive oil and wine vinegar if necessary.
4 Garnish the salad with tomato wedges and ripe olives.

Cooked lentil salad

Do not worry if you have not soaked the lentils – the soaking merely shortens the cooking time. Just cook them, straight from the packet or jar, until they are soft but not mushy.

soaking overnight, cooking and cooling lentils, then 10 minutes

Serves 4–6
225 g /8 oz continental lentils
30 ml /2 tbls olive oil
1 Spanish onion, finely chopped
1 garlic clove
1 bay leaf
5 ml /1 tsp salt
15 ml /1 tbls wine vinegar
freshly ground black pepper

For the dressing
½ Spanish onion, finely chopped
60 ml /4 tbls finely chopped fresh parsley
5 ml /1 tsp mustard
salt
freshly ground black pepper
90 ml /6 tbls olive oil
juice of ½ lemon
For the garnish
anchovy fillets, tomato wedges and black olives

1 Soak the lentils overnight in cold water to cover. Drain.
2 Heat 30 ml /2 tbls of the olive oil in a saucepan and sauté the finely chopped onion until transparent. Add the garlic, bay leaf, salt, lentils and 1.4 L /2½ pts water, bring to the boil and simmer for 30–60 minutes, or until just tender. Drain the lentils and leave them to cool.

Crab Louis

Serve this delicious sauce with other seafood cocktails too!

10 minutes,
plus chilling

Serves 4–6
500 g /1 lb cooked crabmeat, flaked
4–6 large tomatoes
lettuce
4 hard-boiled eggs, sliced
For the sauce
300 ml /10 fl oz Mayonnaise (see recipe)
30 ml /2 tbls tomato ketchup
a dash of Tabasco, or Worcestershire sauce
45 ml /3 tbls olive oil
15 ml /1 tbls wine vinegar
30 ml /2 tbls finely grated onion
30 ml /2 tbls finely chopped fresh parsley
90 ml /6 tbls thick cream, whipped
salt and freshly ground black pepper
a pinch of cayenne pepper
15–30 ml /1–2 tbls stuffed olives, chopped

1 Blend together the mayonnaise, tomato ketchup, Tabasco or Worcestershire sauce, olive oil, wine vinegar, finely grated onion, finely chopped parsley and whipped cream. Season to taste with salt and freshly ground black pepper and a pinch of cayenne pepper. Stir in the chopped stuffed olives, and chill for 1–2 hours.
2 Before serving, add the flaked crabmeat.
3 Cut the tomatoes in half. Place two halves on each individual salad plate. Pile the crab salad on the tomatoes and garnish with lettuce and sliced hard-boiled eggs.

Italian tuna and bean salad

10 minutes,
plus 1 hour marinating

Serves 4–6
400 g /14 oz canned white kidney beans in brine
30 ml /2 tbls finely chopped onion
30 ml /2 tbls finely chopped fresh parsley
1 garlic clove, finely chopped
100 g /3½ oz canned tuna fish, drained and broken into chunks
12 small onion rings
12 black olives
flat-leaved parsley, lettuce leaves or watercress, to garnish
For the dressing
90 ml /6 tbls olive oil
30 ml /2 tbls wine vinegar
2.5 ml /½ tsp Dijon mustard
salt and freshly ground black pepper

1 Drain the beans and rinse with cold water. Drain again and toss gently in a salad bowl with the finely chopped onion, parsley and garlic.
2 Beat the first 3 ingredients for the dressing together with a fork until they form an emulsion. Add salt and freshly ground black pepper to taste. Pour this over the beans and

Italian tuna and bean salad

toss gently. Allow the beans to marinate in this dressing for at least 1 hour, turning once or twice.
3 Transfer the beans to a rectangular hors d'oeuvre dish with a slotted spoon. Arrange tuna chunks on the top of the dish and garnish with onion rings and black olives. **Arrange flat-leaved parsley, lettuce leaves or watercress round the dish.**

● Tuna is equally good served in Moroccan style. Place in a screw-top jar 45 ml /3 tbls wine vinegar, 75 ml /5 tbls olive oil, ½ garlic clove, finely chopped, 1.5 ml /¼ tsp each ground cumin, ginger, cinnamon, paprika and cayenne pepper and salt to taste. Shake the jar to mix. Drain and flake 200 g /7 oz can of tuna and place it in a bowl with ½ Spanish onion, finely chopped. Toss with the dressing. Pile the mixture into a bowl lined with lettuce leaves and garnish with quarters of hard-boiled egg and tomato, and black olives.

Sardine-stuffed lemons

This very simple pâté of mashed sardines and cream cheese is transformed by its elegant presentation, in lemon cases.

30 minutes,
plus chilling

Serves 4
4 large fresh lemons
200 g /7 oz canned sardines or tuna fish, in oil
175 g /6 oz Philadelphia cream cheese
90 ml /6 tbls soured cream
2.5 ml /½ tsp Dijon mustard
5 ml /1 tsp very finely chopped onion
1.5 ml /¼ tsp salt
2.5 ml /½ tsp paprika
freshly ground black pepper
a pinch of cayenne pepper
1 egg white
4 sprigs fresh thyme, bay leaves, or chopped parsley, to garnish

1 Cut off the tops of the lemons and reserve. Dig out the pulp with a grapefruit knife and/or small spoon. Remove the pips and reserve the pulp and juice of 1 lemon. Trim the bottoms of the lemons so they stand upright. Cut any excess pith from the insides of the lemons.
2 Mash the sardines or tuna fish to a smooth paste with the cream cheese, soured cream and mustard, and add the finely chopped onion, salt and paprika; season to taste with freshly ground black pepper and cayenne pepper. Strain the reserved lemon juice and pulp into the mixture.
3 Beat the egg white until stiff and fold into the mixture. Season to taste. Stuff the lemons, piling the mousse up slightly in each lemon. Top with the lemon caps and chill until you are ready to serve them.
4 Before serving, tuck a sprig of thyme, a bay leaf, or some parsley in each lemon.

Japanese radish and watercress salad

10 minutes,
plus 2 hours chilling

Serves 4–6
2 bunches watercress
1 bunch radishes
2 celery stalks
For the soy dressing
90 ml /6 tbls olive oil
2.5 ml /½ tsp sugar
30 ml /2 tbls wine vinegar
15 ml /1 tbls soy sauce
freshly ground black pepper
a pinch of monosodium glutamate (see below)

1 Wash and trim the watercress, discarding any yellow leaves. Dry thoroughly and chill, wrapped in a damp towel, in the refrigerator.
2 Wash and trim the radishes and cut across each radish making thin slices almost through the radish. Drop into a bowl of iced water to open out into 'accordions' (see picture on page 48). Slice the celery.
3 To make the soy dressing, combine the olive oil, sugar, wine vinegar and soy sauce. Season to taste with freshly ground black pepper and a pinch of monosodium glutamate, to bring out the full flavour.
4 Just before serving, place the watercress in a salad bowl; add the radishes and celery. Pour on the dressing and toss until every ingredient glistens.

● Monosodium glutamate, or MSG, is a type of salt that stimulates the taste buds.

Japanese radish and watercress salad,
Sardine-stuffed lemons

Smoked trout appetizer

25 minutes

Serves 6
3 smoked trout
6 slices white bread
90 ml /6 tbls thick cream
15–30 ml /1–2 tbls grated horseradish
finely chopped fresh parsley
6 crisp lettuce leaves
6 slices firm tomato
6 large black olives, stoned and halved
6 lemon wedges

1 Skin and fillet the smoked trout, and cut each fillet in two. Toast the bread slices on both sides and remove the crusts.
2 Whisk the thick cream; add 15–30 ml / 1–2 tbls iced water and whisk again until firm. Fold in the grated horseradish to taste to make horseradish chantilly cream.
3 Spread each slice of toast with horseradish cream and arrange 2 pieces of trout diagonally on top. Sprinkle with a pinch of finely chopped parsley. Cut each slice of toast in half from corner to corner, so there is one fillet on each half.
4 Serve 2 toast triangles per person on individual plates garnished with lettuce, tomato, black olives, and lemon wedges.

Tomato salad with beans and cucumber

Serves 4
175 g /6 oz green beans
salt
5 medium-sized tomatoes
1 medium-sized cucumber
For the dressing
1.5 ml /¼ tsp Dijon mustard
15 ml /1 tbls wine vinegar
salt and freshly ground black pepper
45 ml /3 tbls olive oil
15 ml /1 tbls finely snipped fresh chives

1   Top and tail the green beans and cut them into 15 mm /½ in lengths. Bring a saucepan of salted water to the boil and blanch the beans for 4 minutes, or until barely tender. Drain, rinse under cold running water and drain again. Leave to get cold.
2   Meanwhile, place the tomatoes in a bowl and cover with boiling water. Leave for 30–60 seconds, then drain and peel off the skins. Quarter and seed the skinned tomatoes, removing any core.
3   Peel the cucumber and cut it in half lengthways. Remove the seeds with a sharp teaspoon. Cut each half into 15 mm /½ in slices.
4   In a serving dish, combine the cold green beans, quartered tomatoes and sliced cucumber.
5   Make the dressing. Put the mustard in a small cup and add the wine vinegar. Season with salt and freshly ground black pepper to taste, add the olive oil and the finely snipped chives. Beat vigorously with a fork or whisk until the dressing emulsifies. Pour the dressing over the salad and serve as soon as possible.

🍴 30 minutes, plus cooling

Warm courgette and potato salad

Serves 4
350 g /12 oz even-sized thick courgettes
450 g /1 lb even-sized potatoes
salt
For the dressing
7.5 ml /1½ tsp Dijon mustard
30 ml /2 tbls wine vinegar
salt and freshly ground black pepper
90 ml /6 tbls olive oil
1 clove garlic, finely chopped
15 ml /1 tbls finely chopped fresh parsley
5 ml /1 tsp dried oregano

1   Wipe the courgettes with a damp cloth. Trim off the ends. Bring a saucepan of salted water to the boil and simmer the courgettes for 15 minutes, or until tender but not mushy. Drain well.
2   Meanwhile, cook the potatoes. Bring a large saucepan of salted water to the boil and simmer the potatoes for about 15 minutes, or until tender when pierced with a fork. Drain well and keep warm.
3   While the vegetables are cooking, prepare the dressing. Put the mustard into a small cup and add the vinegar. Season to taste with salt and freshly ground black pepper and add the olive oil, finely chopped garlic and parsley and dried oregano. Beat with a fork until the mixture emulsifies.
4   Cut the warm cooked vegetables into 5 mm /¼ in dice and combine them in a salad bowl.
5   Pour the emulsified dressing over the warm vegetables. Toss gently but thoroughly until well coated and serve immediately.

🍴 25 minutes

Carrot and redcurrant salad

Serves 4
500 g /1 lb carrots
225 g /8 oz redcurrants
10–15 ml /2–3 tsp caster sugar
juice of 1 lemon
salt and freshly ground black pepper
1 small lettuce

1   Scrape the carrots well, or peel them if necessary. Grate them coarsely. Place them in a bowl.
2   Wash and drain the redcurrants thoroughly, then strip them from their stalks. Toss them in the bowl with the coarsely grated carrots.
3   Flavour to taste with sugar and lemon juice, and season with salt and freshly ground black pepper. Mix well to blend the flavours and seasoning. Chill thoroughly.
4   Carefully wash the lettuce in cold water, discarding any damaged leaves. Dry the leaves individually and wrap them in a clean cloth. Chill until needed in the salad compartment of your refrigerator.
5   Just before serving, arrange a bed of lettuce in a serving dish and spoon in the chilled carrot and redcurrant salad. Serve immediately.

15 minutes, plus chilling

Orange appetizer salad with black olives

Serves 4
4 ripe oranges
1 curly endive or small cos lettuce
12 black olives, stoned
pinch of cayenne pepper or 1.5 ml /¼ tsp paprika
For the dressing
90 ml /6 tbls olive oil
30 ml /2 tbls lemon juice
30 ml /2 tbls finely chopped fresh parsley
salt and freshly ground black pepper

1   Peel the oranges carefully, removing all the pith, and slice thinly crossways. Place in a bowl and chill for 1 hour.
2   To make the dressing, combine the olive oil, lemon juice and finely chopped parsley in a bowl, and season with salt and freshly ground black pepper to taste. Beat with a fork until the mixture forms an emulsion, then chill.
3   Wash the curly endive or lettuce, shake dry, wrap in a clean tea-towel and leave to chill.
4   When ready to serve, toss the endive or lettuce in a bowl with half the chilled dressing. Arrange the tossed endive or lettuce in a salad bowl. Toss the orange slices in the remaining dressing and arrange on top of the endive or lettuce in an overlapping circle, 25 mm /1 in from the edge of the bowl. There should be a fringe of endive or lettuce showing around the edge of the salad bowl.
5   Garnish the orange slices with black olives and sprinkle with cayenne pepper or paprika to taste. Serve immediately.

20 minutes, plus chilling

FINGER FOOD & DIPS

Temptingly attractive, finger food does not have to be saved for a party. For something a little different, break with tradition and serve a selection as the appetizer at your next dinner party.

Don't always feel that you automatically have to sit your guests down for their first course – there can be occasions when it is easier to serve the appetizer with the pre-dinner drinks. For instance, if you have quite a large crowd in for a meal, you may find it easier to make a selection of food that can be eaten conveniently with drinks, rather than having to set and clear away a first course prior to being able to organize for your main course. Or perhaps you have a main-course dish which needs a fair amount of last-minute preparation, in which case the atmosphere may be more relaxed if you leave your guests to mingle, rather than leaving them at the table while you disappear into the kitchen.

If you are going to serve a selection of finger food, make sure that most of the recipes can be prepared in advance. Also bear in mind the presentation – colours and garnishes should be complementary, especially if a varied selection is served on one large dish.

A dip makes an excellent appetizer. Serve it with pre-dinner drinks or sit your guests down and serve a selection at the table – they can be a great ice breaker as every one has to dip in. Remember to match your starter to the rest of the meal. If you have a substantial main course to follow, a dip served with raw vegetables would be ideal. If you use warmed pitta bread, as suggested for the Aubergine dip (see recipe), the starter will be quite filling.

Another bonus when serving finger food is the lack of washing up. Give your guests napkins and they should be able to manage without any more equipment! Do remember, though, that if you are serving hot finger food that it should be warmed through but not piping hot: burnt fingers or frantic juggling acts will not be appreciated.

Danish open sandwiches

The word *smorrebrod* means 'buttered bread' in Danish; add a selection of delicious toppings and you have the open sandwich which is a popular midday meal in Scandinavia but which also makes a delicious starter. Here I give you a choice of three toppings, each of which will make four portions, allowing one slice per person.

 30 minutes for each topping

Serves 4
4 slices crustless bread
salt and freshly ground black pepper
lemon wedges, to serve

For the cornucopia topping
50 g /2 oz butter
½ shallot, finely chopped
2.5 ml /½ tsp Dijon mustard
a large pinch of dried thyme
12 slices Parma ham
1 tomato
4 green olives, stoned
8 sprigs of watercress
3 hard-boiled eggs, sliced into 12

For the smoked salmon topping
65 ml /2½ fl oz thick cream
5 ml /1 tbls iced water
freshly grated horseradish
4 slices smoked salmon
12 sprigs fresh dill
2 hard-boiled eggs, sliced into 8
black caviar or lumpfish roe

For the smoked chicken topping
15–22.5 ml /1–1½ tbls finely chopped
 watercress
50 g /2 oz butter
lemon juice'
8 thin slices smoked chicken
8 grapefruit segments
4 slices avocado,
 dipped in lemon juice
4 sprigs of watercress

For the cornucopia topping
1 Beat the butter until creamy, then beat in the shallot, mustard and thyme, with salt and pepper to taste. Spread 4 slices of bread with mustard butter, then place 1 slice of ham neatly on top.
2 Cut the tomato into 8 wedges. Roll the remaining ham into horns, arrange 2 on each slice of bread and tuck 2 wedges of tomato in between the ham rolls. Garnish with an olive and sprigs of watercress and overlap 3 slices of hard-boiled egg on top of the ham. Serve with lemon wedges.

For the smoked salmon topping
1 Whip the cream until it forms soft peaks. Add the iced water and whisk again until thick and fluffy. Fold in grated horseradish to taste and season lightly with salt.
2 Spread 4 slices of bread with the horseradish cream, then cover each slice with 1 piece of smoked salmon and fold the 2 ends to the centre. Place 3 sprigs of fresh dill on each slice and mask the stems of the dill with 2 overlapping slices of hard-boiled egg per sandwich. Sprinkle with caviar or lumpfish roe. Serve with lemon wedges.

For the smoked chicken topping
1 Pound the chopped watercress in a mortar with the butter. Blend in the lemon juice and salt and pepper to taste. Cover and chill in the refrigerator to firm up slightly.
2 Spread the watercress butter over 4 slices of bread, then lay 2 pieces of chicken on each slice. Top each sandwich with 2 grapefruit segments and 1 slice of avocado. Garnish with watercress and serve with lemon wedges.

Prawn bouchées

 1½ hours

Makes 36
500 g /1 lb made-weight puff pastry,
 defrosted if frozen
1 beaten egg for glazing
40 g /1½ oz butter
30 ml /2 tbls finely chopped onion
30 ml /2 tbls flour
425 ml /15 fl oz hot milk
½ bay leaf
6 black peppercorns
a good pinch of freshly grated nutmeg
2 shallots, finely chopped
150 ml /5 fl oz dry white wine
15 ml /1 tbls finely chopped fresh parsley
30 ml /2 tbls thick cream
15 ml /1 tbls cognac
Tabasco sauce
175 g /6 oz boiled, peeled prawns, defrosted
 if frozen
salt and freshly ground black pepper
To serve
lettuce leaves, shredded
a few whole prawns, to garnish

1 Roll the pastry to an even thickness of 5 mm /¼ in. Use a sharp 4 cm /1½ in fluted metal cutter to cut circles of pastry.
2 Transfer the circles to a damp baking sheet. Mark 20 mm /¾ in rounds in the centre of each circle but do not cut right through. Brush with beaten egg and leave to rest in a cool place for 15 minutes. Heat the oven to 200C /400F /gas 6.
3 Bake in the centre of the oven for 20 minutes, until risen and golden. With the point of a knife, gently ease away the centre circle. Reserve the caps. With a teaspoon scrape away any soft pastry and return the cases to the oven for 2–3 minutes to dry out. Transfer to a cooling tray.
4 Melt the butter in a small saucepan over a moderate heat. Add the onion and sauté gently until soft and transparent.
5 Add the flour and cook gently, stirring constantly, for 2–3 minutes. Remove from the heat and gradually stir in a quarter of the hot milk. Return to the heat and gradually bring to the boil, stirring constantly. Still stirring, gradually add the remaining milk and bring to the boil.
6 Add the bay leaf, peppercorns and nutmeg. Cook, stirring occasionally, for 30 minutes or until reduced to 275 ml /10 fl oz.
7 Meanwhile, place the chopped shallots in a small saucepan with the wine and reduce to 15 ml /1 tbls. Add to the sauce with the parsley, cream, cognac and a dash of Tabasco.
8 Roughly chop the prawns and add to the sauce. Add salt and freshly ground black pepper.
9 Ten minutes before serving, heat through the bouchée cases and caps in a 180C /350F /gas 4 oven. Then fill with the hot sauce and replace the caps. Arrange lettuce around the bouchées and dot with the whole prawns. Serve immediately.

Danish open sandwiches

Smoked cod's roe dip

20 minutes,
plus chilling

Serves 6
150 g /5 oz smoked cod's roe
1 garlic clove, crushed
75 ml /5 tbls olive oil
150 ml /5 fl oz yoghurt
100 g /4 oz cottage or cream cheese
15 ml /1 tbls lemon juice
30 ml /2 tbls freshly chopped parsley
freshly ground black pepper
pink or red food colouring (optional)
raw vegetables and cocktail biscuits, to serve

1 Pour boiling water over the smoked cod's roe, leave to soak for 5 minutes, then drain. Peel away the skin.
2 If you have a blender, you can make the dip in a matter of seconds. Alternatively, beat the mixture in a bowl with a fork: break up the roe, add the garlic and beat well. Gradually pour in the olive oil, beating all the time. Beat in the yoghurt and cheese and, when the mixture is smooth, stir in the lemon juice and parsley and season to taste with freshly ground black pepper. If the mixture is very pale, add food colouring.
3 Turn the dip into a serving bowl, cover and chill. Serve with 'dip sticks' of crisp, raw carrots, green pepper strips and cauliflower florets, and with cocktail biscuits.

Avocado dip

Guacamole is one of those dips that every cook seems to make differently. To determine the balance of flavours just right for you, you will need to do a lot of very pleasant tasting!

20 minutes

Serves 6
1 large ripe avocado
175 g /6 oz cottage cheese
1 large ripe tomato, skinned and chopped
1 small onion, finely chopped
lemon or lime juice
1–2 drops Worcestershire sauce
1–2 drops Tabasco or other chilli sauce
salt
To serve
celery sticks and/or potato or corn crisps for dipping

1 Halve the avocado, removing the stone and flesh. Mash the flesh to a coarse consistency. Mix in the cottage cheese, tomato and onion and add the lemon or lime juice, Worcestershire sauce, Tabasco or chilli sauce and salt to taste. Alternatively, for a smoother consistency, purée the ingredients briefly in a blender.
2 Serve the guacamole in a bowl surrounded with celery sticks and/or potato or corn crisps for dipping.

Little Provençal pies

1 hour

Makes 16 pies
700 g /1½ lb made-weight shortcrust pastry, defrosted if frozen
8 anchovy fillets, finely chopped
1 small onion, finely chopped
1 garlic clove, finely chopped
60 ml /4 tbls olive oil
30 ml /2 tbls finely chopped fresh parsley
225 g /8 oz cooked ham or veal, finely chopped
1 medium-size egg, separated
salt and freshly ground black pepper
1 egg yolk, lightly beaten, for glazing

1 Heat the oven to 190C /375F /gas 5. Roll the pastry out 3–6 mm /⅛–¼ in thick and, using a 7.5 cm /3 in plain biscuit cutter, cut out 32 small pastry circles. Use a small decorative cutter to cut a small shape from the centre of half of the pastry rounds.
2 Put the anchovy fillets, onion, garlic and olive oil in a mortar and pound to a smooth paste with a pestle.
3 In a large mixing bowl beat the parsley into the anchovy mixture with the ham or veal. Add enough of the egg yolk to bind the mixture – it must not be too wet. Taste and season carefully with salt and pepper.
4 Place about 15 ml /1 tbls of the anchovy mixture in the centre of each of the 16 whole pastry rounds. Brush the edges with egg white and cover with the remaining pastry

Smoked cod's roe dip

rounds, pressing the edges well together and fluting them with the back of a knife.
5 Brush the pastry tops with lightly beaten egg yolk and bake in the oven for about 20 minutes, or until golden.

Aubergine dip

This aubergine dip has a real flavour of the Middle East. Served with warm pitta bread, it is a tasty and substantial appetizer.

20 minutes

Serves 6
2 medium-sized aubergines
45–60 ml /3–4 tbls tahini (sesame paste)
juice of 1–2 lemons
2 garlic cloves, crushed
a sprinkling of olive oil
salt and freshly ground black pepper
To garnish
30 ml /2 tbls finely chopped fresh parsley
1 tomato, skinned, seeded and chopped
warm pitta bread, to serve

1 Heat the grill to high. Grill the aubergines, turning at intervals, until they are soft and the skins are black and blistered all over. Using a tea-towel to protect your hands, peel the aubergines and squeeze out and discard as much of the juice as you can.
2 Put the pulp in a blender with the tahini, lemon juice, garlic and a sprinkling of olive oil. Season to taste with salt and freshly

round black pepper and purée to a light cream, adding a little water if the consistency is too thick.

Alternatively, pass the aubergine pulp through a vegetable mill and then beat in the other ingredients. Taste and add more crushed garlic, lemon or salt if wished.

Garnish the dip with the chopped parsley and tomato and serve it with the warmed pitta bread.

Cocktail cheese puffs

🔪 1 hour

Makes 40 puffs
85 g /3 oz butter, plus extra for greasing
5 ml /1 tsp salt
pinch of white pepper
pinch of nutmeg
100 g /4 oz flour, sifted
3 medium-sized eggs, beaten
100 g /4 oz Gruyère cheese, grated
1 medium-sized egg, beaten, for glazing

For the fillings
225 g /8 oz full fat cream cheese
60 ml /4 tbls thick cream
60 ml /4 tbls finely snipped chives
freshly ground black pepper
225 g /8 oz smoked salmon trimmings
125 ml /4 fl oz soured cream
10 ml /2 tsp lemon juice
sprigs of parsley

1 Heat the oven to 200C /400F /gas 6. Butter 2 baking sheets.
2 Bring 275 ml /10 fl oz water to the boil. Add the butter and seasonings and boil until the butter has melted. Quickly remove from the heat and immediately stir in all the flour. Beat with a wooden spoon until smooth.
3 Return the pan to a low heat and beat vigorously for 1–2 minutes, until a smooth ball is formed which leaves the sides of the pan without sticking.
4 Remove the pan from the heat and make a well in the centre. Pour a little of the eggs into the well and beat to incorporate. Continue to beat in the rest of the eggs, a little at a time, until they have all been incorporated and the mixture is smooth.
5 Beat the cheese into the choux pastry

and season to taste. Fit a piping bag with a medium-sized plain nozzle and fill the bag with the cheese choux pastry. Holding the bag vertically, pipe out small bun shapes, about 1 tablespoonful in size, onto the buttered sheets, 2.5 cm /1 in apart. Brush the puffs with the beaten egg to glaze.
6 Bake the choux puffs for 15 minutes, then reduce the heat to 190C /375F /gas 5 and cook for a further 10 minutes. Remove from the oven and make very small slits in the puffs to allow the steam to escape, then cool completely on racks.
7 Meanwhile, make the 2 fillings. Beat the cream cheese until it is light and fluffy, then beat in the thick cream. Add the chives and season with black pepper. Set aside.
8 Pound the salmon trimmings to a smooth paste and stir in the soured cream. Add the lemon juice and season to taste with black pepper.
9 Not long before serving, split open the cold puffs and fill half of them with the cream cheese filling and half with the smoked salmon filling. Garnish the Cocktail cheese puffs with sprigs of parsley.

Cocktail cheese puffs

Curry chicken liver crescents

Makes 12 crescents
75 g /3 oz butter, plus extra for greasing
75 g /3 oz full fat cream cheese
75 g /3 oz flour
For the filling
100 g /4 oz chicken livers
30 ml /2 tbls butter
5 ml /1 tsp lemon juice
2.5–5 ml /½–1 tsp curry powder
salt and freshly ground black pepper
1 hard-boiled egg, finely chopped
15 ml /1 tbls finely chopped fresh parsley

1 In a medium-sized mixing bowl, combine the butter and cream cheese and stir until well blended. Sieve in the flour and blend in with a fork. Knead the dough until smooth and form into a ball; wrap in cling film and chill in the refrigerator for 1 hour.
2 Meanwhile, prepare the filling. Sauté the chicken livers in the butter for about 5 minutes until they are lightly browned, cool and chop finely. In a mixing bowl, combine the chopped chicken livers with the lemon juice and curry powder to taste. Season with salt and freshly ground black pepper. Add the chopped egg and parsley and mix well.
3 On a floured surface, roll out the dough thinly to a 30 × 20 cm / 12 × 8 in rectangle. Cut into 6 × 10 cm /4 in squares. Cut each square in half diagonally to make 12 triangles. Place 5 ml /1 tsp of filling in the centre of each triangle. Roll up each triangle from the wide edge to the point and twist the ends to seal in the filling. Bend the ends inwards to form a crescent shape. Place on a greased baking sheet; cover with foil and refrigerate until ready to bake.
4 Heat the oven to 230C /450F /gas 8.
5 Bake the crescents for 10 minutes until golden brown. Serve hot.

⌇⌇ 1 hour 50 minutes, including
1 hour chilling

Raw vegetable appetizer with two dips

Serves 4–6
½ green pepper, seeded
½ red pepper, seeded
2 radishes
2 medium-sized carrots
1 head of chicory
12 button mushrooms, wiped
12 slices of cucumber
sprig of watercress
For the herbed cheese dip
175 g /6 oz cottage cheese
60 ml /4 tbls soured cream
15 ml /1 tbls lemon juice
60 ml /4 tbls finely snipped chives
salt and ground black pepper
For the Provençal anchovy dip
45 g /1¾ oz canned anchovy fillets, drained
1 garlic clove, roughly chopped
45 ml /3 tbls olive oil
25 ml /1 tsp lemon juice
45 ml /3 tbls thick mayonnaise
45 ml /3 tbls thick cream
freshly ground black pepper
paprika

1 To make the herbed cheese dip, combine the cottage cheese and soured cream in a bowl and mix well. Press the mixture through a sieve, then add the lemon juice and blend in an electric blender until smooth. Return the blended mixture to the bowl. Reserve some chives for decoration, add the rest to the mixture and season to taste with salt and freshly ground black pepper. Transfer to a serving bowl and sprinkle the remaining chives over the top. Chill until ready to serve.
2 To make the Provençal anchovy dip, place the drained anchovy fillets with the roughly chopped garlic in a small bowl or mortar, and pound to a pulp. Add the olive oil, lemon juice, mayonnaise and thick cream, mix well and season with freshly ground black pepper to taste. Transfer to a serving bowl and sprinkle with paprika. Chill until ready to serve.
3 Cut the green and red peppers into 12 strips each. Cut each radish into 6 pieces, and cut each carrot into 6 sections lengthways. Separate the chicory leaves.
4 Just before serving, group all the vegetables around the outside of a serving platter, and place the two bowls of dips in the centre. Place a sprig of watercress between the two bowls and serve. Alternatively, place the vegetables, in colourful clumps, in a basket, and serve the two bowls of dip beside it.

⌇ 45 minutes,
plus chilling and arranging

Toast batons with tapenade

Makes 24
50 g /2 oz black olives, stoned, plus extra to garnish
25 g /1 oz canned anchovy fillets, drained
25 g /1 oz canned tuna fish, drained
5 ml /1 tsp Dijon mustard
25 g /1 oz capers
60 ml /4 tbls olive oil
15 ml /1 tbls brandy
freshly ground black pepper
4 large hard-boiled eggs
softened butter
8 slices white bread with crusts removed, toasted

1   Using a mortar and pestle, pound the stoned black olives, drained anchovy fillets and tuna, Dijon mustard and the capers to a smooth paste. Alternatively, use a food processor.
2   Press the mixture through a sieve into a bowl, using the back of a wooden spoon. Beat in the olive oil a little at a time, then stir in the brandy and season to taste with freshly ground black pepper.
3   Slice the hard-boiled eggs in half lengthways and remove the yolks. Chop the whites into small dice. Sieve the yolks into the tapenade mixture, then add the diced egg whites and stir to blend.
4   Butter the toast and cut each slice lengthways into 3 batons.
5   Spread the tapenade mixture evenly over the batons of toast, piling it up a little. Arrange on a serving plate. Garnish with halved black olives, if wished, and serve as canapés.

● *Tapenade* is a Provençal paste used as a sauce with many appetizers and savouries. It takes its name from *tapeno*, the local dialect word for caper.

Pepper and Mozzarella strip

Serves 6
100 g /4 oz made-weight puff pastry, defrosted if frozen
15 g /½ oz butter
15 ml /1 tbls oil
¼ Spanish onion, thinly sliced
1 red pepper, thinly sliced
salt and freshly ground black pepper
75 g /3 oz Mozzarella cheese, thinly sliced
melted butter
black olives

1   Heat the oven to 200C /400F /gas 6.
2   Roll out the pastry to a rectangle 40 × 7.5 cm /16 × 3 in and 3 mm /⅛ in thick. Lay it on a dampened heavy-duty baking sheet and chill in the refrigerator for 30 minutes.
3   Meanwhile, in a large heavy saucepan, heat the butter and oil. Cook the onion slowly for 10–15 minutes, until golden, stirring frequently with a wooden spoon to ensure it colours evenly. Add the red pepper and cook for a further 10 minutes. Season to taste with salt and freshly ground black pepper, and leave to cool.
4   Remove the pastry from the refrigerator and spread with the onion and pepper mixture, not quite to the edge. Lay the thin Mozzarella slices over the top.
5   Fold the outer edges of the pastry over to just touch the mixture. Brush the edges with a little melted butter and press them down firmly to seal. Bake in the oven for 20–30 minutes or until the pastry edges are golden. Cut into 6 pieces, garnish with black olives and serve immediately.

20 minutes

1¼ hours,
including chilling

SEAFOOD STARTERS

From a simple appetizer of canned sardines and hard-boiled eggs – an ideal store-cupboard standby – to elegant ramekins of mixed seafood in a cream sauce, fish and shellfish make delicious starters for all occasions.

The simplest seafood starters are those that require no recipes and no cooking at all: a jar of chilled black caviar on a bed of crushed ice served with hot toast, a dozen oysters or a plateful of thinly sliced smoked salmon with brown bread and butter. All any of these need is a generous supply of lemon wedges – and a large bank balance!

For those of us with rather less money and a bit of time, there is vast scope for preparing tempting appetizers from fresh, frozen or canned fish and shellfish.

Some of my favourites are classics: British potted shrimps – tiny, tasty boiled shrimps embedded in finely spiced butter, French Coquilles St Jacques au gratin – poached scallops in a richly flavoured mushroom sauce served in their shells, and Greek Taramasalata – salty smoked cod's roe softened with olive oil, bread and lemon juice to make a pink paste tasting of the sea.

Some shellfish come complete with their own serving dishes: scallops; mussels – cook them in dry white wine until their shells open, then cover the tender flesh with herby, garlicky 'snail' butter and bake, in the half shell, until bubbling; and crabs – extract both the white and dark meats from a fleshy cooked crab, moisten them with a lemony mayonnaise and pile them back into the shell, decorating prettily with finely chopped hard-boiled egg and parsley.

Or use vegetables or fruit as edible containers: hollowed-out ripe tomatoes can be filled with salt cod, prawns, canned tuna or leftover cooked fish in mayonnaise or vinaigrette; large flat mushroom caps can be stuffed with crabmeat and baked, then served with Mornay sauce; and luscious avocado halves blend perfectly with crabmeat and red pepper salad.

Mussel and celery salad

🍴🍴 preparing the mussels, then 30 minutes plus cooling

Serves 6
1 kg /2 lb or 2 pt mussels
15 ml /1 tbls finely chopped shallots
sprig of thyme
sprig of parsley
bay leaf
salt
75 ml /3 fl oz dry white wine
1 head of celery
30 ml /2 tbls wine vinegar
90–120 ml /6–8 tbls olive oil
coarse salt and freshly ground black pepper
1 garlic clove, finely chopped
15 ml /1 tbls finely chopped fresh parsley
5 ml /1 tsp finely snipped fresh chives
1.5 ml /¼ tsp dried marjoram

1 Sharply tap any mussels that are open and discard those which do not close. Pull away the beards, then, with a hard scrubbing brush, scrub the mussels clean under cold running water. Scrape off any encrustations with a sharp knife. Drop each cleaned mussel in a bowl of clean cold water.
2 Place the mussels in a large saucepan together with the shallots, thyme, parsley, bay leaf, salt and wine. Cover the pan and shake over a high heat for 3–5 minutes, until the shells open.
3 Strain the mussels into a colander and discard any that are still closed. When cool enough to handle, remove the mussels from their shells.
4 Cut the celery into 15 mm /½ in slices, reserving a few leaves for the garnish. Blanch the sliced celery in boiling, salted water for 3–5 minutes. Drain, refresh under cold water, drain again and reserve.
5 In a bowl, combine the vinegar and oil and season with coarse salt and pepper. Add the garlic, parsley, chives and marjoram and beat with a fork until the mixture emulsifies.
6 Pat the celery dry with absorbent paper and add to the dressing, along with the mussels. Stir to mix. Transfer the salad to a serving dish, garnish with the reserved celery leaves and serve.

Avocado with crab

🍴 15 minutes

Serves 4
2 ripe avocados
juice of ½ lemon
75 g /3 oz fresh, frozen or canned crabmeat, drained, defrosted if frozen
½ red pepper, finely chopped
lettuce leaves, to garnish
For the dressing
15 ml /1 tbls lemon juice
45 ml /3 tbls olive oil
2.5 ml /½ tsp Dijon mustard
¼ garlic clove, crushed
30 ml /2 tbls tomato chutney
15 ml /1 tbls finely chopped fresh parsley
salt and freshly ground black pepper

1 Divide the lettuce leaves among 4 individual plates. Cut the avocados in half, remove the stones and sprinkle each half with lemon juice. Arrange on the lettuce.
2 Flake the crabmeat with a fork and add the red pepper. Mix gently.
3 To make the dressing, mix together the lemon juice, oil, mustard, garlic, chutney, parsley and salt and freshly ground black pepper to taste.
4 Gently stir the dressing into the crabmeat and pepper mixture, then spoon into the avocado halves. Serve immediately.

Marinated pepper and prawn salad

🍴🍴 30 minutes, then 30 minutes marinating

Serves 4
olive oil
1 large green pepper, halved
1 large red pepper, halved
250 g /8 oz boiled, peeled prawns, defrosted if frozen
15 ml /1 tbls freshly chopped parsley, to garnish
For the vinaigrette
90 ml /6 tbls olive oil
30 ml /2 tbls red wine vinegar
1 garlic clove, finely chopped
15 ml /1 tbls finely chopped fresh parsley
salt and freshly ground black pepper

1 Heat the grill without the grid to high.
2 Brush the grid of the grill pan with a little olive oil and lay the peppers on the grid side by side, skin side up. Brush with olive oil and cook 12.5 cm /5 in from the heat for 7–10 minutes, or until the skins are well browned and blistered. Leave until cool enough to handle, then peel. Using a sharp knife, slice into thin strips. Place the strips in a shallow serving dish.
3 Prepare the vinaigrette. In a bowl, combine the oil, wine vinegar, garlic and parsley. Season to taste with salt and pepper. Beat with a fork until the mixture emulsifies. Pour the dressing over the pepper strips and leave to marinate in a cool place for 30 minutes.
4 To serve, add the pepper strips to the prawns. Toss to mix, garnish with a sprinkling of finely chopped fresh parsley and serve immediately.

Sardine and egg appetizer

🍴 20 minutes

Serves 4
225 g /8 oz canned sardines in oil
2 eggs, hard-boiled
30 ml /2 tbls finely chopped fresh parsley
4 tomatoes, thinly sliced
salt and freshly ground black pepper
1 lemon, cut into wedges

1 Drain the sardines and pat them with absorbent paper to remove any remaining oil. Arrange them together closely, side by side, on a rectangular serving platter.
2 Separate the yolks of the eggs from the whites and sieve them separately.
3 Garnish the sardines with the sieved white, yolk and chopped parsley, in strips.
4 Overlap the tomato slices around the sardines and season the tomatoes to taste with salt and freshly ground black pepper. Garnish with lemon wedges and serve.

Mussel and celery salad

Creamy seafood ramekins

🔪🔪 1 hour

Serves 8
butter
2 shallots, finely chopped
4 large mushrooms, finely chopped
500 g /1 lb turbot or sole fillet, skinned
8 scallops, shelled
salt and freshly ground black pepper
juice of 1 lemon
600 ml /1 pt thick cream
1 chicken stock cube
beurre manié, made by mashing together
    25 g /1 oz butter and 30 ml /2 tbls flour
250 g /8 oz boiled, peeled prawns, defrosted
    if frozen
2 egg yolks
8 lemon twists, to garnish
8 unshelled prawns, to garnish

1   Heat the oven to 220C /425F /gas 7. Generously butter a flameproof casserole.
2   Place half the finely chopped shallots and mushrooms in the bottom of the casserole. Place the turbot or sole fillet and the scallops on top and sprinkle with the remaining shallots and mushrooms. Season to taste with salt and freshly ground black pepper, then sprinkle the lemon juice over.
3   Butter a piece of foil large enough to fit over the casserole; cover with this, then the lid. Heat the casserole for 1 minute on top of the stove, then transfer to the oven and cook for 15 minutes.
4   Meanwhile, put 450 ml /16 fl oz thick cream in a saucepan. Crumble in the chicken stock cube. Bring to the boil very carefully, then simmer for 5 minutes to reduce slightly, stirring with a wooden spoon.
5   Whisk in the beurre manié a little at a time and simmer for a further 5 minutes, or until thickened, stirring occasionally. Season to taste with salt and pepper.
6   With a slotted spoon, transfer 1 scallop to each of 8 ramekins. Remove the fish from the casserole with the slotted spoon. Cut it evenly into cubes and divide it between the ramekins.
7   Heat 25 g /1 oz butter in a small frying-pan and sauté the prawns for 2–3 minutes, or until heated through, shaking the pan occasionally. Add the sautéed prawns to the ramekins.
8   Add the fish cooking liquid and vegetables to the cream sauce and stir until well blended. Spoon the sauce over the seafood in the ramekins and keep warm in a bain marie.
9   Meanwhile, in a bowl, whisk the remaining thick cream until it forms soft peaks, then beat in the egg yolks.
10   A few minutes before serving, heat the grill to high. Spoon about 15 ml /1 tbls of the whisked cream and egg yolk mixture into each ramekin. Place the ramekins under the hot grill until the tops are golden brown. Serve immediately, garnished with lemon twists and unshelled prawns.

Devilled whitebait

🔪 25 minutes

Serves 4
oil for deep frying
60–90 ml /4–6 tbls flour
salt and freshly ground black pepper
cayenne pepper
500 g /1 lb whitebait
1 lemon, cut into wedges, to garnish

1   With the frying basket in place, heat the oil in a deep-fat frier to 190C /375F. At this temperature a 25 mm /1 in cube of day-old white bread will take 50 seconds to turn crisp and golden.
2   Sprinkle the flour onto a large plate. Season generously with salt, freshly ground black pepper and cayenne pepper.
3   Toss the whitebait in seasoned flour, shaking off the excess. Place half the fish in the hot basket and deep fry for 3–4 minutes, or until crisp and lightly golden. Drain the whitebait on absorbent paper. Place them on a heated plate and keep hot while you fry the remaining whitebait.
4   Season the fried fish with salt and freshly ground black pepper to taste and arrange on a heated serving dish, garnished with lemon wedges. Serve immediately.

Coquilles St Jacques au gratin

🔪🔪 making fish stock, then 1¼ hours

Serves 4
12 shelled scallops, with corals
1 small onion, sliced
bouquet garni
300 ml /10 fl oz dry white wine
salt and freshly ground black pepper
75 g /3 oz butter
1 medium-sized onion, finely chopped
175 g /6 oz button mushrooms, finely
    chopped
30 ml /2 tbls finely chopped fresh parsley
30 ml /2 tbls freshly grated
    Parmesan cheese
60 ml /4 tbls fresh white breadcrumbs
flat-leaved parsley, to garnish
For the fish velouté sauce
7.5 g /¼ oz butter
7.5 ml /½ tbls flour
150 ml /5 fl oz boiling fish stock (page 11)
salt and freshly ground white pepper
lemon juice

1   Make the fish velouté sauce: melt the butter in a small pan, add the flour and cook for a few minutes. Gradually add the boiling

sh stock and salt and white pepper to taste, ien cook, stirring vigorously until smooth. educe the heat and cook gently, stirring ccasionally and skimming from time to me, until it is reduced to 60 ml /4 tbls. lavour with lemon juice, strain through a ne sieve and reserve.

Cut away the black translucent line ehind the coral of each scallop. Place the callops in a saucepan with the sliced onion, ouquet garni and wine and season with a ttle salt and black pepper.

Bring to the simmer, then poach gently r just 5 minutes. Remove the scallops from ie pan with a slotted spoon and slice in half orizontally.

In a clean pan, melt 50 g /2 oz butter nd cook the chopped onion for 5–7 iinutes, or until soft, stirring occasionally. dd the chopped mushrooms and cook for a irther 3–4 minutes. Add the chopped arsley, the strained sauce and the halved callops. Adjust the seasoning and spoon the iixture into 4 well-scrubbed scallop shells r individual flameproof dishes.

Heat the grill to high. Sprinkle the rated Parmesan and breadcrumbs over the callops and dot with the remaining butter. rill for 2–3 minutes, until browned. arnish with flat-leaved parsley and serve at nce.

reamy seafood ramekins

Crab-stuffed mushrooms

 1 hour 20 minutes

Serves 4
8 large flat mushroom caps, weighing about
  250 g /8 oz
40 g /1½ oz butter
60 ml /4 tbls finely chopped onion
175 g /6 oz fresh, frozen or canned
  crabmeat, drained, defrosted if frozen
90 ml /6 tbls fresh white breadcrumbs
1 egg, beaten
30 ml /2 tbls thick cream
30 ml /2 tbls finely chopped fresh parsley
salt and freshly ground black pepper
a pinch of cayenne pepper
15 ml /1 tbls lemon juice
15 ml /1 tbls olive oil
For the mornay sauce
15 g /½ oz butter
15 ml /1 tbls flour
175 ml /6 fl oz milk, warmed
45 ml /3 tbls thick cream
1.5 ml /¼ tsp dry mustard
25 g /1 oz freshly grated Parmesan cheese
25 g /1 oz freshly grated Gruyère cheese
salt and freshly ground black pepper

1 Heat the oven to 375F /190C /gas 5.
2 Cut off the mushroom stalks and discard them or reserve for use in another recipe.
3 Melt ⅓ of the butter in a small saucepan. Cook the chopped onion for 7–10 minutes, or until soft, stirring occasionally. Leave to cool.
4 In a bowl, combine the crabmeat,

Crab-stuffed mushrooms

breadcrumbs, beaten egg, thick cream, chopped parsley and cooled onion. Mix until well blended. Season to taste with salt and black and cayenne pepper. Stir in the lemon juice. Set aside.
5 Heat the remaining butter and the olive oil in a large frying-pan. When the foaming subsides, sauté the mushroom caps for 2–3 minutes each side, or until lightly browned, turning them carefully with a spatula.
6 Select a shallow ovenproof dish large enough to take the mushroom caps in 1 layer. With a slotted spoon, remove the sautéed mushrooms from the pan and lay them side by side in the dish, hollow sides up. Stuff the caps with the crab mixture, shaping it into neat domes with your fingers or a spoon. Cover with foil and bake for 15 minutes, or until the mushrooms are tender and the crab mixture is heated through.
7 While the mushrooms are in the oven, prepare the mornay sauce: in a small, heavy-based saucepan, melt the butter over a low heat. Stir in the flour, then cook, stirring, for 1–2 minutes, or until the roux is thick and smooth but not coloured.
8 Remove the pan from the heat and add the warmed milk gradually, stirring vigorously. Return to a low heat and cook, stirring, until the sauce begins to thicken. Stir in the cream, mustard and Parmesan and Gruyère cheeses. Season to taste with salt and freshly ground black pepper, then simmer gently for a further 5 minutes. Cover and keep warm until the mushrooms are cooked.
9 To serve, place 2 stuffed mushrooms on each of 4 heated serving plates. Top with a few spoonfuls of sauce and serve at once.

Smoked fish rolls

 30 minutes

Serves 6
225 g /8 oz smoked trout fillet
20 ml /4 tsp horseradish sauce
90 ml /6 tbls thick cream
1.5 ml /¼ tsp cayenne pepper
5 ml /1 tsp lemon juice
2 bunches of watercress
12 thin slices smoked salmon (about 400 g /
* 14 oz)*
12 lemon twists, to garnish
thin slices of buttered brown bread, to serve

1   Skin the smoked trout fillet, place it in a large bowl and flake it. Add the horseradish sauce and thick cream and stir well, until the mixture is fairly smooth and creamy. Add the cayenne pepper and lemon juice and stir in.
2   Finely chop enough watercress leaves to give 30 ml /2 tbls, and add to the trout. Pluck neat sprigs from the remaining watercress and reserve for the garnish.
3   Put about 22.5 ml /1½ tbls of the smoked trout mixture on 1 end of each slice of smoked salmon. pat the mixture into a cigar shape, then roll up the salmon around it.
4   To serve, place the smoked fish rolls on a long serving platter and garnish each roll with a lemon twist. Place thinly sliced, buttered brown bread down the centre of the platter and surround with sprigs of watercress.

Potted shrimps

⫴ making clarified butter,
  then 30 minutes, plus cooling

Serves 4
450 g /1 lb boiled, peeled shrimps, defrosted
* if frozen*
100 g /4 oz butter
a pinch of ground mace
a pinch of cayenne pepper
freshly grated nutmeg
salt and freshly ground black pepper
225 g /8 oz clarified butter (see below)
lettuce leaves (optional)
4 lemon wedges (optional)
hot toast and chilled butter, to serve

1   Pat the shrimps dry with absorbent paper to remove any moisture.
2   Melt the butter in a saucepan. Add the shrimps and heat them through slowly over a gentle heat, tossing occasionally. Season with mace, cayenne pepper, nutmeg, a little salt and pepper to taste. The shrimps should be highly flavoured.
3   Divide the buttered shrimps among 4 ramekins and leave them to become cold.
4   Pour clarified butter into the ramekins to cover the shrimps completely. Cool, then chill. The potted shrimps can be stored in the refrigerator for several days.
5   Serve the shrimps in the ramekins, if wished, or turn out onto individual plates lined with lettuce leaves and garnished with a lemon wedge. Serve with hot toast and chilled butter.

Smoked fish rolls

● To clarify butter, put it in a small, heav based saucepan and melt it very slowly. T butter will foam and the foam will sink the bottom. Pour the clear butter careful into a bowl without disturbing the sedimen Keep in the refrigerator and use as needed.

Blue cheese prawn cocktail

⫴ 30 minutes,
  plus chilling

Serves 4–6
500 g /1 lb boiled, peeled prawns,
* defrosted if frozen*
juice of ½ lemon
½ chicken stock cube
freshly ground black pepper
a pinch of cayenne pepper
8 small lettuce leaves
30 ml /2 tbls finely chopped
* fresh parsley, to garnish*
4–6 tomato roses (page 48), to garnish
For the dressing
90–120 ml /6–8 tbls tomato ketchup
60 ml /4 tbls thick cream
30 ml /2 tbls finely chopped onion
60 ml /4 tbls lemon juice
5 ml /1 tsp Worcestershire sauce
a dash of Tabasco sauce
65 g /2½ oz Danish blue cheese,
* crumbled*

1   Place the prawns in a flat dish. Heat the lemon juice in a small pan and dissolve half the chicken stock in it. Pour this over the prawns. Add freshly ground black pepper and cayenne pepper to taste. Toss well, then cool and chill.
2   Make the dressing: in a bowl, combine the tomato ketchup, thick cream, chopped onion, lemon juice, Worcestershire sauce, Tabasco sauce and crumbled Danish blue cheese. Mix well and chill.
3   Arrange the lettuce leaves in old-fashioned open champagne or cocktail glasses so that they line the sides of the glass. Drain the prawns. Mix them with the blue cheese dressing and place in the lettuce-lined glasses. Sprinkle with finely chopped parsley and garnish with the tomato roses. Serve immediately.

Tuna Waldorf salad

This salad of winter vegetables and fruit, first served at the Waldorf-Astoria Hotel in New York, is made more substantial by the addition of canned tuna fish.

 20 minutes

Serves 6
300 g /11 oz canned tuna fish, drained
4–6 celery stalks, sliced
75 g /3 oz walnuts, broken or chopped
250–350 ml /9–12 fl oz mayonnaise (page 49)
lemon juice
salt and freshly ground black pepper
a pinch of cayenne pepper
3 tart dessert apples
crisp lettuce leaves

1   Flake the tuna into bite-sized pieces and combine with the sliced celery and walnut pieces. Stir in enough mayonnaise to bind the ingredients together lightly. Season to taste with lemon juice, salt, freshly ground black pepper and cayenne.
2   Core, but do not peel, the apples; cut into 5–10 mm /¼–½ in cubes and toss in lemon juice to prevent discoloration. Stir the apple cubes into the tuna mixture.
3   Line 6 individual serving plates with lettuce leaves. Divide the tuna and apple mixture equally among them and serve immediately.

Pecan salmon roll

 20 minutes, plus chilling overnight

Serves 4–6
250 g /8 oz cold poached salmon or canned salmon, drained
100 g /4 oz cream cheese
½ small onion, grated
30 ml /2 tbls lemon juice
30 ml /2 tbls grated horseradish
salt and freshly ground white pepper
50 g /2 oz pecan nuts, finely chopped
30 ml /2 tbls finely chopped fresh parsley
melba toast, to serve

1   If using poached salmon, skin, flake and remove any bones. Work the flesh in a blender with the cream cheese, grated onion, lemon juice and grated horseradish until smooth. Season to taste with salt and white pepper.
2   Using wet hands, shape the mixture into a 15 cm /6 in long cylinder, then roll it in cling film. Refrigerate overnight.
3   Carefully remove the cling film. Spread the chopped pecan nuts and parsley on separate plates. Roll the salmon in the pecans, then in the parsley. Arrange on a dish, slice and serve with melba toast.

Mussels with snail butter

 preparing the mussels, then 1 hour

Serves 4
24 mussels, about 1 kg /2 lb or 2 pt
25 g /1 oz butter
¼ Spanish onion, finely chopped
1 celery stalk, finely chopped
freshly ground black pepper
10 ml /2 tsp lemon juice
150 ml /5 fl oz dry white wine
French bread, to serve
For the snail butter
225 g /8 oz softened butter
2 garlic cloves, finely chopped
30 ml /2 tbls finely chopped fresh parsley
30 ml /2 tbls finely snipped fresh chives
freshly ground black pepper

1   Sharply tap any mussels that are open; discard those which do not close. Pull away the beards, then, with a hard scrubbing brush, scrub the mussels clean under cold running water. Scrape off any encrustations with a sharp knife, then drop each cleaned mussel into a bowl of clean, cold water.
2   In a large saucepan, melt the butter and cook the finely chopped onion and celery over a moderate heat for about 10 minutes, or until softened, stirring occasionally.
3   Add the mussels. Season with freshly ground black pepper to taste and sprinkle with lemon juice. Add the dry white wine. Cover the pan tightly and cook over a high heat, shaking the pan frequently, for about 5 minutes, or until the shells open. Discard any mussels that have not opened.
4   Heat the oven to 200C /400F /gas 6. Remove and discard the top half of each mussel shell. Place the mussels in their half shells in an ovenproof serving dish.
5   Prepare the snail butter. Beat the softened butter until light and creamy. Stir in the finely chopped garlic, parsley and snipped chives. Season to taste with freshly ground black pepper.
6   Spread some snail butter over each mussel in the half shell and smooth with a knife. Bake for 10 minutes, or until the butter is bubbling. Serve immediately with French bread.

● This garlic-flavoured herb butter is traditionally served with snails, hence its name.

Mussels with snail butter

Curried crab ramekins

🔪 cooking the rice,
then 45 minutes

Serves 6
25 g /1 oz butter
1 small green pepper, finely chopped
½ small onion, finely chopped
15 ml /1 tbls flour
15 ml /1 tbls mild curry powder
300 ml /10 fl oz milk
30 ml /2 tbls thick cream
salt and freshly ground black pepper
50 g /2 oz long-grain rice, cooked
350 g /12 oz fresh, frozen or canned
crabmeat, drained
15 ml /1 tbls finely chopped fresh parsley
60 ml /4 tbls fresh white breadcrumbs

1   Heat the oven to 220C /425F /gas 7.
2   In a saucepan, melt 15 g /½ oz butter. Reserve a little green pepper for the garnish, and cook the onion and remaining green pepper over a moderate heat for 10 minutes, or until tender, stirring occasionally. Stir in the flour and curry powder and gently cook over a low heat for 2–3 minutes, stirring occasionally.
3   Meanwhile, bring the milk to the boil. Add the milk to the saucepan, stirring constantly with a wire whisk to prevent lumps forming. Bring to the boil, then reduce the heat and simmer for 2–3 minutes, or until very slightly thickened – the sauce should be thin at this stage.
4   Add the thick cream and season to taste with salt and freshly ground black pepper.

Curried crab ramekins

Stir in the cooked rice, crabmeat and parsley. Correct the seasoning.
5   Spoon the mixture into 6 × 150 ml /5 fl oz ovenproof ramekins. Sprinkle the tops with breadcrumbs and dot with the remaining butter. Bake for 5 minutes, or until lightly browned. Sprinkle a little of the reserved green pepper over each ramekin and serve immediately.

Cod mayonnaise

This quick but elegant starter is a delightful way of using leftover fish.

🔪 30 minutes

Serves 4
500 g /1 lb leftover cooked cod or other
white fish, skinned
2 large tomatoes
2 × 15 mm /½ in slices unpeeled cucumber
90 ml /6 tbls finely chopped onion
60 ml /4 tbls finely chopped fresh fennel
or dill
30 ml /2 tbls finely chopped fresh parsley
15–30 ml /1–2 tbls lemon juice
salt and freshly ground black pepper
425 ml /15 fl oz mayonnaise (page 49)
16 lettuce leaves
sprigs of fennel or dill, to garnish

1   Cut each tomato into 8 wedges and cut each wedge in half. Cut each cucumber slice into 8 wedges. Cut the fish into chunks, being careful to remove all the bones.
2   Combine the fish in a bowl with the finely chopped onion and all but 15 ml /1 tbls of the mixed fresh herbs. Add lemon juice to taste, season generously with salt and pepper and toss together gently.
3   Reserve about 30 ml /2 tbls mayonnaise for the garnish and add the rest to the fish. Mix gently.
4   Arrange 4 lettuce leaves on each individual serving plate and top with a mound of the fish mayonnaise. Stud each serving with pieces of tomato and cucumber and top with a piped swirl of mayonnaise. Sprinkle with the remaining herbs and garnish with sprigs of fennel or dill.

Cod mayonnaise

Californian avocado

20 minutes

Serves 4–6

large ripe avocados, peeled and sliced
ice of 3 lemons
eggs, hard-boiled
0 g /8 oz boiled, peeled prawns, defrosted
  if frozen
lt and freshly ground white pepper
0 ml /5 fl oz mayonnaise (page 49)
-12 large prawns in their shells, to garnish

Sprinkle the avocado slices with the juice
2 lemons to prevent discoloration.
rrange on 4–6 individual serving plates.

Reserve 2 of the hard-boiled egg yolks.
ice the remaining eggs and the egg whites
ngthways and place them on the individual
ates with the avocado.

Season the prawns with salt and freshly
ound white pepper and pile onto the
ates.

Add the remaining lemon juice to the
ayonnaise and blend well. Fit a piping bag
ith a star nozzle and fill with mayonnaise.
ipe the mayonnaise on top of the prawns,
rming elegant peaks.

Sieve the reserved egg yolks through a
ylon sieve over the mayonnaise. Garnish
ch individual plate with 2 prawns and
rve immediately.

Marinated herring appetizer

preparing fish, 45 minutes,
then 12 hours or more chilling

Serves 4
4 fresh herrings, scaled and cleaned,
  with gills and head removed
For the marinade
30 ml /2 tbls finely chopped fresh parsley
1 Spanish onion, finely chopped
4–6 carrots, thinly sliced
12 coriander seeds
4 bay leaves
90 ml /6 tbls olive oil
150 ml /5 fl oz dry white wine
30 ml /2 tbls white wine vinegar
salt and freshly ground black pepper
a pinch of cayenne pepper
lemon juice
For the garnish
4 thin orange slices, cut into quarters
30 ml /2 tbls finely chopped fresh parsley

1 Place the fish in a shallow flameproof casserole and reserve.
2 For the marinade, combine the parsley, onion, carrots, coriander seeds and bay leaves in a large, heavy-based saucepan. Add the olive oil and dry white wine and bring to the boil. Reduce the heat and simmer until the onion is transparent.

3 Add the wine vinegar, then season generously with salt and freshly ground black pepper and add cayenne pepper to taste. Bring the marinade back to the boil and pour over the herrings.
4 Place the casserole over a low heat and bring the marinating liquid slowly to the boil. Poach the fish gently for 15 minutes, remove from the heat and leave to cool.
5 Using a fish slice, carefully transfer the herrings to a shallow earthenware or porcelain dish. Pour over the marinade, cover the dish and chill in the refrigerator for at least 12 hours. Remove from the refrigerator 2 hours before serving to take the chill off.
6 Just before serving, carefully transfer the herrings to a shallow serving dish and pour over the marinade and a few drops of lemon juice. Garnish the herrings with quartered slices of orange, then sprinkle with the chopped parsley and serve.

● Ask the fishmonger to prepare the fish, or do it yourself at home. To scale, hold the fish by its tail and draw the blunt edge of a knife firmly from the tail to the head; rinse to remove loose scales. To clean, make a slit along the belly from the gills halfway to the tail with a sharp knife. Scrape out the insides, rinse, then rub the cavity with salt and scrape away any black skin. Cut off the gills, then the head.

Californian avocado

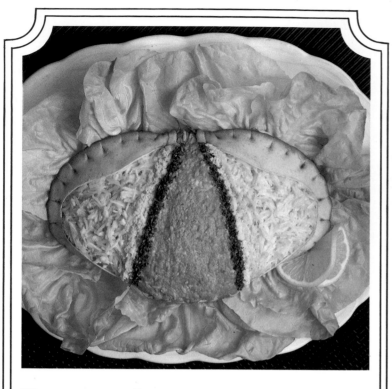

Dressed crab

Serves 4
1.1 kg /2½ lb cooked crab, in the
   shell
olive oil, for brushing
mayonnaise (page 49)
lemon juice

salt and ground black pepper
1 egg, hard-boiled and shelled
15 ml /1 tbls very finely
   chopped fresh parsley
lettuce leaves, to serve
1 thin lemon slice, to garnish

1   Place the crab on its back with the tail end facing you. Twist the
claws sharply inwards, to break them off. Hold the crab steady
with your thumbs under the tail flap and push downwards until the
body breaks away from the shell. Keeping the white and dark meats
separate, scoop out all the meat, discarding the mouth, stomach sac
and grey lungs. Twist off the legs and dig out the meat with a
skewer. Crack the claws and remove the meat. Add the leg and claw
meat to the white meat. Weigh the white meat, make a note of the
weight and put the meat in a bowl. Repeat with the dark meat,
putting it in a separate bowl.
2   Wash and scrub the shell. Trim it back to the line which appears
round the border using flat-nosed pliers, or break off the rough
edges neatly with a hammer. Brush with olive oil.
3   Flavour the mayonnaise to taste with lemon juice. Using 45 ml /
3 tbls mayonnaise to each 100 g /4 oz white meat, carefully fold the
mayonnaise into the white meat. Season with salt and pepper.
4   For each 100 g /4 oz dark meat, measure 30 ml /2 tbls
mayonnaise. Strain any excess juice from the dark meat into the
mayonnaise, then fold into the dark meat, and season.
5   Spoon the meat into the shell, with the dark meat in the centre
and the white meat in 2 panels on either side.
6   Press the egg white through a fine sieve into a bowl, then rinse
and dry the sieve and press the egg yolk into a separate dish.
7   Using a knife to help you make neat decorative lines, press the
blade into the white flesh on one side of the dividing line between
the different-coloured meats and tilt it away from the brown crab
meat. Dribble half the sieved egg yolk across the crab in a thin line
close to the knife blade. Move the knife to the other side of the line
of yolk and repeat with half the egg white. Move the knife again and
repeat with half the parsley. The result is a very thin tricolour
stripe. Repeat on the other side. Keep chilled until ready to serve.
8   To serve, arrange a bed of lettuce leaves on a plate and put the
dressed crab in the centre. Garnish with a thin slice of lemon. Each
person spoons one quarter of the crab meat out of the shell, taking
half the white meat and a quarter of the brown meat.

 1 hour

Prawn and cucumber salad

Serves 4
250 g /8 oz boiled, peeled prawns, defrosted if frozen
1 cucumber
salt
30–45 ml /2–3 tbls lemon juice
150 ml /5 fl oz mayonnaise (page 49)
15–30 ml /1–2 tbls tomato ketchup
60–90 ml /4–6 tbls thick cream
30–60 ml /2–4 tbls diced green pepper
freshly ground black pepper
a dash of Tabasco sauce
30 ml /2 tbls freshly chopped parsley

1   Drain the prawns well and dry on absorbent paper. Reserve.
Peel the cucumber, cut in half lengthways and, using a small spoon,
scoop out and discard the seeds. Cut the seeded cucumber into
chunks about 25 mm /1 in thick, then cut each slice lengthways into
5 mm /¼ in strips. Sprinkle with salt and lemon juice and chill in the
refrigerator for 10–15 minutes.
2   Drain the cucumber strips well. In a bowl, combine the
mayonnaise, ketchup and cream and blend thoroughly. Then stir in
the diced green pepper, prawns and cucumber strips and toss.
Season to taste with salt, freshly ground black pepper and Tabasco.
Pile the salad onto a serving plate, sprinkle over the parsley and
serve.

 15 minutes,
plus chilling

Taramasalata

Serves 4–6
6 thin slices of white bread
¼ Spanish onion, grated
1–2 garlic cloves, crushed
juice of 1 lemon, more if needed
175 g /6 oz jar of smoked cod's roe
120–150 ml /8–10 tbls olive oil
15 ml /1 tbls finely chopped fresh parsley, to garnish
green olives, to garnish
hot toast or pitta bread, to serve

1   Trim the crusts from the bread. Soak the slices in cold water for a few minutes, then squeeze out as much moisture as possible. Place the bread in a blender and add the grated onion, garlic, lemon juice and cod's roe. Blend to a smooth, pink paste.
2   Remove the centre of the lid of the blender and, with the blender at a moderate speed, trickle in 120 ml /8 tbls of the olive oil. Taste and add more lemon juice if the mixture seems too bland, or more olive oil if it is still very strongly flavoured.
3   Turn the mixture into a serving bowl. Sprinkle with finely chopped parsley, garnish with green olives, and serve with hot toast or pitta bread.

● In the traditional recipe for taramasalata, the cod's roe had to be pounded slowly and painfully in a mortar until it finally turned to a smooth paste. Nowadays the combination of an electric blender and potted roes, which are much softer and creamier to begin with, allows you to make this classic Greek hors d'oeuvre in a matter of minutes.
● Try stuffing the mixture into 5 cm /2 in lengths of crisp celery for a party nibble.

 20 minutes

Provençal salad of salt cod

Serves 6
350 g /12 oz dried salt cod fillets
6 large, ripe tomatoes
salt and freshly ground black pepper
150 ml /5 fl oz well-flavoured mayonnaise (page 49)
1 garlic clove, finely chopped
1–2 anchovy fillets, finely chopped
15 ml /1 tbls finely chopped fresh basil or tarragon
60 ml /4 tbls finely chopped fresh parsley
15 ml /1 tbls finely chopped capers
5 ml /1 tsp lemon juice

1   Soak the cod fillets overnight in a bowl of cold water, changing the water once or twice.
2   Drain the cod and put it in a saucepan. Cover with cold water, bring to the boil, then drain and return to the saucepan. Cover with fresh cold water and bring to the boil again. Turn off the heat and allow the fish to steep in the hot water for 10 minutes – but do not overcook or the fish will toughen.
3   Strain the cod, remove the skin and bones and flake the fish, then leave to cool completely.
4   To prepare the tomato cases, remove the top of each tomato, making zigzag cuts with a sharp knife, and carefully scoop out all the pulp and seeds. Season with salt and freshly ground black pepper and turn upside down to drain until ready to use.
5   In a bowl combine the mayonnaise with the chopped garlic, anchovy fillets, basil or tarragon, 30 ml /2 tbls of the chopped parsley, the chopped capers and the lemon juice.
6   Toss the flaked fish lightly in the sauce until well coated. Pile the fish mixture into the tomato cases and garnish with the remaining finely chopped parsley.

● Salted cod is a staple food in Portugal and right around the Mediterranean. Once it has been soaked it is easy to prepare for this tempting appetizer.

overnight soaking,
then 45 minutes, plus cooling

EGG & CHEESE STARTERS

Quick to cook and always at hand, eggs and cheese can be used to create an enormous range of starters – from a colourful but simple salad to an elegant soufflé or poached eggs set in aspic.

Eggs and cheese can be teamed up to make a variety of delicious starters or, equally well, they can be used separately. Eggs are particularly versatile as they can be served in many different ways and with a variety of textures, depending on the method of cooking.

Quick egg ideas

Eggs can be hard boiled, cut in half and stuffed with fish, paté, herbs or a sauce.
Curried eggs can be made by mashing the hard-boiled yolk with very finely chopped onion, concentrated curry paste, finely chopped ham and mayonnaise and spooning it back into the egg-white halves.
Canned anchovy fillets can be sliced and mashed with egg yolk and a pinch of dry mustard and spooned into the whites.
Slice or chop hard-boiled eggs and add to a sauce which can be reheated and served with cooked leeks, asparagus or cauliflower. Alternatively, add the egg to the sauce, top with breadcrumbs or grated cheese, brown under the grill and then serve on its own as a starter.
Scrambled eggs make a surprisingly rich starter before a light main course. Scrambled eggs are very simple to prepare but must be done at the last minute as they need to be cooked with great care – they must not be overcooked or they will become stiff, lumpy and indigestible.

Elegant egg starters

Individual starters can be served in an edible shell of vegetables, bread or pastry cases.
Globe artichokes can be cooked filled with sauce and topped with an egg: cook until tender, then scoop out the choke. Fill with a white or tomato sauce, top with a poached egg and spoon more sauce over the top.
Bread cases can be baked until crisp, then filled with chopped grilled bacon. Top with a poached egg and cover with a white or cheese sauce.
Baked eggs can be cooked in cocottes or ramekins, topped with thick cream and a sprinkling of fresh herbs, if wished. Season with salt and pepper just before serving.
Eggs and cheese can be combined to make individual soufflés or one large one to serve four to six people. Almost any type of cheese, from a soft curd cheese to a hard cheese, can be mixed with eggs to make one large omelette suitable for serving up to four people as a starter.

Quick cheese ideas

Cheese combines well with fruit, particularly apple or pineapple. It can also be used as a tasty filling for fried sandwiches and crêpes, in pastry for savoury tartlets or in a mille-feuille (see recipe). Mix crumbled blue cheese into salads or use soft cheeses to stuff tomatoes or courgettes.

Eggs mimosa

hard boiling and cooling the eggs, then 20 minutes

Serves 4
6 hard-boiled eggs
100 g /4 oz boiled, peeled prawns, defrosted if frozen
15 ml /1 tbls lemon juice
a pinch of cayenne pepper
175 ml /6 fl oz mayonnaise (page 49)
For the garnish
8 lettuce leaves, washed and dried
2 tomatoes, quartered
8 black olives

1 Shell the cold hard-boiled eggs and cut each in half lengthways. Remove the yolks. Push 2 yolks through a sieve and reserve for the garnish. Reserve the remaining yolks for use in another recipe.
2 In a bowl, mix the boiled, peeled prawns, the lemon juice, and a pinch of cayenne pepper to taste, until blended. Carefully fill the cavity of each egg white with the prawn mixture, using a teaspoon.
3 On 4 individual plates, arrange 2 lettuce leaves, with 2 tomato wedges. Place 3 egg halves flat side down on each plate.
4 If the mayonnaise is very thick, put it in a bowl. Add 15–30 ml /1–2 tbls boiling water and beat well.
5 With a large metal spoon, coat each egg half with mayonnaise. Sprinkle with the reserved sieved egg yolk, garnish with 2 black olives and serve.

● This popular starter takes its name from the early-flowering Mediterranean mimosa. Its flowers are bright yellow and have a crumbly texture not unlike sieved hard-boiled egg yolk!

Ham and cheese fritters

3 hours, including 2 hours chilling

Serves 6
275 ml /10 fl oz milk
40 g /1½ oz butter
105 ml /7 tbls flour
100 g /4 oz Cheddar cheese, freshly grated
salt and freshly ground black pepper
a pinch of cayenne pepper
a pinch of freshly grated nutmeg
75 g /3 oz lean ham, diced
2 eggs, lightly beaten
50 g /2 oz fresh white breadcrumbs
oil for deep frying
sprigs of watercress, to garnish

1 In a saucepan, bring the milk to the boil. Set aside.
2 In a heavy-based saucepan, heat the butter. Stir in 45 ml /3 tbls flour, then cook over a low heat for 2–3 minutes, stirring.
3 Pour in the milk and stir vigorously with a wire whisk. Bring to the boil and simmer for 3 minutes, stirring frequently.
4 Remove from the heat and beat in the cheese. Season to taste with salt and pepper. Stir in a pinch each of cayenne pepper and nutmeg. Stir in the diced ham.
5 Line a 30 × 20 cm /12 × 8 in baking tin with cling film.
6 Spread the mixture evenly in the tin, then leave to get cold and chill for 2 hours.
7 Sprinkle the remaining flour on a flat plate. Put the lightly beaten eggs into a shallow dish and the fresh white breadcrumbs into a separate shallow dish.
8 With a floured knife, cut the chilled mixture into 24 rectangles. Lift each one with a palette knife and coat in flour, shaking off the excess. Dip in the beaten egg, then toss in the fresh white breadcrumbs.
9 Lay the rectangles on a tray lined with cling film and chill for at least 10 minutes.
10 About 20 minutes before serving, heat the oil in a deep-fat frier to 190C /375F. (A bread cube will brown in 50 seconds.)
11 Fry the fritters a few at a time for 1½ minutes, or until golden. Drain on absorbent paper and transfer to a heated dish; keep hot. Decorate with watercress and serve.

Egg and anchovy salad

hard boiling and cooling the eggs, then 15 minutes

Serves 4
2 crisp lettuces
3 hard-boiled eggs
50 g /2 oz canned anchovy fillets, drained
2 large tomatoes, blanched, skinned, seeded and cut into even-sized strips
For the vinaigrette
45 ml /3 tbls olive oil
15 ml /1 tbls wine vinegar
salt and freshly ground black pepper

1 Prepare the lettuces. Wash well under cold running water, discarding any damaged leaves. Drain the leaves well and wrap in a tea-towel to dry. Arrange in a serving bowl.
2 Shell the hard-boiled eggs. Halve lengthways, then cut lengthways into quarters. Place the quartered eggs on top of the lettuce leaves, yolk side up.
3 Cut each anchovy fillet into 3. In a small bowl, combine the anchovy pieces with the tomato strips, tossing lightly.
4 Arrange the anchovy and tomato mixture evenly on top of the quartered eggs.
5 Prepare the vinaigrette. In a small bowl, combine the olive oil, wine vinegar, salt and pepper. Beat with a fork until mixture emulsifies.
6 Just before serving, pour the vinaigrette over the salad.

Eggs mimosa

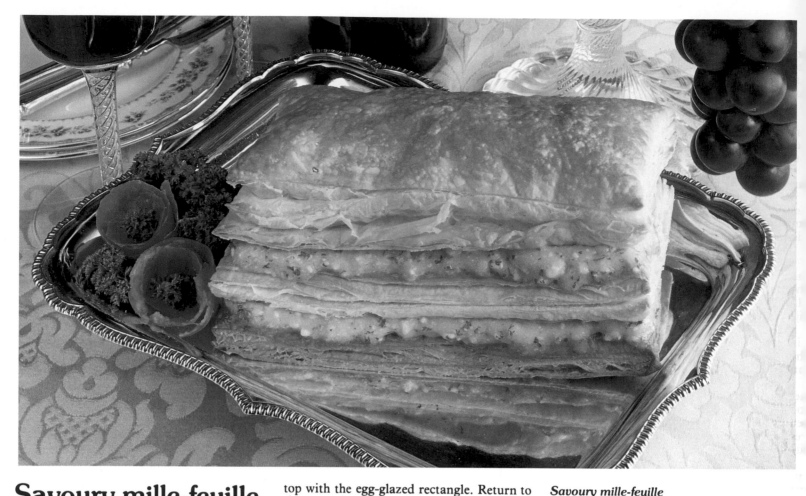

Savoury mille-feuille

🔪🔪 1 hour, plus cooling time
and 5–10 minutes reheating

Serves 8
200 g /7 oz ready-made puff pastry,
  defrosted if frozen
100 g /4 oz blue cheese
50 g /2 oz butter, softened
15 ml /1 tbls freshly chopped parsley
1 egg yolk
30 ml /2 tbls thin cream
freshly ground black pepper
beaten egg mixed with milk, to glaze

1 Divide the pastry into 3 and roll each piece into a rectangle 10 × 20 cm /4 × 8 in. Carefully roll each piece of pastry over the rolling pin and unroll onto a dampened pastry sheet. Prick 2 with a fork. Place all 3 in the refrigerator for 30 minutes.
2 Meanwhile, heat the oven to 200C / 400F /gas 6 and make the filling: beat the cheese until soft and then beat in the softened butter and parsley. Beat the egg yolk with the thin cream and mix into the cheese mixture. Season with the pepper.
3 Remove the pastry rectangles from the refrigerator and brush the unpricked rectangle with the beaten egg and milk glaze. Bake the pastry for 20 minutes, or until lightly golden and puffy. Cool the rectangles on a wire rack. Lower the oven to 190C /375F /gas 5.
4 Spread one unglazed rectangle with half the blue cheese mixture. Cover with the other unglazed rectangle and spread that with the remaining cheese mixture. Finally

top with the egg-glazed rectangle. Return to the oven for 5–10 minutes, or until pastry and filling are heated through.

Sophie's salad

🔪🔪 30 minutes, plus chilling

Serves 6
2 large green peppers
2 large red peppers
6 firm tomatoes
salt and freshly ground black pepper
6 hard-boiled eggs, shelled
90 g /3½ oz canned anchovy fillets,
  drained
about 24 black olives, stoned and halved
For the herb dressing
2 garlic cloves, finely chopped
15 ml /1 tbls finely chopped fresh parsley
15 ml /1 tbls finely chopped fresh tarragon
15 ml /1 tbls finely chopped fresh chervil
15 ml /1 tbls finely snipped fresh chives
120 ml /8 tbls olive oil
45 ml /3 tbls white wine vinegar
salt and freshly ground black pepper

1 Heat the grill to high.
2 Make the herb dressing. In a bowl, combine the garlic, herbs, oil and vinegar. Season to taste with salt and freshly ground black pepper. Beat until the dressing emulsifies.
3 Place the peppers 7.5 cm /3 in from the heat and grill for about 10 minutes, turning them, until the skin on all sides has blistered and blackened.

Savoury mille-feuille

4 Leave the charred peppers to cool, then peel off the skins.
5 Slice the tomatoes thickly. Cover the bottom of a large flat serving dish with the tomato slices. Season with salt and pepper. Sprinkle with a quarter of the dressing.
6 Cut each skinned pepper into 10–12 strips lengthways and remove any seeds.
7 Lay the green pepper strips over the tomatoes. Season with salt and pepper. Sprinkle with dressing. Repeat with the red pepper strips.
8 Slice the eggs into rings and cover the red peppers with a layer of egg slices. Pour over the remainder of the dressing.
9 Cut each anchovy fillet into fine strips with a sharp knife. Arrange in a fine lattice over the egg rings. Garnish with olives and chill in the refrigerator for at least 30 minutes.

Cheese soufflé

🔪🔪 50 minutes

Serves 4
butter, stale breadcrumbs and grated
  Parmesan cheese for the dish
300 ml /10 fl oz milk
40 g /1½ oz butter
45 ml /3 tbls flour
4 eggs, separated
75 g /3 oz strong Cheddar cheese, grated
salt and freshly ground black pepper
10 ml /2 tsp Dijon mustard
1 egg white

Heat the oven to 190C /375F /gas 5.

Grease a 1.4 L /2½ pt soufflé dish generously with butter, paying particular attention to the inside rim of the dish, then dust all over with stale breadcrumbs and Parmesan cheese.

Bring the milk to the boil.

Melt the butter in a heavy-based saucepan; blend in the flour and stir over a low heat with a wooden spoon for 2–3 minutes to make a pale roux.

Add the boiled milk gradually to the roux, stirring vigorously with a wire whisk to prevent lumps forming. Bring to the boil and simmer over a moderate heat for about 2 minutes longer, stirring, until the sauce is thick and smooth.

Remove the pan from the heat and beat in the egg yolks, one at a time. Pour the sauce into a large bowl, add the grated Cheddar cheese and season generously with salt and freshly ground black pepper and the Dijon mustard.

Select another large bowl and make sure it is spotlessly clean and dry. Put all the egg whites in it, add a pinch of salt and whisk until stiff but not dry.

Fold the whisked egg whites into the cheese sauce with a large metal spoon, working as quickly and lightly as possible. Gently spoon the soufflé mixture into the prepared dish and lightly level off the top with the back of the spoon.

Cook in the oven for 25–30 minutes, or until the soufflé is well puffed and golden brown. Serve immediately.

Oeufs en cocotte with cream and herbs

15 minutes

Serves 4

butter for greasing
60 ml /4 tbls thick cream
10 ml /2 tsp French mustard
salt and freshly ground black pepper
15 ml /1 tbls finely chopped fresh parsley
15 ml /1 tbls finely chopped fresh tarragon
15 ml /1 tbls finely snipped fresh chives
4 eggs, at room temperature
bundle of chives, to garnish (optional)

Heat the oven to 170C /325F /gas 3.

Butter 4 individual cocottes, ramekins or tiny soufflé dishes.

In a small saucepan, combine the thick cream with the French mustard. Season to taste with salt and freshly ground black pepper.

Stir in the finely chopped parsley and tarragon and the finely snipped chives, then place over a low heat until smooth and warm.

Break an egg into each cocotte, without breaking the yolks.

Put the cocottes in a roasting tin. Pour in enough boiling water to come halfway up the side of the cocottes.

Cook over a low heat on top of the stove

for 2 minutes, or until the water simmers gently.

8 Pour the cream and herb mixture over the eggs and cover the tin with foil.

9 Transfer the tin to the oven and cook for 5–6 minutes, or until the whites are set and the yolks still runny. Garnish each dish with a small bundle of chives, if wished. Serve immediately.

Italian omelette

30 minutes for the sauce,
plus 10 minutes for the omelette

Serves 3–4
For the tomato sauce
15 ml /1 tbls olive oil
30 ml /2 tbls finely chopped onion
400 g /14 oz canned tomatoes
1.5 ml /¼ tsp dried basil
1.5 ml /¼ tsp sugar
salt and freshly ground black pepper
For the omelette
75 g /3 oz ricotta cheese
30 ml /2 tbls thick cream
30 ml /2 tbls grated Parmesan cheese
25 g /1 oz Gruyère cheese, grated
90 ml /6 tbls green beans, cooked and diced
30 ml /2 tbls coarsely chopped fresh parsley
6 medium-sized eggs
salt and freshly ground black pepper
25 g /1 oz butter
30 ml /2 tbls olive oil

Italian omelette

1 First prepare the tomato sauce. Heat the olive oil in a small, heavy-based saucepan, add the finely chopped onion and sauté for 3–4 minutes until soft and golden. Then add the canned tomatoes, with their juices, the dried basil and the sugar. Season lightly with salt and freshly ground black pepper.

2 Simmer the sauce for about 20 minutes until reduced and thickened, stirring and mashing occasionally with a wooden spoon. Remove the pan from the heat and press the contents through a fine nylon sieve. Correct the seasoning and keep the sauce hot.

3 Prepare the omelette mixture. In a bowl, beat together the ricotta cheese with the cream and grated Parmesan and Gruyère. Stir in the diced green beans and coarsely chopped parsley, then season to taste with salt and freshly ground black pepper.

4 In a separate bowl, stir the eggs vigorously with a fork until thoroughly blended. Pour onto the ricotta mixture and mix well. Taste and correct the seasoning.

5 Place an omelette pan 20 cm /8 in diameter over high heat. Add the butter and olive oil and swirl over the base and sides of the pan. When the fat is hot but not coloured, pour in the omelette mixture. Leave for 1 minute, then stir with the flat part of a fork 2–3 times. Reduce heat to medium-low. With a palette knife, lift the far edge of the omelette and tilt the pan so that the raw egg runs onto the base. As soon as the omelette is set and golden underneath but still very moist on top, slide it out of the pan onto a heated serving plate. Serve immediately with the hot tomato sauce.

Grilled apple croustades

 20 minutes

Makes 6
2 small dessert apples
50 g /2 oz butter
6 large slices white bread
6 slices of salami with the skin removed
6 slices of Cheddar cheese, cut in rounds
paprika

1   Heat the grill. Peel and core the apples with an apple corer or sharp pointed knife. Slice each apple into 3 even-sized rings about 10 mm /½ in thick.
2   Melt 25 g /1 oz butter in a frying-pan, then add the apple rings. Brown the rings on both sides. Remove them with a slotted spoon and drain on absorbent paper.
3   Using a pastry cutter or glass, stamp out a circle 6–7.5 cm /2½–3 in in diameter from each slice of bread. Heat the remaining butter in the frying-pan and when sizzling add the bread circles. Brown on both sides. Remove the croûtons with a slotted spoon and drain on absorbent paper.
4   Place an apple ring on each fried croûton of bread. Cover each with a slice of salami and top with a round of Cheddar cheese. Sprinkle each apple croustade with a small pinch of paprika and grill until golden brown and bubbling. Serve the grilled apple croustades immediately.

Poached eggs en brioche

30 minutes

Serves 6
6 small brioches
melted butter
60 ml /4 tbls white wine vinegar
6 eggs
30 ml /6 tsp red caviar
For the hollandaise sauce
lemon juice
salt
freshly ground white pepper
4 egg yolks
100 g /4 oz softened butter, cut into 4 pieces

1   Heat the oven to 170C /325F /gas 3.
2   Make the hollandaise sauce. In the top pan of a double boiler, combine 5 ml /1 tsp lemon juice with 15 ml /1 tbls cold water and salt and ground white pepper to taste. Add the egg yolks and 1 piece of butter and stir the mixture rapidly and constantly with a wire whisk over hot but not simmering water until the butter has melted and the mixture starts to thicken.
3   Whisk in the second piece of butter. When it has melted, add a third piece, stirring from the bottom of the pan until it has melted. Stir in the remaining butter.
4   Remove the top pan from the heat and

Grilled apple croustades

continue beating for 2–3 minutes, then return to the hot water and continue beating for 2 more minutes. By this time an emulsion should have formed and the sauce will be thick. Add a few drops of lemon juice, strain and keep over warm (not hot) water.
5   Remove the top from each brioche and hollow out the middle with a teaspoon to make a cavity big enough to hold a poached egg. Brush the brioche cases with melted butter and heat for 6–8 minutes in the oven.
6   Meanwhile, pour 7.5 cm /3 in water into a large saucepan. Add the vinegar and bring to the boil, then reduce heat to a simmer.
7   Break an egg into a cup and slip it into the water. Repeat with 2 more eggs. Poach the eggs for 3–4 minutes.
8   Transfer them to a bowl of warm water to keep warm. Poach the remainder.
9   Place the brioches on a heated serving dish. Drain the eggs on absorbent paper and trim neatly. Put an egg in each brioche cavity. Spoon over a little hollandaise sauce and top with 5 ml /1 tsp red caviar. Serve with the remaining sauce.

Eggs cooked like tripe

20 minutes

Serves 6
600 ml /1 pt milk
½ chicken stock cube, crumbled
250 g /8 oz medium-sized onions, sliced
25–40 g /1–1½ oz butter
30 ml /2 tbls cornflour
salt and freshly ground black pepper
a pinch of cayenne pepper
a pinch of grated nutmeg
6 hard-boiled eggs, cut into quarters

1   Heat the milk in a saucepan and dissolv the crumbled chicken stock cube in it.
2   In a medium-sized flameproof casserol sauté the sliced onions gently in the butt for 10 minutes until tender but not browne Add the cornflour and mix well. Gradual stir in the flavoured milk and bring to t boil, stirring continuously. Simmer for minutes, stirring occasionally. Seaso generously with salt, black pepper, cayenr pepper and freshly grated nutmeg.
3   Stir in most of the quartered hard-boil eggs, reserving a few for garnish, and he through.
4   Pour the creamy egg mixture into cocottes or ramekins. Garnish with th reserved quarters of hard-boiled egg, eithe as they are or finely chopped.

● This creamy egg casserole, *oeufs à la trip* contains no tripe but is cooked in a crean onion sauce which is a well known way cooking tripe.

Fried Mozzarella sandwiches

The Italian title of this dish, 'Mozzarella in carrozza', literally means 'Mozzarella in a carriage', a very grand name for a poor man's dish, since Mozzarella cheese and oil are plentiful and cheap in Italy. If Italian Mozzarella is unavailable, Bel Paese is a better substitute than other Mozzarellas.

🍴 35 minutes

Serves 4

8 large slices of 1 or 2 day-old white bread, crusts removed
200 g /7 oz Italian Mozzarella or Bel Paese cheese
salt and freshly ground black pepper
vegetable oil for frying
300 ml /11 fl oz milk
2 medium-sized eggs
75 g /3 oz flour

1 Halve all the bread slices. Cut the Mozzarella or Bel Paese cheese into 10 mm / ½ in thick slices and divide the slices into 8 portions. Lay each portion over a half slice of bread, sprinkle with salt and freshly ground black pepper and cover with another half slice of bread.
2 Put enough oil in a frying-pan to come 10 mm /½ in up the side of the pan and turn the heat to high. Pour the milk into a shallow dish. Place the eggs in another shallow dish and beat them with a little salt and pepper. Place the flour on a large, flat plate. Very quickly dip each sandwich into the milk. Lightly coat with flour and then dip in the beaten eggs, letting any excess egg flow back into the dish. Make sure all the sandwiches are coated evenly
3 When the oil is very hot but not smoking, slip the sandwiches, a few at a time, into the pan. When they have turned a deep golden brown on the underside, about 5 minutes, turn them over and brown the other side. Drain the sandwiches on absorbent paper, sprinkle with salt and serve at once. Fry the remaining sandwiches and serve immediately.

Scrambled eggs provençale

🍴 30 minutes

Serves 4

8 canned, drained anchovy fillets
4 × 5 mm /¼ in thick slices of white bread
25–40 g /1–1½ oz butter
15 ml /1 tbls olive oil
4 eggs
15 ml /1 tbls thin cream, milk or water
salt and freshly ground black pepper
a pinch of cayenne pepper
4 plump black olives, stoned and quartered
15 ml /1 tbls finely chopped fresh parsley

1 Heat the oven to 150C /300F /gas 2. Slice the anchovy fillets in half lengthways.
2 Use a biscuit cutter about 8 cm /3¼ in in diameter to cut the bread into rounds. Heat all but 15 g /½ oz butter and the olive oil in a saucepan until foaming stops, then fry the bread gently until golden on both sides. Drain on absorbent paper. Transfer to a baking tray and put in the oven to keep warm.
3 Break the eggs into a bowl. Add the cream, milk or water, and salt, freshly ground black pepper and cayenne pepper to taste. Mix lightly.
4 Melt 15 g /½ oz butter in a saucepan over gentle heat. Add the eggs and scramble them, stirring constantly with a wooden spoon, until the egg mixture is cooked but still creamy and slightly moist.
5 Remove the fried bread rounds from the oven and put on individual heated plates. Spoon the scrambled eggs onto the fried bread rounds. Garnish with a lattice-work of anchovy strips. Dot each portion with four pieces of olive and garnish with a pinch of finely chopped parsley. Serve immediately.

Egg and celery salad in tomato cases

🍴 hard boiling and cooling the eggs, then 30 minutes

Serves 6

6 large tomatoes
salt
freshly ground black pepper
3 hard-boiled eggs
3 celery stalks, thinly sliced
150 ml /5 fl oz mayonnaise (page 49)
5 ml /1 tsp Dijon mustard
15 ml /1 tbls lemon juice
a pinch of cayenne pepper
15 ml /1 tbls finely chopped fresh parsley
15 ml /1 tbls finely chopped fresh chives

1 Slice the rounded bottom end of each tomato with a very sharp knife and hollow out the middle with a sharp teaspoon, reserving seeds and juice for another dish if wished. Season inside each tomato cavity with salt and freshly ground black pepper to taste. Leave them to draw, upside-down on absorbent paper, until needed.
2 Shell the hard-boiled eggs and chop them finely.
3 In a bowl, combine the chopped hard-boiled eggs, sliced celery, mayonnaise, Dijon mustard and lemon juice. Season with salt and freshly ground black pepper and a pinch of cayenne pepper to taste. Stir until all the filling ingredients are well mixed together. Taste and correct seasoning, if necessary.
4 Fill each tomato cavity with the egg and celery salad, piling it up well. Sprinkle the top of the filling with finely chopped parsley and chives and serve immediately.

Scrambled eggs provençale

Deep-fried cheese crêpes

Serves 4
crêpe batter (see page 94)
For the filling
25 g /1 oz butter
30 ml /2 tbls flour
300 ml /10 fl·oz milk
120 g /4½ oz Gruyère cheese, diced
salt and freshly ground black pepper
a pinch of paprika
2 medium-sized egg yolks, beaten
oil for greasing
For deep frying
fat or oil for deep frying
1 medium-sized egg, beaten
50 g /2 oz breadcrumbs

1   While the batter is resting, make the filling. Melt the butter in a saucepan, stir in the flour until well blended and cook, stirring, for 5 minutes, or until lightly coloured. Whisk in the milk until smooth and cook, stirring occasionally, for 10 minutes, or until the sauce has thickened.
2   Add the diced Gruyère cheese and continue cooking until the cheese melts. Season to taste with salt and freshly ground black pepper and paprika. Remove the mixture from the heat and beat in the egg yolks.
3   Pour the mixture into an oiled square or rectangular shallow baking dish or tin about 25 × 15 cm /10 × 6 in and leave to cool and set.
4   Make 8 crêpes from the crêpe batter (see Herb and spinach crêpes, step 3, page 93). Heat the oil in a deep-fat frier to 180C / 350F: at this temperature a cube of bread will brown in 60 seconds.
5   Cut the filling mixture into 8 rectangles. Put a cheese rectangle into the middle of one crêpe. Fold over two sides, brush with beaten egg to seal and fold over the top and bottom. Treat the other crêpes in the same way. Dip the cheese crêpes in beaten egg and brush all over. Then coat carefully and thoroughly in breadcrumbs.
6   Deep fry the crêpes for 1½ minutes, or until golden brown. Drain on absorbent paper and serve immediately.

 2½ hours including resting batter and cooling the filling, then 1 hour

Moroccan egg and pepper appetizer

Serves 4
25 g /1 oz butter
15 ml /1 tbls olive oil
1 Spanish onion, thinly sliced
1 large red pepper
1 large yellow pepper
1-2 small dried hot chillies
coarse salt
freshly ground black pepper
4 eggs

1   Select a heavy-based sauté pan with a tight-fitting lid. Heat the butter and olive oil in the pan. When the foaming subsides, add the sliced onion and sauté over a high heat for 2-3 minutes, or until it starts to colour, stirring occasionally with a wooden spoon.
2   Meanwhile, core, seed and slice the peppers. Core, seed, and dice the chillies.
3   Reduce the heat and add the prepared peppers and chillies. Cook gently for 10–12 minutes, or until the peppers are soft but not mushy, stirring occasionally. Season to taste with coarse salt and freshly ground black pepper.
4   Using the back of a spoon, make 4 depressions in the vegetables. Break an egg into each hollow. Cover the pan with a lid and cook over a low heat for about 4 minutes, or until the eggs have set. Serve immediately.

● The Moroccan name of this hot and substantial appetizer is *chachouka*.

 20 minutes

Baked egg and bacon

Serves 4
butter for greasing
15–30 ml /1–2 tbls olive oil
60 ml /4 tbls finely chopped bacon
60 ml /4 tbls finely chopped fresh parsley
salt and freshly ground black pepper
4 eggs
60 ml /4 tbls thick cream

1   Heat the oven to 170C /325F /gas 3.
2   Butter 4 individual ramekins, soufflé dishes or cocottes.
3   In a small frying-pan, heat the olive oil and sauté the finely chopped bacon until crisp. Drain it well on absorbent paper and mix with the finely chopped parsley. Season to taste with salt and freshly ground black pepper.
4   Sprinkle the base of each ramekin with a little of the bacon mixture and break an egg carefully into each one.
5   Bake in the oven for 12–15 minutes, or until the whites are just setting but the yolks are still runny.
6   Swirl 15 ml /1 tbls thick cream over the top of each egg and serve immediately.

30 minutes

Eggs in aspic

Serves 6
850 ml /1½ pt aspic (see below)
45 ml /3 tbls Madeira
6 thin slices cooked carrot
sprigs of tarragon or parsley
6 medium-sized eggs
6 thin slices ham
For the garnish
6 small lettuce leaves
6 sprigs watercress or parsley
12 black olives
6 tomato roses or wedges (see page 48)

1   Warm the aspic until it liquefies, then stir in the Madeira. Pour a thin layer over the base of each of 6 individual ramekins, large enough to hold an egg. Refrigerate for 20 minutes, or until set.
2   Cut the carrot slices into flower shapes and arrange them on top of the aspic; surround them with small pieces of tarragon or parsley, to make 'leaves'. Spoon a 6 mm /¼ in layer of liquid aspic over them and chill again until set.
3   Meanwhile poach the eggs lightly for 3 minutes. Allow the eggs to cool and trim the edges neatly. Put one in each ramekin and fill to the brim with aspic. Chill until set.
4   Cut the ham slices to the diameter of the ramekins and fit them in each ramekin, over the top of the solid aspic. Melt the remaining aspic and spoon a little over the ham. Chill until ready to serve.
5   To unmould, plunge each ramekin into hot water for 1–2 seconds, then invert each one over a small individual plate. Hold the plate and ramekin together and shake gently until you feel the aspic loosen and settle onto the dish. If you are not serving them immediately, return the aspic eggs to the refrigerator.
6   Just before serving, garnish each plate with a lettuce leaf, a sprig of watercress or parsley, 2 black olives and a tomato rose or wedge.

● To save time, you can make aspic from powdered gelatine and good quality canned consommé; mix according to the instructions on the gelatine packet. You can also serve a smaller number of eggs in aspic on a single large serving plate. To do this, invert each ramekin onto a small damp plate and slide the aspic onto the damp serving dish. Garnish as above.

1½ hours

VEGETABLE STARTERS

A vegetable starter makes one of the most attractive beginnings to a meal. Raw or cooked vegetables can be used; they are light and fresh and can be mixed with other ingredients for contrasting flavour.

Most vegetable starters need very little preparation or cooking, but they need careful attention to detail. Cutting and presentation are all important.

Lettuces can be used whole or shredded and there is no end to the additions you can make to your green salad for texture, colour and flavour. Diced celery, crisp green pepper or aniseed-flavoured fennel, or a touch of finely chopped onion or shallot add 'crunch appeal', while tomato, cucumber, radishes, mushrooms, avocado, nuts, raisins, crumbled bacon, diced ham or cheese, hard-boiled egg or black olives can be added for colour and flavour.

Raw vegetables can be sliced, shredded or grated and served with mayonnaise or vinaigrette. All kinds of subtle flavours can be added to stuffed and baked vegetables when they are served as a dish on their own. Fillings can range from simple sauces to minced meat and vegetables mixed with breadcrumbs or rice.

Choose vegetables that are crisp and fresh looking. No amount of attention will restore flavour, texture and goodness to a wilted vegetable that is past its prime.

Spicy cooked cucumber salad

30 minutes,
plus 4 hours marinating

Serves 4
1 large cucumber, washed
15 ml /1 tbls salt
30 ml /2 tbls sugar
1 red pepper
30 ml /2 tbls sesame seed oil
4 thin slices fresh ginger root, shredded
60 ml /4 tbls rice vinegar or wine vinegar
15 ml /1 tbls thick (dark) soy sauce

1 Cut the cucumber in half lengthways and scoop out the seeds with a metal spoon. Cut each half into 4 cm /1½ in lengths, then slice each length into 5 mm /¼ in strips. Sprinkle them with salt and half the sugar, then leave to stand for at least 15 minutes.
2 Meanwhile, cut the red pepper into the same size strips as the cucumber. Rinse the cucumber strips under cold running water, drain and dry with a tea-towel.
3 In a wok or frying-pan, heat the oil and add the cucumber and red pepper strips and the shredded fresh ginger. Stir-fry over a high heat for 2–3 minutes, or until slightly softened. Transfer to a bowl.
4 Add the rice vinegar or wine vinegar, the remaining sugar and the soy sauce to the vegetables. Toss until well coated. Transfer to a serving dish and leave to marinate for at least 4 hours in the refrigerator.

Raw mushroom and bacon salad

10–15 minutes,
plus 2 hours chilling

Serves 6
500 g /1 lb button mushrooms
45 ml /3 tbls lemon juice
120 ml /8 tbls olive oil
60 ml /4 tbls finely chopped onion
salt
freshly ground black pepper
4 slices back bacon
15 g /½ oz butter
15 ml /1 tbls finely chopped fresh chives
30 ml /2 tbls finely chopped fresh parsley

1 Remove the stalks from the mushrooms and reserve for another dish. Wipe the caps clean with a damp cloth; do not peel. Slice the caps thinly and place in a salad bowl with the lemon juice and olive oil. Add the onion, salt and freshly ground black pepper to taste. Toss the mushrooms carefully until evenly coated, then cover the bowl and chill in the refrigerator for 2 hours.
2 In the meantime, remove and discard the rind from the bacon. Slice the bacon across into thin strips. Melt the butter in a frying-pan over a moderate heat, add the strips of bacon and sauté until crisp. using a slotted spoon, remove the bacon from the pan; drain and leave to cool.
3 Just before serving, remove the mushrooms from the refrigerator; pour off any excess dressing or add a little more olive oil and lemon juice as necessary. Scatter over the freshly chopped herbs and crisp bacon strips and serve.

Asparagus with walnuts

30 minutes

Serves 4
500 g /1 lb asparagus, trimmed
salt
60 ml /4 tbls walnut oil
a pinch of cayenne pepper
50 g /2 oz walnuts, finely chopped
60 ml /4 tbls freshly chopped parsley

1 Tie the asparagus into 4 bundles. Bring a deep pan of salted water to the boil and put in the asparagus, leaving the tips above the water. Cover with the lid or a dome of aluminium foil and boil gently for 15 minutes, or until tender.
2 Drain the asparagus and put one bundle on each of 4 warm serving plates. Remove the strings.
3 Spoon 15 ml /1 tbls walnut oil over each bundle and sprinkle with a little cayenne pepper. Divide the walnuts and the parsley among the plates and serve at once.

Easy salad appetizer

boiling the eggs,
then 30 minutes, plus chilling

Serves 4–6
275 g /10 oz large fresh broccoli heads
salt
3 medium-sized tomatoes
3 hard-boiled eggs
6–8 lettuce leaves
150 ml /5 fl oz natural yoghurt
7–15 ml /½–1 tbls curry paste
6 thin lemon slices
12–18 ripe black olives, stoned
2.5 ml /½ tsp dried basil
125 ml /4 fl oz vinaigrette (see page 50)

1 Cut away any stalks and large leaves from the broccoli; rinse the heads in cold water. Cook in boiling, salted water for 5–10 minutes, until tender but still crisp. Drain and refresh under cold running water.
2 Cut the tomatoes in half across and the hard-boiled eggs in half lengthways.
3 Using a rectangular dish, place the lettuce leaves around the edges, leaving one corner free. Arrange the halved tomatoes and hard-boiled eggs alternately on the lettuce leaves.
4 Mix the yoghurt and curry paste in a small bowl, then place it in the corner of the dish of salad. Fill the centre of the dish with broccoli and tuck slices of lemon in among the heads. Place the olives around the bowl. Chill until ready to serve.
5 Just before serving, add the dried basil to the vinaigrette dressing and pour it over the tomatoes, eggs and lettuce leaves.

Carrot and orange appetizer salad

30 minutes,
plus chilling

Serves 4
90 ml /6 tbls mayonnaise
20 ml /4 tsp lemon juice
finely grated zest of 2 oranges
500 g /1 lb carrots, coarsely grated
salt and freshly ground black pepper
15 ml /1 tbls finely chopped fresh parsley

1 In a bowl combine the mayonnaise, lemon juice and grated orange zest, mixing with a wooden spoon. Stir in the grated carrot and season with salt and freshly ground black pepper to taste. Chill.
2 Pile the salad into individual dishes; sprinkle with the parsley and serve.

Spicy cooked cucumber salad

Chinese vegetable salad

 40 minutes,
plus 2 hours chilling

Serves 4
8 radishes
2 large carrots
4 celery stalks
8 spring onions
4 large lettuce leaves
For the dressing
45 ml /3 tbls olive oil
10 ml /2 tsp lemon juice
5 ml /1 tsp soy sauce
5 ml /1 tsp sugar
a pinch of monosodium glutamate (optional)
freshly ground black pepper

1   Have ready a large bowl of water with
ice cubes in it. With a small, sharp knife
trim the radishes; make 4 cuts parallel to the
radish on 4 sides to make petals. Then pare
the skin of the centre tip so that it is white
and the radish resembles a flower. Drop the
radish flowers into iced water.
2   Slice the carrots thinly lengthways and
cut into thin 4 cm /1½ in strips. Add to the
bowl of iced water.
3   Cut the celery stalks into thin strips
lengthways, then into 4 cm /1½ in lengths.
Add to the bowl of iced water.
4   Trim the roots of the spring onions and
cut off the green parts to make them about
6.5 cm /2½ in long, including the white
bulbs. Then make 3 or 4 cuts 25 mm /1 in
long at the stalk end, taking care not to
separate the onion strips completely. Add
to the bowl of water.
5   Leave the bowl of vegetables to soak in
the refrigerator for at least 2 hours, during

Chinese vegetable salad

which time they will all curl up most
attractively.
6   Just before serving, beat the ingredients
for the dressing together in a bowl until they
form an emulsion.
7   To serve, drain the chilled vegetables
and pat dry thoroughly with a clean tea-
towel. Toss them in the prepared dressing
and arrange in a bowl lined with lettuce
leaves, making sure the radishes point
upwards. Serve immediately.

Celeriac salad remoulade

50 minutes,
plus chilling time

Serves 6
2 celeriac roots, each about 225 g /8 oz
salt
30 ml /2 tbls lemon juice
freshly ground black pepper
paprika, to garnish
For the sauce remoulade
275 ml /10 fl oz mayonnaise (see page 49)
15 ml /1 tbls finely chopped fresh tarragon
15 ml /1 tbls finely chopped fresh basil or
   chervil
15 ml /1 tbls finely chopped fresh parsley
1 garlic clove, crushed
2.5–5 ml /½–1 tsp dry mustard
5 ml /1 tsp capers
2 small gherkins, finely chopped
5 ml /1 tsp pounded anchovy fillets, or
   anchovy paste
2 hard-boiled eggs, finely chopped

1   Scrub the celeriac roots with a stiff
brush under running water to remove dirt.

2   Bring a large pan of salted water to the
boil. Add the lemon juice. Submerge the
roots in the water and boil gently for about
30 minutes, or until tender but still on the
crisp side when pierced with a skewer.
3   Peel the celeriac roots. Slice and cut into
strips 5 cm /2 in long and 5 mm /¼ in thick.
Place them in a bowl and cover.
4   Make up the sauce remoulade by mixing
all the ingredients together. Chill the sauce,
then fold in the prepared celeriac. Season to
taste, decorate with a little paprika and then
serve.

Cauliflower niçoise

 45 minutes

Serves 4–6
1 large cauliflower
salt
6 anchovy fillets, finely chopped
12 black olives, stoned and finely chopped
45 ml /3 tbls finely chopped fresh parsley
1 garlic clove, finely chopped
15 ml /1 tbls finely chopped capers
90 ml /6 tbls olive oil
30 ml /2 tbls wine vinegar
freshly ground black pepper
anchovy fillets, cut into strips (optional)

1   Remove the leaves from the cauliflower.
Trim the stems and cut any bruised pieces
away. Break or cut into florets. Bring a large
pan of salted water to the boil and poach the
florets for about 5 minutes, or until barely
tender. Drain and place them in a bowl of
cold, salted water for 30 minutes. Drain
again.
2   Mix the finely chopped anchovies, olives,
parsley, garlic and capers with the olive oil
and wine vinegar in a large mixing bowl.
Add the florets and season.
3   To serve, arrange the florets in a serving
dish. Pour over dressing and garnish with
anchovy fillets, if wished.

Hot spinach-stuffed tomatoes

45 minutes

Serves 6
6 large tomatoes
500 g /1 lb fresh spinach
25 g /1 oz softened butter
90 ml /6 tbls thin cream
salt and freshly ground black pepper
2 anchovy fillets, chopped
15 ml /1 tbls toasted breadcrumbs
butter for greasing
15–30 ml /1–2 tbls olive oil

1   Heat the oven to 170C /325F /gas 3.
2   Slice the tops off the tomatoes and scoop
out the insides carefully; reserve them for
another dish.
3   Wash the spinach several times, discarding any damaged leaves. Remove the stems,
drain and shake off excess moisture.

In a large saucepan, cook the spinach in the water that clings to its leaves after washing. Stir continuously over a medium heat until the spinach wilts, about 2 minutes. Drain and squeeze out any excess moisture and chop finely.

While the spinach is still hot, combine it with the softened butter and the thin cream in a dry pan. Season with salt and pepper. Spoon into the tomatoes. Top with chopped anchovies and the breadcrumbs.

Lightly grease a shallow baking dish and stand the stuffed tomatoes in it. Drizzle olive oil over each tomato and bake in the oven for about 15 minutes, or until the tomatoes are just beginning to soften and the stuffing has heated through. Serve.

Sliced tomato and onion appetizer

15 minutes

Serves 4–6
4 medium-sized ripe, firm tomatoes
1 small Spanish onion
small sprig of parsley, to garnish
For the dressing
5 ml /1 tsp caster sugar
15 ml /1 tbls wine vinegar
45 ml /3 tbls olive oil
salt and freshly ground black pepper

1 Cut the tomatoes into very thin slices and discard the end slices of each.
2 Slice the onion as thinly as possible.
3 On a serving dish, arrange overlapping, alternating slices of tomato and onion.
4 Prepare the dressing. In a small bowl, combine the caster sugar, wine vinegar and olive oil. Season with salt and pepper, then beat with a fork until the mixture emulsifies.
5 Pour the dressing over the tomato and onion slices and serve immediately, garnished with a small sprig of parsley.

Montpellier appetizer

1¼ hours

Serves 6
3 large tomatoes
450 g /1 lb large button mushrooms
30 ml /2 tbls fresh white breadcrumbs
salt and freshly ground black pepper
crusty French bread, to serve (optional)
For the butter
45 ml /3 tbls finely chopped fresh parsley
30 ml /2 tbls finely chopped fresh fennel
45 ml /3 tbls finely chopped fresh tarragon
2 garlic cloves, crushed
6 canned anchovy fillets, pounded
15 ml /1 tbls made mustard
225 g /8 oz butter, softened

1 Cut the tomatoes across in half, scoop out the seeds, turn the tomato halves upside down and drain.
2 Peel the mushrooms and cut off the stalks. Finely chop these and reserve.
3 For the butter, put the herbs in a mortar and pound with the pestle. Add the crushed garlic, anchovy fillets and mustard and mix well. In a large bowl, whisk the herb mixture into the softened butter.
4 Divide the butter mixture into 2 and mix the chopped mushroom stalks into one half of the mixture.
5 Heat the oven to 190C /375F /gas 5.
6 Grease a large roasting pan with some of the butter mixture (the half without the mushrooms) and lay the tomatoes in the pan.
7 Fill the tomatoes with the mushroom stalk and butter mixture and sprinkle 5 ml / 1 tsp breadcrumbs over the top of each one. Put in the oven and bake for 25 minutes.
8 Remove the pan from the oven and add the mushroom caps. Spread the plain butter mixture over the mushrooms, sprinkle them and the tomatoes with salt and freshly ground black pepper and return to the oven for a further 10 minutes.
9 To serve, carefully transfer a tomato half to each of 6 individual plates. Place 6 mushroom caps on each plate and pour over some of the juice. Serve immediately, with crusty French bread, if wished.

Montpellier appetizer

Creamed aubergine salad

Serves 4
8 large courgettes
salt
45 ml /3 tbls oil
1 small onion, finely chopped
100 g /4 oz ham, finely chopped
100 g /4 oz fresh white breadcrumbs
30 ml /2 tbls freshly chopped parsley
5 ml /1 tsp dried thyme
15 ml /1 tbls lemon juice
freshly ground black pepper
1 medium-sized egg, beaten
butter for greasing
parsley sprigs, to garnish
For the cheese sauce
25 g /1 oz butter
25 g /1 oz flour
275 ml /10 fl oz milk
100 g /4 oz Cheddar cheese, grated
a pinch of grated nutmeg
salt and freshly ground black pepper

1 Hollow out the centres of the courgette by pushing an apple corer into each end Heat the oven to 190C /375F /gas 5.

2 Boil the hollowed-out courgettes i salted water for 10 minutes to blanch them Drain thoroughly and pat the courgettes dr with absorbent paper.

3 Heat the oil in a frying-pan, add th onion and fry for 5 minutes, or until soft Remove from the heat and stir in the ham breadcrumbs, parsley, thyme and lemo juice. Season to taste with salt and freshl ground black pepper, then bind all th

Stuffed courgettes

Creamed aubergine salad

🥄 draining aubergines,
🔪 then 30 minutes, plus chilling

Serves 4
1 large aubergine
salt and freshly ground black pepper
45 ml /3 tbls olive oil
200 ml /7 fl oz mayonnaise (see page 49)
200 ml /7 fl oz yoghurt
1 small onion, finely chopped
7.5 ml /1½ tsp dried marjoram
5 ml /1 tsp honey
5 ml /1 tsp horseradish sauce
5 ml /1 tsp lemon juice
a pinch of cayenne pepper
pitta bread, to serve

1 Wipe the aubergine with a damp cloth; do not peel. Cut it in half and chop each half into very fine strips. Put on a plate, sprinkle liberally with salt and leave to drain for 30 minutes.

Creamed aubergine salad

2 Put the aubergine strips into a colander and thoroughly rinse under cold running water. Pat dry with absorbent paper.

3 Put 45 ml /3 tbls olive oil in a large frying-pan over a medium heat and, when very hot, add the aubergine. Cook for 10 minutes, stirring occasionally. Remove from the pan and drain on absorbent paper. Leave to cool.

4 In a large bowl, mix the mayonnaise with the yoghurt. Add the onion, marjoram, honey, horseradish and the lemon juice and mix thoroughly. Add the cold aubergine, season to taste with salt and freshly ground black pepper, mix well and put in the refrigerator to chill for 30 minutes.

5 Pile onto a serving dish, sprinkle a pinch of cayenne pepper over the top and serve with piping hot pitta bread.

Stuffed courgettes

🔪 1 hour

gredients together with the beaten egg.
Carefully stuff the hollowed-out
ourgettes with the filling. Arrange the
ourgettes in a lightly buttered dish, cover
ith foil and bake for 30 minutes.
Meanwhile, make the cheese sauce. Melt
e butter in a saucepan and, using a
ooden spoon, stir in the flour. Cook over
oderate heat for 2 minutes, then remove
om the heat. Add the milk gradually, stir-
ng until thick and smooth. Add the cheese,
pinch of nutmeg and salt and pepper to
ste. Heat until the cheese has melted into
e sauce.

Remove the courgettes from the oven
d divide them among 4 small plates. Pour
little of the sauce over each serving and
rnish with parsley sprigs. Serve
mediately.

Bean and bacon salad

🍴 50 minutes

Serves 4
50 g /12 oz whole French beans
50 g /12 oz new potatoes
lt and freshly ground black pepper
5 g /1 oz butter
25–275 g /8–10 oz streaky bacon, trimmed
  and cut in strips
Spanish onion, finely chopped
) ml /2 tbls finely chopped fresh parsley

For the vinaigrette
30 ml /2 tbls wine vinegar or lemon juice
salt and freshly ground black pepper
mustard powder (optional)
120 ml /8 tbls olive oil
30 ml /2 tbls finely chopped onion

1 Trim and wash the beans. Wash the
potatoes without peeling them. Put the
beans and potatoes in separate pans of
boiling salted water. Boil the beans for
15–20 minutes and the potatoes for about
25 minutes, or until they are tender.
2 Meanwhile, melt the butter in a deep
frying-pan or sauté dish and sauté the bacon
strips for about 3 minutes, until crisp and
golden. Remove with a slotted spoon and set
aside. Add the finely chopped onion and
sauté for about 7 minutes, or until soft.
3 When the beans are cooked, drain them
thoroughly and place in a salad bowl. Drain
the potatoes, peel and cut into 5 mm /¼ in
thick slices. Add to the beans and season
lightly with salt and freshly ground black
pepper. Mix in the sautéed onions.
4 To make the vinaigrette, combine either
the wine vinegar or lemon juice with salt
and pepper to taste. Add a little mustard, if
desired. Add the olive oil and beat with a
fork until the dressing thickens and
emulsifies. Stir in the chopped onion.
5 Pour the vinaigrette dressing over the
warm beans and potatoes and toss gently
until well mixed. Leave to cool.
6 Just before serving, transfer the salad to
serving plates. Sprinkle with the bacon
strips and finely chopped parsley.

Mushroom beignets

🍴🍴 2½ hours including resting batter

Serves 4–6
225 g /8 oz firm white button mushrooms,
  wiped, with stems trimmed and
  halved if large
45 ml /3 tbls dry white wine
30 ml /2 tbls lemon juice
salt and freshly ground black pepper
oil for deep frying
For the beer batter
150 g /5 oz flour
pinch of salt
30 ml /2 tbls olive oil
200 ml /7 fl oz light beer
1 large egg white
For the tomato sauce
25 g /1 oz butter
30 ml /2 tbls olive oil
100 g /4 oz prosciutto, coarsely chopped
1 Spanish onion, finely chopped
2 garlic cloves, finely chopped
400 g /14 oz canned tomatoes
60 ml /4 tbls tomato purée
2 bay leaves
45 ml /3 tbls finely chopped fresh parsley
1.5 ml /¼ tsp oregano
1 small strip of lemon zest
45 ml /3 tbls dry white wine
salt and freshly ground black pepper

1 To make the beer batter, sift the flour
and salt into a mixing bowl and make a well
in the centre. Pour in the olive oil and
gradually add the beer, stirring with a
wooden spoon to incorporate the flour from
the sides of the well. The batter should be
smooth and slightly thick. Leave to rest for 2
hours. Meanwhile, make the tomato sauce.
2 In a heavy saucepan, heat the butter and
olive oil and gently sauté the prosciutto and
finely chopped onion and garlic for about 10
minutes, or until the vegetables are soft and
golden. Sieve the canned tomatoes in their
juice and add to the pan, together with the
tomato purée, bay leaves, parsley, oregano,
lemon zest and dry white wine. Mix well,
season to taste and bring to the boil, stirring.
Cover and simmer very gently, stirring
occasionally, for 1 hour, or until reduced to
a thick sauce.
3 Prepare the mushrooms: place them in a
saucepan with the dry white wine, lemon
juice and salt and pepper to taste. Simmer
for about 10 minutes, until the mushrooms
are tender but still very firm.
4 Drain the mushrooms thoroughly and
leave to become cold. Dry thoroughly with
absorbent paper, then season generously with
salt and freshly ground black pepper.
5 Heat the oil in a deep-fat frier to 190C /
375F, or until a cube of bread turns brown
in 50 seconds.
6 Whisk the egg white until stiff; fold
lightly into the batter.
7 Dip the mushrooms into the batter, a
few at a time. Shake off excess batter and
deep fry for 4–5 minutes, or until a rich
golden colour. Drain thoroughly on absorbent paper and serve immediately
accompanied by the tomato sauce.

Stuffed tomato appetizer

🔪 40 minutes, plus chilling

Serves 4
4 large tomatoes
salt and freshly ground black pepper
bouquets of parsley, to garnish
For the stuffing
90 ml /6 tbls cooked rice (see below)
½ green pepper, seeded and chopped
75 g /3 oz cooked mussels, shelled and
*   halved, or bottled mussels, halved*
juice of ½ lemon
30 ml /2 tbls olive oil
15 ml /1 tbls finely chopped fresh parsley
4 stuffed olives, sliced

1   Cut the stalk end off each tomato and reserve. Scoop out the pulp and seeds. Season inside with salt and black pepper. Chill in the refrigerator.
2   Meanwhile, prepare the stuffing. In a bowl, combine the cooked rice, chopped green pepper and halved mussels. Sprinkle over the lemon juice and olive oil. Stir in the finely chopped parsley and sliced olives. Season with salt and pepper.
3   Pile the stuffing into the tomato cases, replace the caps and garnish with parsley.

● For extra flavour, add a pinch of powdered saffron or turmeric when cooking the rice.

Stuffed tomato appetizer

Anchovy and potato salad

🔪 1¼ hours, including cooling

Serves 4
6 medium-sized new potatoes
salt
120 ml /8 tbls dry white wine
freshly ground black pepper
30 ml /2 tbls olive oil
30 ml /2 tbls wine vinegar
2 shallots, finely chopped
5 ml /1 tsp finely snipped fresh chives
2 garlic cloves, crushed
1 small green pepper, halved, seeded and
*   sliced*
3 medium-sized tomatoes, blanched,
*   skinned, seeded and quartered*
75 g /3 oz black olives, stoned
12 anchovy fillets, cut lengthways into fine
*   strips*
15 ml /1 tbls finely chopped fresh parsley

1   Boil the potatoes in salted water, about 15–20 minutes, until tender but still firm. Cool, peel and cut into slices. Place them in a mixing bowl.
2   Bring the dry white wine to the boil in a small saucepan and pour over the potato slices. Season generously with salt and freshly ground black pepper. Allow to cool.

3   In a large bowl, combine the olive ⊙ wine vinegar, finely chopped shallots, chi and crushed garlic. Beat with a fork ur the mixture emulsifies. Season with salt a freshly ground black pepper to taste. A the sliced pepper, quartered tomato stoned black olives and potato slices. Adjː the seasoning and toss carefully, taking c: not to break the potato slices.
4   Arrange the potato salad on a servi platter. Lay the anchovy fillets diagonaː across the salad and sprinkle with chopp parsley in fine lines to form a lattice with t anchovy strips. Serve immediately.

● If new potatoes are not available, use ⊙ ones, but boil the potatoes in the jacke then leave them to cool completely in the water before peeling carefully.

Creamed mushrooms

🔪 20 minutes

Serves 4
500 g /1 lb small button mushrooms
25 g /1 oz butter
15 ml /1 tbls lemon juice
salt
cayenne pepper
300 ml /10 fl oz thick cream
15 ml /1 tbls butter, softened
15 ml /1 tbls flour
freshly ground black pepper
sprigs of parsley, to garnish
triangles of toasts, to serve

1   Trim stalks and wipe mushrooms.
2   Combine the mushrooms, butter, lemː juice, 2.5 ml /½ tsp salt and a pinch cayenne pepper in a medium-sized saucepaː Cover the pan and cook over a medium heː for 5 minutes, stirring from time to timː Add the cream and bring gently to the boilː
3   Beat the softened butter and the floː together to form a *beurre manié* and add ː a little at a time, to the mushroom aː cream mixture. Simmer for 2–3 minutɛ Correct the seasoning with salt, freshː ground black pepper and a hint of cayenː pepper. Garnish with parsley and serː immediately with triangles of toast.

Lettuce hearts La Napoule

🔪 20 minutes, plus chilling
   and dressing

Serves 4
2 small heads of lettuce
90–120 ml /6–8 tbls olive oil
30–45 ml /2–3 tbls wine vinegar
2.5 ml /½ tsp paprika
150 ml /5 fl oz thick cream
coarse salt and freshly ground black pepper
For the garnish
2 hard-boiled eggs
30 ml /2 tbls finely chopped fresh parsley

Remove the outer leaves of the lettuces that you are left with the hearts. Reserve ?e outer leaves to use in another recipe. ash the lettuce hearts and cut each heart :o quarters. Drain well and pat dry in a ?an cloth. Gather up the edges of the cloth d shake to remove any remaining ɔisture from the lettuce. Roll the lettuce in dry cloth and chill in the salad compart- :nt of the refrigerator for at least 1 hour, until you are ready to assemble the salad.

To make the dressing, place the olive oil a bowl with the wine vinegar, paprika, ick cream and coarse salt and freshly ɔund black pepper to taste. Whisk until ick and creamy. Chill until ready to use.

To prepare the garnish, separate the lks from the whites of the hard-boiled gs. Rub the yolks through a sieve. Finely op the egg whites.

To assemble the salad, place 2 quarters lettuce heart on each of 4 salad plates. ask each quarter of lettuce with dressing, en garnish a third of each plate with opped egg white, a third with sieved egg lk and a third with parsley.

This luxurious green salad comes from the hing town of La Napoule outside Cannes France. The salad is not tossed but simply asked with the creamy dressing.

₃russels sprout oleslaw

45 minutes

rves 4
'5 g /8 oz Brussels sprouts
lt
small red-skinned apple, cored and thinly sliced
ml /1 tbls sultanas
g /2 oz shelled walnuts, coarsely chopped
-8 radishes, sliced
ml /6 tbls mayonnaise (see page 49)
ml /3 tbls olive oil
ml /2 tbls lemon juice
eshly ground black pepper
r the garnish
-3 tomatoes, sliced crossways
hard-boiled eggs, sliced crossways
-45 ml /2-3 tbls freshly chopped parsley

Cut off the stem ends from the Brussels routs and remove any wilted or damaged tside leaves. Soak the sprouts in cold ater with a little salt for 15 minutes. rain, then dry and shred finely.

In a large bowl, combine the shredded routs, the thinly sliced apple, sultanas, the arsely chopped walnuts and the sliced dishes. Thin the mayonnaise with the olive l and lemon juice. Add the mayonnaise to e bowl. Season with salt and freshly ound black pepper to taste and toss until e sprouts, apple, sultanas, nuts and dishes are evenly coated with dressing.

Serve the Brussels sprout coleslaw on a sh surrounded by alternate tomato and ard-boiled egg slices and sprinkled with nely chopped parsley.

Italian pepper appetizer with lemon

30 minutes, then cooling and chilling

Serves 6
8 sweet red, green or yellow peppers
olive oil
6-8 canned anchovy fillets, drained
3 garlic cloves, finely chopped
45 ml /3 tbls finely chopped fresh parsley
10 ml /2 tsp lemon juice
salt and freshly ground black pepper (optional)

1 Heat the grill to moderate. Brush the peppers all over with olive oil
2 Place the peppers side by side in the grill pan and grill steadily under a moderate heat for about 10 minutes, or until their skins blister and blacken all over, and the peppers become rather limp. Turn the peppers regularly to ensure they cook evenly.
3 Plunge the grilled peppers into a large bowl of cold water. Leave them for about 2 minutes, then drain and peel. The skins will peel off easily from the cooked peppers if they have been grilled in an even way.
4 Slice the peppers in half. Cut out the core and rinse out the seeds under cold running water. Pat each piece of pepper dry with absorbent paper or a clean tea-towel. Cut each pepper across into 4.
5 Cut the anchovy fillets into 5 mm /¼ in lengths and combine them in a deep serving dish with the peppers and finely chopped garlic and parsley. Toss until well mixed.
6 In a small saucepan, heat 60 ml /4 tbls olive oil and the lemon juice. When it is very hot, pour the dressing over the peppers and mix lightly to coat. Leave to become cold, then chill. As it cools, the hot dressing will develop and blend the flavours together in a way that a simple cold dressing could never do.
7 Season lightly with salt and freshly ground black pepper, if wished, and serve the peppers chilled.

● This dish is so strongly flavoured that you are unlikely to need either salt or pepper, but taste and judge for yourself.
● The slow, steady grilling helps bring out the flavour of the peppers – make sure the heat stays moderate.
● If available, use a mixture of red, green and yellow peppers. The colour combination is very attractive.

Italian pepper appetizer with lemon

Stuffed tomatoes

Serves 8–10
For tuna tomatoes
8–10 large tomatoes, skinned
salt
2–4 garlic cloves, peeled
275 ml /10 fl oz thick mayonnaise
freshly ground black pepper
2 × 215 g /7½ oz cans tuna fish
2 celery stalks, finely chopped
8–10 crisp lettuce leaves
finely chopped fresh parsley
3 hard-boiled eggs, quartered
75 g /3 oz black olives, stoned
parsley sprigs, to garnish
gherkins, cut into 'fan' shapes

For the cheese tomatoes
8–10 large tomatoes, skinned
salt
175 g /6 oz cottage cheese, sieved
90–120 ml /6–8 tbls thick cream
30 ml /2 tbls finely chopped
* onion*
10 ml /2 tsp Worcestershire
* sauce*
45–60 ml /3–4 tbls lemon juice
75–100 g /3–4 oz Roquefort or
* other blue cheese, crumbled*
finely chopped fresh parsley
freshly ground black pepper
2 medium-sized egg whites

Tuna tomatoes
1 Cut a thin slice from the top of each tomato. Using a small metal spoon, carefully scoop out the pips and the pulp. Sprinkle the cavities with salt, turn upside down and cover loosely with foil; leave to drain for at least 30 minutes.
2 Place the garlic, to taste, in a bowl or mortar and crush or pound to a paste, then blend into the mayonnaise. Season generously.
3 Drain and flake the tuna. Reduce the tuna with half the garlic mayonnaise to a smooth purée in an electric blender. Turn the tuna purée into a bowl and stir in the chopped celery. Add a little more garlic mayonnaise, if necessary, and check the seasoning.
4 Rinse the tomato cavities and pat dry. Fill the tomatoes with the tuna mixture. Just before serving, arrange the lettuce leaves on a wide, shallow plate and place a stuffed tomato on each one. Spoon or pipe a dab of garlic mayonnaise on the top of each tomato and garnish with a sprig of parsley. Garnish the edge of the dish with hard-boiled egg, black olives, parsley sprigs and gherkin 'fans'.
Cheese tomatoes
1 Prepare tomatoes as above.
2 Combine the sieved cottage cheese, thick cream, finely chopped onion, Worcestershire sauce and lemon juice and whisk or beat until smoothly blended. Blend in the crumbled Roquefort or other blue cheese, to taste, and 60 ml /4 tbls parsley. Season with pepper. Whisk the egg whites until stiff and fold into the cheese mixture.
3 Just before serving, fill the tomatoes with the cheese mixture. Arrange on a serving plate and sprinkle with more parsley.

1 hour

Grilled aubergine slices

Serves 4
2 medium-sized ripe aubergines
salt
45 ml /3 tbls olive oil
2 garlic cloves, finely chopped
oil for greasing
25 g /1 oz Gruyère cheese, freshly grated
freshly ground black pepper

1 Wash the aubergines and wipe them dry. Trim off the stem ends and slice each aubergine into rounds about 5 mm /¼ in thick. Score the cut surfaces lightly with a sharp knife, and rub each slice on one side with salt. Leave the aubergines, salted sides downwards, in a colander for at least 30 minutes to allow the salt to draw out the bitter juices.
2 Drain the aubergine rounds thoroughly, squeezing them lightly to get rid of as much moisture as possible. Wipe them dry with absorbent paper. In a small bowl mix together the olive oil and the garlic.
3 Heat the grill to high. Lightly grease a large baking sheet. Place the aubergine rounds on the baking sheet and sprinkle each with a little of the olive oil and garlic mixture and top with freshly grated Gruyère cheese. Season with freshly ground black pepper.
4 Place the baking sheet 7.5 cm /3 in from the grill and cook for 5–7 minutes, or until aubergines are soft through and golden brown on top. Drain quickly and carefully on absorbent paper and serve immediately.

● This appetizer also makes an attractive side dish for veal and poultry. With a tomato sauce and perhaps deep fried or poached eggs it will also make a simple supper dish.

45 minutes

Celery hearts appetizer salad

Serves 4
2 heads of celery
1 chicken stock cube, crumbled
15 ml /1 tbls salt
275 ml /10 fl oz vinaigrette (see page 50)
2.5 ml /½ tsp paprika
a pinch of cayenne pepper
150 ml /5 fl oz thick cream
1 hard-boiled egg
15 ml /1 tbls finely chopped fresh parsley

1   Remove the outer stalks of the celery, trim the top third off the remaining stalks and reserve. Cut the hearts in half lengthways and wash. Put the celery hearts in a saucepan with the trimmings, the crumbled chicken stock cube and salt; cover with cold water and bring slowly to the boil. Simmer for 10 minutes, remove from the heat and leave in the hot water for 5 minutes. Drain and cool.
2   Arrange the celery hearts in a flat dish, spoon over half the vinaigrette and leave the celery to marinate for at least 1 hour.
3   In a bowl combine the remaining vinaigrette with the paprika, a pinch of cayenne pepper and the thick cream. Mix well using a small wire whisk.
4   Separate the yolk from the white of the hard-boiled egg, rub the yolk through a wire sieve and reserve. Rub the white through the sieve and reserve.
5   To serve, drain the celery hearts and reserve the marinade. Place the hearts on a flat surface and brush them with a little of the reserved marinade. To garnish the hearts, use a wide-bladed knife held diagonally across one third of the heart. Sprinkle up to the knife with the sieved egg white. Garnish the next third with the sieved egg yolk, again using the knife to mark the division. Garnish the remaining third with the finely chopped parsley.
6   With a spatula, carefully lift the hearts onto a serving dish. Pour the creamed dressing down the side of the dish without disturbing the garnish and serve immediately.

⏲ 25 minutes, 1 hour marinating,
then 15 minutes

Flat mushrooms à la bordelaise

Serves 4
350 g /12 oz flat mushrooms
90 ml /6 tbls olive oil
3 cloves garlic, crushed
45 ml /3 tbls finely chopped fresh parsley
salt and freshly ground black pepper
sprig of flat-leafed parsley, to garnish (optional)

1   Wipe the mushroom caps with a damp cloth and remove the stems, reserving them for another recipe.
2   Heat the olive oil in a heavy-based frying-pan large enough to take the mushrooms in one layer. Put the mushrooms side by side, stalk-side down, into the pan and cook over a moderate heat for 3 minutes.
3   Turn the mushrooms over carefully with a palette knife and sprinkle the tops with the crushed garlic and finely chopped parsley. Season with salt and freshly ground black pepper to taste. Sauté for a further 2–3 minutes, or until the mushrooms are tender.
4   Transfer the mushrooms to a heated serving dish, parsley-side up, and serve immediately, garnished with flat-leaved parsley, if wished.

⏲ 15 minutes

SUBSTANTIAL STARTERS

The Italians often start a meal with pasta; why don't you? You can make a tasty sauce in the time it takes for the spaghetti to cook. Or try spinach crêpes with a cheesy filling, or a creamy prawn tart.

Some of the most delicious starters are fairly hefty – crêpes, pasta and pulses, quiches and tartlets, spareribs and potato salads make substantial beginnings, and should be followed by a light main course and dessert. Some of them can make a light meal accompanied by a green salad.

Filled and rolled crêpes make an elegant appetizer. You can make the crêpes well in advance and keep a supply in your refrigerator or freezer. I suggest using courgette and sweetcorn fillings and giving your guests one of each, but they are also delicious with diced cooked chicken or turkey or flaked fish or shellfish in a rich, creamy sauce.

You can make simple starter salads from store-cupboard ingredients and a few leftovers: plain boiled rice (white or brown), macaroni or other pasta, lentils and other pulses make good bases. Toss in a vinaigrette dressing (if you can do this while they're still warm, so much the better) and season generously with salt and freshly ground black pepper. Then add diced cooked meat, poultry or fish, chopped hard-boiled egg, nuts, chopped fruit or vegetables such as spring onions, green or red peppers, celery, avocado, apple, raisins – try serving a whole selection for a good contrast of colours, textures and flavours.

French mushroom tartlets

🍴 1 hour

Serve 8
500 g /1 lb made-weight shortcrust pastry, defrosted if frozen
For the mushroom filling
500 g /1 lb white button mushrooms
50 g /2 oz butter
30 ml /2 tbls olive oil
15 ml /1 tbls flour
salt and freshly ground black pepper
a good pinch of cayenne pepper
60 ml /4 tbls Madeira
3 medium-sized egg yolks
300 ml /10 fl oz thick cream
finely chopped fresh parsley, to garnish

1 Roll out the pastry 3 mm /⅛ in thick and use it to line 8 fluted tartlet tins, approximately 10 cm /4 in across the top and 10 mm /½ in deep. Press the pastry well into the sides and run your rolling pin across the tops of the tins to trim off any excess pastry. Prick the pastry bases with a fork and then leave the pastry to relax in

the refrigerator for at least 30 minutes.
2 While the pastry is relaxing, neatly trim the stem ends off the mushrooms. Heat the butter and olive oil in a large, heavy-based frying-pan and sauté the mushrooms for 3 minutes. Sprinkle with the flour and season with salt, freshly ground black pepper and cayenne pepper to taste. Add the Madeira and toss thoroughly. Remove the pan from the heat.
3 Heat the oven to 200C /400F /gas 6. Line the pastry cases with foil and beans and bake for 10 minutes, then lower the heat to 180C /350F /gas 4 and remove the foil and beans. Bake for a further 5 minutes, or until set and golden. Keep warm.
4 Meanwhile, whisk the egg yolks lightly in the top pan of a double boiler, then blend in the thick cream. Place the pan over gently simmering water and stir with a wooden spoon for 10–15 minutes, until the mixture begins to thicken.
5 Add the contents of the pan of mushrooms to the sauce and continue to stir for a further 10–15 minutes, until the sauce is thick. Do not allow the sauce to boil, or it will curdle. Adjust the seasoning.
6 Unmould the warm pastry cases onto heated individual serving plates. Divide the mushroom mixture among the cases, sprinkle with the finely chopped parsley and serve at once.

● The pastry cases for these elegant tartlets can be baked a day in advance, stored overnight in an airtight tin, then reheated in their tartlet tins at 150C /300F /gas 2 for about 5 minutes.

French mushroom tartlets

Spaghetti with oil and garlic

Spaghetti con olio e aglio is a traditional Roman dish, as delicious as it is quick and simple to prepare.

15 minutes

Serves 4
salt
45 ml /3 tbls olive oil, more if needed
250 g /8 oz spaghetti or linguine
40 g /1½ oz butter
30 ml /2 tbls finely chopped fresh parsley
2 garlic cloves, finely chopped
freshly ground black pepper
60—90 ml /4—6 tbls freshly grated Parmesan cheese
15 ml /1 tbls finely chopped fresh parsley, to garnish

1 Bring a large pan of salted water to the boil. Add 5 ml /1 tbls olive oil, then the spaghetti or linguine. Cook until *al dente* – tender but still firm. Drain the cooked pasta and keep warm.
2 Meanwhile, in a large saucepan heat 25 g /1 oz butter and the remaining olive oil. When the foaming subsides, sauté the 30 ml /2 tbls parsley and the garlic, stirring frequently with a wooden spoon for 1—2 minutes. Do not allow the garlic to colour.
3 Add the drained pasta to the oil and garlic mixture and stir until thoroughly coated, adding a little more olive oil if necessary. Season to taste with salt and freshly ground black pepper.
4 Turn the pasta into a heated serving dish. Sprinkle with freshly grated Parmesan cheese, dot with the remaining butter, sprinkle with finely chopped parsley and serve immediately.

Artichoke heart, prawn and potato salad

A garnish of prawns in their shells makes all the difference, visually, to this salad with its curry-flavoured dressing.

40 minutes, plus cooling

Serves 4—6
4 medium-sized waxy new potatoes
salt
6 large canned artichoke hearts, rinsed and drained
150 ml /5 fl oz dry white wine
freshly ground black pepper
175 ml /6 fl oz mayonnaise (see page 49)
5 ml /1 tsp curry paste
a pinch of cayenne pepper
4 hard-boiled eggs, quartered
30 ml /2 tbls finely chopped fresh parsley
50 g /2 oz black olives, stoned, to garnish
12 boiled prawns in their shells, to garnish

Artichoke heart, prawn and potato salad

1 Scrub the potatoes well, but do not peel them. Bring a saucepan of salted water to the boil, add the potatoes and boil for 20 minutes, or until just tender. They are ready as soon as you can pierce them with a fork.
2 Meanwhile, dry the canned artichoke hearts on absorbent paper and dice them.
3 Drain the potatoes. Return them to a dry pan and toss them briefly over a low heat to get rid of any excess moisture. Peel them as soon as they are cool enough to handle. Dice the cooked new potatoes and place them in a large bowl.
4 In a small saucepan, bring the dry white wine to the boil and pour it over the warm diced potatoes. Season to taste with salt and black pepper and leave to cool.
5 In a bowl, combine the mayonnaise with the curry paste and a pinch of cayenne pepper and stir to blend.
6 Add the diced artichoke hearts, quartered hard-boiled eggs and finely chopped parsley to the diced potatoes. Stir lightly to mix, taking care not to break up the diced potatoes or egg quarters, then stir in the curry-flavoured mayonnaise. Correct the seasoning, adding more salt, freshly ground black pepper, cayenne pepper or curry paste to taste.
7 To serve, transfer the salad to a serving platter or 4—6 individual plates. Garnish with the stoned black olives and the boiled prawns in their shells.

Green pasta and olive salad

Serve this unusual salad as an appetizer or as an accompaniment to cold meats.

15 minutes, plus cooling

Serves 4
salt
175 g /6 oz tagliatelle verdi
90 ml /6 tbls olive oil
1 garlic clove, crushed with a pinch of salt
freshly ground black pepper
20 green olives, stoned and finely chopped
60 ml /4 tbls freshly chopped parsley
15 ml /1 tbls freshly chopped basil (optional)
30 ml /2 tbls chopped capers
1—2 ripe tomatoes, cut into wedges, to garnish

1 Bring a large pan of lightly salted water to the boil. Drop in the tagliatelle verdi and cook until it is just tender, then drain it.
2 In a bowl, mix together the olive oil, crushed garlic and freshly ground black pepper. Fold in the warm tagliatelle and set aside to cool.
3 When the tagliatelle is cold, fold in the chopped olives, herbs and capers. Divide the salad among 4 small serving plates, garnish with the tomato wedges and serve.

Creamy prawn tart

making and relaxing pastry,
then 1 hour 10 minutes

Serves 6
125 g /4 oz flour
2.5 ml /½ tsp garlic salt
1.5 ml /¼ tsp celery salt
1.5 ml /¼ tsp dry mustard
65 g /2½ oz butter, in small dice
30 ml /2 tbls iced water
125 g /4 oz cream cheese
125 ml /4 fl oz thick cream
50 ml /2 fl oz top of the milk
2 medium-sized eggs
1 medium-sized egg yolk
15 ml /1 tbls tomato purée
salt and freshly ground black pepper
50 g /2 oz spring onions, finely chopped
25 g /1 oz butter
30 ml /2 tbls dry vermouth
*125 g /4 oz boiled, peeled prawns, defrosted
   if frozen*
6 thin rings of red pepper, to garnish
a sprig of parsley, to garnish

1   Make the pastry: sift the flour, garlic
salt, celery salt and dry mustard into a bowl.
Add the butter and cut it with 2 knives until
the mixture resembles coarse breadcrumbs,
then rub the butter into the flour until the
mixture resembles fine crumbs.
2   Add the iced water and press the dough

Creamy prawn tart

into a ball with your fingertips. Wrap in a
polythene bag and place in the refrigerator
to relax for 30 minutes or more.
3   Roll out the pastry thinly and use to line
a 20 cm /8 in flan ring, pressing well into the
sides. Prick the bottom with a fork and put
the flan case into the refrigerator to relax for
30 minutes or more.
4   Heat the oven to 200C /400F /gas 6.
Line the case with foil and beans and bake
for 10 minutes, then remove the foil and
beans and bake for a further 8 minutes.
5   Meanwhile, beat the cream cheese, thick
cream, top of the milk, eggs and egg yolk
with the tomato purée and salt and freshly
ground black pepper to taste.
6   Reserving some chopped spring onion
for garnish, cook the remainder in the butter
over medium heat for 3 minutes. Add the
dry vermouth and quickly reduce to 15 ml /1
tbls. Reserve 6 prawns for garnish; add the
rest to the pan and toss until all the liquid
has evaporated.
7   Lower the oven heat to 170C /325F /gas
3. Arrange the prawn mixture over the
bottom of the flan case. Pour the cream
mixture carefully on top and bake for 10–15
minutes, until slightly set. Arrange the red
pepper rings on top and return to the oven
for 25–30 minutes, or until firm.
8   Let the tart set for 5 minutes before
removing it from the flan ring. Serve hot or
cold, garnished with the reserved prawns,
chopped spring onions and a sprig of
parsley.

Chick-peas vinaigrette

overnight soaking, cooking
chick-peas, then 15 minutes

Serves 4
175 g /6 oz chick-peas, soaked overnight
6 spring onions, finely chopped
30 ml /2 tbls finely chopped fresh parsley
*200 g /7 oz canned tuna fish, drained and
   flaked*
salt and freshly ground black pepper
For the vinaigrette
120 ml /8 tbls olive oil
30 ml /2 tbls red wine vinegar
15 ml /1 tbls lemon juice
1 garlic clove, crushed
salt and freshly ground black pepper

1   Drain the soaked chick-peas. Place in a
saucepan with water to cover. Bring to the
boil, then reduce the heat and simmer for
1–2 hours, or until tender, according to the
quality and age of the chick-peas.
2   Drain the cooked chick-peas and rinse
under cold running water. Drain thoroughly
and transfer to a bowl, adding the spring
onions, parsley and flaked tuna fish.
3   Make the vinaigrette: in a bowl, combine
the olive oil, red wine vinegar, lemon juice,
crushed garlic, salt and pepper to taste. Beat
with a fork until the mixture emulsifies.
4   Pour the vinaigrette over the chick-peas
and toss to mix. Adjust the seasoning, if
necessary, then transfer to a serving bowl
and serve immediately.

Chick-peas vinaigrette

Herb and spinach crêpes

2 hours standing,
then 1¼ hours

Serves 4–6
50 g /2 oz flour
2.5 ml /½ tsp salt
2 medium-sized eggs, beaten
75 ml /5 tbls melted butter
150 ml /5 fl oz milk
225 g /8 oz frozen spinach, defrosted, well
drained and finely chopped
30 ml /2 tbls finely chopped fresh tarragon,
basil or chives
oil for greasing crêpe pan
butter for greasing baking dish
30–60 ml /2–4 tbls freshly grated Parmesan
cheese
300 ml /10 fl oz hot Fresh tomato sauce (see
page 101)
For the cheese filling
450 g /1 lb cottage cheese
125 ml /4 fl oz soured cream
2 medium-sized eggs, beaten
50 g /2 oz grated Gruyère cheese
30–60 ml /2–4 tbls freshly grated Parmesan
cheese
30–60 ml /2–4 tbls finely chopped fresh
herbs (parsley, chives and, when
available, tarragon)
salt and freshly ground black pepper
freshly grated nutmeg

1 First make the batter. Sift the flour and salt into a mixing bowl. Stir in the eggs. Gradually add 30 ml /2 tbls of the melted butter, the milk and 60–90 ml /4–6 tbls water and stir gently until smooth. Strain the batter through a fine sieve, add the finely chopped spinach and the chopped fresh herbs. The batter should be the consistency of thin cream – add a little water if it is too thick. Leave the batter to stand for at least 2 hours.
2 Meanwhile, combine the ingredients for the cheese filling, seasoning to taste with salt, black pepper and grated nutmeg. Refrigerate for at least 1 hour.
3 Make the crêpes: heat a heavy frying-pan 12–15 cm /5–6 in in diameter. When very hot, rub it with oiled absorbent paper. Spoon 30 ml /2 tbls batter into the pan and tilt it so the batter coats the surface thinly. Cook over a moderate heat for 1 minute, or until bubbles start to form underneath. Turn the crêpe with a palette knife and cook for 1 minute. Place on a plate while you cook the remaining crêpes (greasing the pan each time); you should have 12. Stack them, cover with a clean folded towel and allow to cool.
4 Heat the oven to 180C /350F /gas 4. Spread each crêpe with 60–75 ml /4–5 tbls of the cheese filling. Roll them and arrange in a well-buttered baking dish.
5 Brush the crêpes with the remaining melted butter and sprinkle with the grated Parmesan cheese. Bake for about 20 minutes, or until the crêpes are heated through. Serve with the hot Fresh tomato sauce served separately in a sauce-boat.

Barbecue spareribs

These American-style spareribs, glazed with a barbecue sauce, make an unusual and attractive starter. To eat them, pick them up with your fingers!

1 hour 50 minutes

Serves 4
1 kg /2¼ lb Chinese-cut pork spareribs
65 ml /2½ fl oz black treacle or molasses
1 garlic clove, crushed
15 ml /1 tbls tomato purée
5 ml /1 tsp American or mild mustard
15 ml /1 tbls cider vinegar
1.5 ml /¼ tsp dried thyme
a good pinch of cayenne pepper
salt and freshly ground black pepper

1 Heat the oven to 190C /375F /gas 5. Cut the spareribs into single ribs.
2 In a small mixing bowl, combine the black treacle or molasses, crushed garlic, tomato purée, mustard, cider vinegar, thyme and cayenne pepper. Stir thoroughly and season well with salt and pepper.
3 Arrange the spareribs in a single layer in a large roasting tin. Brush them lightly with a little of the barbecue sauce, then roast in the oven for 30 minutes.
4 Using tongs, take the spareribs out of the tin and pour off all the fat which has collected. Return the ribs to the tin and spoon over the remaining sauce. Roast for a further hour, basting frequently, until the ribs are glazed and golden brown.

Avocado pancakes

 45 minutes

Serves 4–6
4 medium-sized eggs
15 ml /1 tbls milk
5–7.5 ml /1–1½ tsp Worcestershire sauce
5 ml /1 tsp salt
1 onion, chopped
40 g /1½ oz flour
1 large, firm avocado, chopped
1 large potato, grated
15 ml /1 tbls lemon juice
freshly ground black pepper
butter for greasing
For the soured cream sauce
125 ml /4 fl oz soured cream
125 ml /4 fl oz yoghurt
freshly ground black pepper
a dash of Tabasco sauce

1 First make the soured cream sauce by combining all the ingredients. Reserve.
2 Put the eggs, milk, Worcestershire sauce, salt and onion into a blender and blend until combined. Add the flour, avocado, potato, lemon juice and pepper and blend for a few seconds at low speed.
3 Heat a heavy frying-pan on a medium heat, lightly grease with butter and pour in about 50 ml /2 fl oz of the batter. Cook until lightly browned on the bottom, then turn carefully and cook until done. Keep the pancake warm while you make the rest in the same way, then serve at once, with the sauce handed round separately.

Courgette and sweetcorn crêpes

This starter will surprise your guests each person receives two different crêpe Ideal for a dinner party, the crêpes ca be assembled a few hours in advanc then simply heated through.

making the crêpes,
then 1¼ hours

Serves 4
100 g /4 oz courgettes
15 g /½ oz butter, plus extra for greasing
salt
freshly ground black pepper
200 g /7 oz canned sweetcorn, drained
finely chopped fresh parsley, to garnish
For the crêpes
75 g /3 oz flour
2.5 ml /½ tsp salt
2 eggs, beaten
30 ml /2 tbls melted butter or oil
150 ml /5 fl oz milk
oil for greasing

Courgette and sweetcorn crêpes

Pasta salad with ham and tomato

Pasta salad with ham and tomato

30 minutes

Serves 6
salt
250 g /9 oz tagliatelle
175 g /6 oz cooked ham, in thick matchstick
strips
350 g /12 oz tomatoes, blanched, skinned,
seeded and quartered
For the dressing
2.5 ml /½ tsp Dijon mustard
30 ml /2 tbls wine vinegar
90 ml /6 tbls olive oil
salt and freshly ground black pepper
15 ml /1 tbls finely chopped fresh parsley
15 ml /1 tbls finely chopped mixed herbs
(such as thyme, fennel and tarragon)

1 Bring a large pan of salted water to the boil. Add the tagliatelle and cook until tender but still firm. Drain the cooked pasta, then refresh it under cold running water. Drain again.
2 Put the Dijon mustard into a bowl. Add the wine vinegar, olive oil, salt and freshly ground black pepper to taste. Beat vigorously with a fork until the mixture emulsifies. Add the finely chopped parsley and mixed herbs and stir until well blended. Add the drained pasta, ham strips and quartered tomatoes. Toss lightly with 2 forks. Add more salt and freshly ground black pepper, if necessary.
3 To serve, spoon the dressed pasta salad into a flat serving dish.

'or the bechamel sauce
'0 g /1½ oz butter
'0 ml /2 tbls finely chopped onion
'0 ml /2 tbls finely chopped ham
'0 ml /2 tbls flour
'25 ml /15 fl oz milk, scalded
chicken stock cube, crumbled
bay leaf
white peppercorns
good pinch of freshly grated nutmeg

First make the crêpe batter: sift the flour
and salt into a bowl. Stir in the eggs and
melted butter or oil, then gradually add the
milk. Strain the batter through a fine sieve,
adding a little water if necessary to give the
batter the consistency of thin cream. Leave
to stand for 2 hours.
2 Meanwhile, make the bechamel sauce:
melt the butter in a small saucepan over a
ow heat. Add the onion and cook, stirring
occasionally, until soft. Stir in the chopped
ham and the flour and cook for 2–3 minutes,
stirring.
3 Add the scalded milk gradually, stirring
vigorously, then add the crumbled stock
cube, bay leaf, peppercorns and nutmeg. Let
the sauce simmer very gently until it is
reduced to about 300 ml /10 fl oz, stirring
from time to time.

4 Make 8 × 15 cm /6 in crêpes following
step 3 in the recipe for Herb and spinach
crêpes (*page 93*). Reserve.
5 Strain the reduced bechamel sauce
through a fine sieve; reserve.
6 Halve the courgettes lengthways, then
slice very thinly. Cook in the butter for 4–5
minutes over a medium heat, stirring, until
lightly browned and tender. Cool slightly,
stir into half of the bechamel sauce and
adjust the seasoning.
7 Stir the drained sweetcorn into the
remaining sauce and adjust the seasoning.
8 Heat the oven to 180C /350F /gas 4.
Divide the courgette mixture evenly among
4 crêpes and roll up. Divide the sweetcorn
mixture among the remaining crêpes and
roll. Place the crêpes in a buttered gratin
dish large enough to hold them in 1 layer.
9 Cover with foil and cook for 10–15
minutes, or until heated through. To serve,
place 1 courgette crêpe and 1 sweetcorn
crêpe on each of 4 heated serving plates and
sprinkle with finely chopped parsley.

Herbed salad
niçoise

40 minutes

Serves 4
500 g /1 lb new potatoes
salt
¼ Spanish onion, sliced into thin rings
200 g /7 oz canned tuna fish
1 green pepper, thinly sliced
4 celery stalks, sliced
2 large, firm tomatoes, blanched, skinned
    and cut into wedges
2 hard-boiled eggs, quartered
50 g /2 oz canned anchovy fillets, drained

Herbed salad niçoise

For the dressing
150 ml /5 fl oz olive oil
30 ml /2 tbls dry white wine
30 ml /2 tbls wine vinegar
2.5 ml /½ tsp Dijon mustard
1 shallot, finely chopped
salt and freshly ground black pepper
15 ml /1 tbls finely chopped fresh parsley
1.5 ml /¼ tsp each dried marjoram, chervil
    and tarragon
For the garnish
12 black olives, stoned
a sprig of flat-leaved parsley

1 Boil the potatoes in their skins in salted
water for about 15–20 minutes until they
are just tender.
2 Meanwhile, prepare the dressing: whisk
together the olive oil, dry white wine, wine
vinegar and mustard until they emulsify.
Stir in the finely chopped shallot and season
with salt and freshly ground black pepper to
taste.
3 Soak the thinly sliced onion rings in cold
water for 10 minutes.
4 As soon as the potatoes are tender, hold
the pan under cold running water until the
potatoes are cool enough to handle. Peel
them and slice into a bowl. Pour 60–75 ml /
4–5 tbls of the dressing over them, mix
gently and leave to cool.
5 Add the herbs to the remaining dressing.
Drain and flake the tuna fish. Drain the
onion rings, pat dry and add to the potatoes,
along with the thinly sliced green pepper,
sliced celery, flaked tuna fish, tomato
wedges, quartered hard-boiled eggs and
anchovy fillets.
6 Add the herb-flavoured dressing and toss
very carefully, taking care not to break the
eggs or potatoes. Garnish with black olives
and a sprig of parsley.

Quiche provençale

Serves 6–8
250 g /9 oz made-weight shortcrust pastry,
    defrosted if frozen
45 ml /3 tbls olive oil
1 Spanish onion, finely chopped
2 garlic cloves, finely chopped
900 g /2 lb tomatoes, blanched, skinned, seeded
    and diced
salt and freshly ground black pepper
2 eggs, lightly beaten
30 ml /2 tbls thick cream
100 g /4 oz freshly grated Gruyère cheese
30 ml /2 tbls finely chopped fresh parsley
1 medium-sized egg white, beaten
10 black olives, halved and stoned

1   Roll out the pastry 3 mm /⅛ in thick and use it to line a 23 cm /9 in fluted pastry case, pressing well into the sides. Prick the base with a fork and place in the refrigerator to relax for at least 30 minutes.
2   Heat the oven to 200C /400F /gas 6. Line the pastry case with foil and beans and bake for 10 minutes. Turn the heat down to 180C /350F /gas 4, remove the foil and beans and bake for 8–10 minutes, until the pastry is dry but not coloured. Remove from the oven and leave it to cool in its tin, but leave the oven turned on.
3   While the pastry case is cooling, make the filling; in a heavy-based saucepan, heat the olive oil. Add the finely chopped onion and sauté over a moderate heat for 7–10 minutes, or until softened, stirring occasionally. Stir in the finely chopped garlic and the prepared tomatoes. Season to taste with salt and freshly ground black pepper and simmer over a moderate heat for about 15 minutes, or until the mixture has reduced to a pulp, stirring frequently. Cool slightly.
4   Stir the beaten eggs, thick cream, freshly grated Gruyère cheese and finely chopped parsley into the tomato and onion mixture until thoroughly combined. Correct the seasoning.
5   Brush the cooled pastry case with beaten egg white and place it, in its tin, on a baking sheet. Pour the filling into the prepared pastry case. Bake for 35–40 minutes, or until set and golden. Decorate with the halved olives, cut side down, and serve as soon as possible.

preparing and relaxing the pastry case,
then 2 hours

Red caviar roll

Serves 4–6
olive oil and flour for baking tin
50 g /2 oz butter
50 g /2 oz flour, sifted
275 ml /10 fl oz hot milk
salt
10 ml /2 tsp caster sugar
a pinch of grated nutmeg
4 eggs, separated

175 g /6 oz full-fat cream cheese
15 ml /1 tbls lemon juice
150 ml /5 fl oz soured cream
freshly ground black pepper
150 ml /5 fl oz thick cream
100 g /4 oz Russian red caviar,
    mixed with 10–15 ml /
    2–3 tsp olive oil if solid
watercress sprigs, to garnish

1   Heat the oven to 200 C /400F /gas 6. Line a 33 × 20 cm /13 × 8 in Swiss-roll tin with foil. Brush with olive oil and dust with flour, shaking out any excess.
2   To make the roll, melt the butter in a small pan. Add 25 g /1 oz flour and stir over a low heat to form a roux. Gradually stir in the hot milk and cook gently, stirring constantly, until the sauce thickens. Bring to the boil and simmer, stirring, for 3–4 minutes.
3   Pour the sauce into a bowl. Beat in a pinch of salt, the sugar and a small pinch of nutmeg. Beat the egg yolks lightly and pour into the sauce in a thin stream, beating constantly. Leave until tepid.
4   Whisk the egg whites with a pinch of salt until stiff but not dry. Fold a quarter into the tepid sauce. Sift the rest of the flour; fold in half. Fold in a third of the remaining egg whites, then the rest of the sifted flour and finally all the remaining egg whites.
5   Pour the mixture into the prepared tin and level out with a spatula. Bake for 5 minutes, then lower the oven temperature to 150C /300F /gas 2 and continue to bake for about 50–55 minutes, or until golden brown and springy to the touch.
6   While the roll is cooking, make the filling. Blend the cream cheese, lemon juice and 30 ml /2 tbls soured cream together. Season to taste with pepper. Whip the thick cream until light and fluffy, then fold into the cheese mixture, followed by 45–60 ml /3–4 tbls red caviar. Correct the seasoning and chill until needed.
7   Line a damp cloth with greaseproof paper. As soon as the roll is baked, turn it out onto the paper and peel off the foil from the back. Trim the crusty edges. Using the cloth and paper lining, roll up loosely, from the long side, like a Swiss roll. Cool.
8   Gently unroll the cold roll. Remove lining and spread with the filling, leaving a 5 mm /¼ in margin, roll up once more. Wrap loosely in a clean tea-towel and chill overnight.
9   Place on a bed of watercress and serve, cut in thin slices and garnished with the rest of the soured cream and red caviar.

2 hours,
then overnight chilling

Pasta and kidney beans

Serves 6
250 g /8 oz dried red kidney beans, soaked overnight
1 beef marrow bone, about 10 cm /4 in long
25 g /1 oz butter
15 ml /1 tbls olive oil
1 Spanish onion, finely chopped
1 garlic clove, finely chopped
60 ml /4 tbls tomato purée
30 ml /2 tbls finely chopped fresh parsley
1.5 ml /¼ tsp cayenne pepper
10 ml /2 tsp dried oregano
175 g /6 oz short cut macaroni
boiling water, if needed
salt and freshly ground black pepper
freshly grated Parmesan cheese, to serve

1   Drain the beans and place them in a large, heavy-based saucepan with the marrow bone. Cover with 1 L /2 pt cold water and bring to the boil. Boil vigorously for 10 minutes, then reduce the heat and simmer gently for 45 minutes–1 hour, or until tender.
2   Heat the butter and olive oil in a small saucepan. Add the finely chopped onion and garlic and cook over a moderate heat for 5–7 minutes, or until soft, stirring occasionally with a wooden spoon.
3   Add the onion and garlic to the kidney beans, along with the tomato purée, finely chopped parsley, cayenne pepper, oregano and macaroni. Cook for a further 10–15 minutes, or until the macaroni is just tender, stirring frequently and adding a little boiling water if necessary. Season to taste with salt and freshly ground black pepper.
4   Transfer the pasta and beans, with their liquid, to a heated serving dish. Sprinkle generously with Parmesan cheese and serve immediately with a bowl of extra Parmesan cheese.

soaking the beans overnight,
then 1½ hours

Croustades of scrambled egg

Serves 6
350 g /12 oz made-weight   *175 g /6 oz ham, finely chopped*
   shortcrust pastry,   *salt*
   defrosted if frozen   *freshly ground black pepper*
175 g /6 oz mushrooms   *7 eggs*
50 g /2 oz butter   *45 ml /3 tbls thick cream*

1   Grease 6 × 9.5 cm /3¾ in brioche moulds, loose-bottomed fluted tartlet tins, 4 cm /1½ in deep and 9.5 cm /3¾ in across the top, or individual Yorkshire pudding tins.
2   Divide the pastry into 6 and roll out each piece thinly. Line the moulds, pressing the pastry into the flutes with the fingertips. Trim off the tops with a knife and prick the bottoms with a fork. Relax in the refrigerator for 30 minutes.
3   Heat the oven to 200C /400F /gas 6. Line the pastry cases with foil and beans. Bake for 10 minutes, carefully remove the beans and foil and return the pastry shells to the oven for a further 8 minutes. Remove from the oven, let the pastry cases set for 2 minutes, then remove from the moulds. Keep warm.
4   While the cases are baking, start the filling. Slice the mushrooms thinly. Melt 25 g /1 oz butter in a saucepan, add the mushrooms and sauté over a medium heat for 3–4 minutes, or until golden. Add the finely chopped ham and season to taste with salt and freshly ground black pepper. Cook for 3 minutes. Remove from the heat.
5   Break the eggs into a bowl. Add salt and freshly ground black pepper to taste and stir well with a fork (don't beat) until the yolks and whites are thoroughly mixed. Stir in the thick cream.
6   Select a heavy frying-pan or saucepan. Add the remaining butter and heat until sizzling but not coloured. Then swirl the butter round so that the bottom and sides of the pan are coated.
7   Pour in all the eggs at once. Set the pan over a very low heat and immediately start stirring with a large wooden spoon. Keep stirring, making sure the spoon reaches the edge of the pan and keeping the whole mass of liquid egg on the move, until the eggs are creamy and almost set.
8   Remove the pan from the heat and fold in the mushrooms and ham. Correct the seasoning if necessary and divide equally among the pastry cases. Arrange on a large serving platter and serve immediately.

lining pastry cases, relaxing,
then 30 minutes

SAVOURY MOUSSES

A light-textured savoury mousse, hot and fluffy or cold and beautifully moulded, adds a touch of elegance as a buffet dish or dinner party starter, and is very satisfying to make.

There are two main varieties of savoury mousse: hot, made with eggs; and cold, set with powdered gelatine or aspic jelly. Both can be flavoured with smooth mixtures of fish, shellfish, meat, cheese or vegetables.

Both hot and cold mousses are often very subtle in flavour and to bring out their full taste I have invented my own Special spice blend: grind to a powder 75 ml /5 tbls white peppercorns and combine with 30 ml /2 tbls paprika, 15 ml /1 tbls each ground bay leaves, dried sage, marjoram, rosemary and mace, and 7.5 ml /1½ tsp each cayenne pepper, ground cinnamon, ground cloves and freshly grated nutmeg.

Avocado mousse

Hot mousses

Hot mousses are quite simple to make. The basic flavouring mixture is combined with eggs, then moulded and baked until it holds its shape. It is then turned out and served hot, sometimes masked with a complementary sauce.

By far the trickiest part of making hot moulded mousses is getting the right balance of seasoning. Not many people relish the idea of tasting a raw mixture, and, as a result they do not taste, and season incorrectly. However, there is a simple way round this: when the mixture is ready to be packed into its baking dish, take a spoonful of it, shape it into a little patty and sauté it in a little butter until cooked through.

Cold mousses

Cold mousses are doubly wonderful: the look great on the day of the party, and ca be prepared the day before.

The base of a cold mousse may be bechamel or velouté sauce, or an eve thicker mixture of butter, flour, milk an egg. This is combined with the flavourin mixture. Alternatively, a bulky flavourin mixture can be used as the base. In this cas liquid aspic, or powdered gelatine dissolve in water, is added for body, and sometime whipped cream and/or stiffly beaten eg whites are folded in for a lighter texture The mixture is then poured into a mould use a soufflé dish, if you wish – and chille in the refrigerator until set.

The base of your mousse must be com pletely cold when you add whipped crean and beaten egg white, otherwise these wil melt, losing all the air you have so carefull beaten into them!

Test your mousse for setting power an flavour before you commit it to the mould. / mousse mixture which does not contai enough gelatine is likely to slither down int

liquid mass as it is being turned out, while
[o]ne that contains too much will be
[u]npleasantly rubbery.

Simply spoon a tiny amount of the
[m]ixture onto a chilled saucer and pop it into
[t]he freezer for a moment or two to set. If the
[se]t mousse is like chewing gum, gently fold
[in] a little wine or stock or a little more
[w]hipped cream or stiffly beaten egg white. If
[t]he mousse is too thin, add a little more
[g]elatine, allowing 2.5 ml /½ tsp gelatine
[p]owder for each 425 ml /15 fl oz mousse
[m]ixture. Dissolve this in a little water and
[fo]ld it into the mousse with a gentle figure-
[o]f-eight movement.

If the mousse lacks flavour, add a little
[m]ore seasoning and some wine, port, sherry,
[M]adeira, lemon juice, onion juice,
[W]orcestershire sauce or Tabasco.

Serving a cold mousse

[A] cold mousse should not be served straight
[f]rom the refrigerator, especially if it has
[b]een left there overnight. Turn it out and
[le]ave it at room temperature for about an
[h]our before serving to take off the chill and
[r]estore softness.

Turning out: select a serving plate large
[e]nough to hold the turned-out mousse. Wet
[it] lightly so that if you do not manage to
[t]urn the mousse onto the centre of the plate,
[y]ou will be able to slide it into position
[w]ithout damaging it.

Run the very tip of a knife between the
[e]dge of the mousse and the rim of the mould
[–] the knife tip should only be inserted a few
[m]illimetres. Rinse a towel in hot water and
[w]ring it out. Hold it around the mould for
[1]–2 seconds only – no longer. This should
[lo]osen the mousse from the mould.

Lay the serving plate upside down on the
[m]ould and, holding the plate and mould
[f]irmly together with both hands, quickly
[in]vert them. Halfway over, give them a
[q]uick jerk, so that if the mousse is being held
[f]ast by an airlock it will be released. When
[t]he mould and plate are completely inverted,
[g]ive them a couple of firm shakes. You will
[f]eel the weight of the mousse transfer itself
[f]rom the mould to the plate.

If the mousse does not slip away from the
[m]ould, repeat the hot, wet towel operation
[a]s before and try again. Do not be tempted
[t]o dip the mould into hot water, which
[w]ould melt away the surface.

When you are sure that the mousse has
[c]ome loose, place the plate and mould on the
[t]able and slowly lift off the mould. If the
[o]uter surface has melted a little, slip it back
[in]to the refrigerator to firm up.

Garnishing: If the mousse has been
[d]amaged on its way out of the mould, some
[t]hick mayonnaise and a little chopped
[p]arsley, used with discretion, will
[c]amouflage all but the most disastrous
[m]ishap.

Alternatively, you can line the mould with
[a]spic, so that it can be turned out complete
[w]ith garnish.

Aspic for garnishing should be on the
[p]oint of setting. If it has set, melt it and pour
[in]to a small bowl. Stand this in a larger bowl
[o]f ice and stir until it begins to turn syrupy.
[It] should have the consistency of unbeaten
[e]gg white.

Unmoulding a cold mousse

Run the tip of a knife around the edge of the
mousse. Hold a hot, damp towel around the
mould for 1–2 seconds, then place a lightly
wetted plate upside down on the mould.

Hold the mould and plate firmly, and
quickly invert them. Halfway over, give a
quick jerk. Invert completely, give 1 or 2
firm shakes, then lift off the mould.

To line a mould, fill a chilled mould with
aspic, then stand in a bowl of ice until the
aspic begins to set around the edges. Use
vegetable shapes for garnishing. Dip them
on the point of a skewer into the aspic and
arrange in the base of the lined mould, then
spoon a little more aspic on top. Chill until
set, then fill the mould with mousse mixture.

Quick aspic jelly

**Making true aspic jelly is a long and
complicated process; here is a quick
version.**

15 minutes

Makes about 600 ml /1 pt
15 ml /1 tbls powdered gelatine
*425 ml /15 fl oz chicken or beef stock, home-
  made or from a cube*
30 ml /2 tbls each Madeira and dry sherry

1   Sprinkle the gelatine over 60 ml /4 tbls
water in a small bowl. Leave for a few
minutes to soften. Do not stir.
2   Strain the stock through a sieve lined
with fine muslin. Transfer the strained stock
to a saucepan and heat to almost boiling.
Add the softened gelatine, and stir until the
gelatine has dissolved completely.
3   Leave the mixture to cool, then stir in
the Madeira and dry sherry.

● A very quick aspic can be made using
packaged savoury aspic powder. Place 600
ml /1 pt water in a saucepan with 45 ml /3
tbls aspic powder and bring slowly to the
boil. Cool before using.
● It is wise to test that the aspic will set
properly by chilling it thoroughly after it is
made and remelting it just before use. If the
aspic fails to set during this test, you still
have time to strengthen it: add a little extra
dissolved powdered gelatine.

Avocado mousse

45 minutes,
plus 2 hours chilling

Serves 6
2 large, ripe avocados
30 ml /2 tbls lemon juice
10 ml /2 tsp finely chopped onion
2.5 ml /½ tsp Tabasco sauce
*275 ml /10 fl oz chicken stock, home-made
  or from a cube*
15 g /½ oz powdered gelatine
150 ml /5 fl oz thick cream
2 medium-sized egg whites
150 ml /5 fl oz mayonnaise (see page 49)
salt and freshly ground black pepper
halved lemon slices, to garnish
cucumber slices and twists, to garnish

1   Peel, stone and chop the avocados. Blend
them in an electric blender with the lemon
juice, chopped onion, Tabasco sauce and
chicken stock until smooth.
2   Sprinkle the gelatine over 45 ml /3 tbls
water in a small bowl. Leave to soften for a
few minutes, then set the bowl in a saucepan
of hot water over a very low heat until
dissolved. Do not stir. Pour the gelatine into
the avocado mixture in a thin stream, stirring constantly. Chill for about 15 minutes,
until the mixture is just setting.
3   Meanwhile, whip the cream until it just
holds its shape but is not stiff. Whisk the egg
whites until they form stiff peaks.
4   Carefully fold the cream into the
avocado mixture, followed by the
mayonnaise and the egg whites. Season with
salt and freshly ground black pepper.
5   Rinse out a 1.1 L /2 pt charlotte mould.
Turn the avocado mixture into the mould.
Cover and refrigerate for about 2 hours.
6   Turn out onto a plate 1 hour before
serving. Garnish the top with halved lemon
slices and cucumber slices and surround
with cucumber twists.

Cold ham and ginger mousse

🔪🔪 1 hour,
plus chilling

Serves 4–6
300 ml /10 fl oz Quick aspic jelly (see recipe)
150 g /5 oz butter
50 g /2 oz flour
salt
6.5 ml /1¼ tsp Special spice blend (see page
98)
1 medium-sized egg, beaten
300 ml /10 fl oz milk
225 g /8 oz cooked ham
10–15 ml /2–3 tsp tomato purée
30 ml /2 tbls Madeira
4–6 pieces stem ginger in syrup, drained and
finely chopped
2 medium-sized egg whites
90 ml /6 tbls thick cream
For the garnish
1 thin slice ham
6–8 × 25 mm /1 in sticks of cooked green
beans, cooked carrot or raw cucumber

1 Chill a 1.1 L /2 pt mould. Use the aspic just on the point of setting – it will be of a syrupy consistency. Spoon 90 ml /6 tbls of the syrupy aspic into the bottom of the chilled mould and refrigerate until set.
2 Prepare the garnish: cut a small flower shape from the thin slice of ham with a biscuit cutter. Dip the ham flower in the syrupy aspic and place it in the middle of the set aspic in the mould. Arrange the sticks of beans, carrot or cucumber around the ham flower, dipping them in the syrupy aspic before laying them in position. Carefully spoon 45 ml /3 tbls of the syrupy aspic over the set aspic and garnish in the mould. Refrigerate until set.
3 Make the mousse: melt 50 g /2 oz of the butter in a small, heavy saucepan. Remove the pan from the heat and mix in the flour. Add the salt to taste and the Special spice blend. Combine the beaten egg with half of the milk and add to the pan, then return the pan to the heat and stir vigorously for about 3 minutes, until the mixture comes clean away from the sides of the pan. Spread the mixture on a plate and chill.
4 Cream the remaining 75 g /3 oz butter until very light and fluffy. Put the ham through the mincer 3 times.
5 Beat the ham into the creamed butter, a little at a time, then beat in the tomato purée and Madeira. If the mixture is not absolutely smooth at this stage, purée it in an electric blender. Beat in the chilled sauce mixture, 90 ml /6 tbls of the syrupy aspic, the remaining milk and the chopped ginger.
6 Whisk the egg whites until stiff but not dry. Whip the cream until it holds its shape in soft peaks. Fold the cream into the ham mixture, followed by the egg whites.
7 Spoon the ham mousse into the mould, then spoon the remaining aspic over the top. Chill in the refrigerator for several hours or overnight, to set.
8 Unmould the mousse onto a flat serving plate 1 hour before serving.

Cold smoked salmon mousses

Here is a delicious way to make a little smoked salmon go a long way. If you want to be extravagant, garnish the mousses with extra smoked salmon.

🔪 30 minutes,
plus chilling

Serves 6–8
225 g /8 oz smoked salmon
150 ml /5 fl oz thin cream
15 ml /1 tbls lemon juice
salt and freshly ground black pepper
freshly grated nutmeg
60 ml /4 tbls Quick aspic jelly (see recipe)
2 medium-sized egg whites
300 ml /10 fl oz thick cream
For the garnish
sprigs of parsley
strips of smoked salmon

Cold smoked salmon mousses

1 Coarsely chop the smoked salmon. Plac[e] it in a blender with the thin cream, lemo[n] juice and a small pinch each of salt, fresh[ly] ground black pepper and freshly grate[d] nutmeg. Be careful not to season th[e] mixture too heavily. Blend the mixture to [a] smooth purée and transfer to a bowl.
2 Use the aspic on the point of setting – [it] will be syrupy in consistency. Beat it int[o] the salmon mixture.
3 Whisk the egg whites until stiff but n[ot] dry. Whip the thick cream until it holds i[ts] shape in soft peaks. Fold the whipped crea[m] into the salmon mixture, followed by the eg[g] whites. Taste, and adjust the seasoning wit[h] a little more lemon juice, salt, pepper o[r] nutmeg, as necessary.
4 Rinse 6–8 individual ramekins, divid[e] the mousse mixture among them, the[n] refrigerate several hours or overnight, to set[.]
5 Remove from the refrigerator 1 hou[r] before serving. Serve in the ramekins, ga[r]nished with parsley sprigs and salmon strip[s].

Hot chicken mousses

1 hour

Serves 8
50 g /2 oz butter, plus extra for greasing
50 g /2 oz flour
275 ml /10 fl oz milk
350 g /12 oz raw chicken meat
50 g /2 oz cooked ham
2 medium-sized eggs
175 ml /6 fl oz thick cream
10 ml /2 tsp tomato purée
45 ml /3 tbls vermouth
pinch of cayenne pepper
5 ml /1 tsp Special spice blend (page 98)
lemon juice
salt and freshly ground black pepper
sprigs of watercress, to garnish
thin strips of red pepper, to garnish

For the Fresh tomato sauce
1 large Spanish onion, finely chopped
1 garlic clove, halved
60 ml /4 tbls olive oil
1 chicken stock cube, crumbled
450 g /1 lb ripe tomatoes, blanched, skinned, seeded and chopped
30 ml /2 tbls tomato purée
salt and freshly ground black pepper
a pinch of cayenne pepper
lemon juice
30 ml /2 tbls finely chopped fresh parsley

1 Heat the oven to 170C /325F /gas 3, and butter 8 individual ovenproof soufflé dishes, 150 ml /5 fl oz in capacity.
2 Melt the butter in a small saucepan, stir in the flour, then cook over a medium heat for 2–3 minutes. Remove the pan from the heat and gradually stir in the milk. Bring slowly to the boil, stirring constantly. Simmer for 1 minute, then remove the pan from the heat.
3 Put the chicken and ham through the finest blade of your mincer 3 times. Place the minced meat in the blender with the eggs, thick cream, tomato purée, vermouth, cayenne pepper and Special spice blend. Blend until smooth. Add the white sauce mixture and lemon juice, salt and pepper to taste, then blend again until smooth.
4 Divide the mixture among the buttered dishes and cook in the oven for 20–25 minutes.
5 Meanwhile, make the Fresh tomato sauce. Sauté the finely chopped onion and halved garlic clove in 30 ml /2 tbls of the olive oil until the onion is soft. Discard the garlic. Add the crumbled stock cube, chopped tomatoes, tomato purée and 150 ml /5 fl oz water, then simmer for 5 minutes.
6 Season to taste with salt, freshly ground black pepper, cayenne pepper and lemon juice. Blend until smooth. Stir in the chopped parsley and the remaining olive oil.
7 Turn out each mousse onto a heated individual serving plate, mask with Fresh tomato sauce and garnish with sprigs of watercress and thin strips of red pepper. Serve immediately, with the rest of the sauce passed around separately.

Stilton mousse

This rich and creamy mousse makes good use of a small piece of Stilton; Roquefort would be equally delicious.

30 minutes, plus chilling

Serves 4–6
7.5 ml /1½ tsp powdered gelatine
100 g /4 oz Stilton, crumbled
2 egg yolks, beaten
90 ml /6 tbls thick cream
1.5 ml /¼ tsp turmeric
1 egg white
oil for greasing
60 ml /4 tbls ground almonds
2–3 black olives, halved and stoned

1 Sprinkle the gelatine over 15 ml /1 tbls cold water in a small bowl and leave to soften. Place the bowl in a saucepan of hot water over a very low heat until dissolved. Do not stir.
2 In a bowl, beat the crumbled Stilton and the egg yolks until smooth. Add 30 ml /2 tbls thick cream and the turmeric and continue beating to blend. Stir in the gelatine.
3 Whisk the egg white until stiff peaks form. In another bowl, lightly whip the remaining thick cream. Fold the whipped cream into the Stilton mixture, then fold in the egg white. Lightly grease a 600 ml /1 pt soufflé dish with oil. Pour mixture into the dish and chill until set, about 1–1½ hours.
4 Meanwhile, heat the grill to high. Place the ground almonds in a small flameproof dish under the grill for 1–2 minutes, until lightly brown. Leave to cool.
5 Remove the mousse from the refrigerator 1 hour before serving. Sprinkle the almonds on a sheet of greaseproof paper. Hold a hot towel around the mould for 1–2 seconds and turn the mousse out onto the paper. Cover the top and sides of the mousse with almonds, using a palette knife. Shake off the excess and transfer the mousse to a serving platter. To serve, mark the top into portions and place half a black olive in the centre of each.

Hot chicken mousses

Seafood and lettuce mousse

Serves 8

275 g /10 oz fresh, frozen or canned crabmeat, defrosted if frozen
  and drained
¼ cucumber, peeled and diced
100 g /4 oz boiled, peeled scampi, defrosted if frozen and chopped
1 lettuce, outer leaves removed, finely shredded
25 g /1 oz powdered gelatine
275 ml /10 fl oz cold fish stock (see page 11)
juice of ½ lemon
salt and freshly ground black pepper
1.5 ml /¼ tsp cayenne pepper
150 ml /5 fl oz thick cream
very thin slices of cucumber, to garnish
lemon wedges and buttered brown bread, to serve

1   Place the drained crabmeat in a large bowl and flake finely with
a fork. Add the diced cucumber, chopped scampi and shredded
lettuce and mix well.
2   Sprinkle the powdered gelatine over 60 ml /4 tbls water in a
small bowl. Leave to soften for a few minutes, then set the bowl in a
saucepan of hot water over a very low heat until dissolved. Do not
stir.
3   In a bowl, combine the cold fish stock, dissolved gelatine, lemon
juice, salt and freshly ground black pepper to taste and the cayenne
pepper.
4   Whip the thick cream until stiff and rinse out a 1.4 L /2½ pt
soufflé dish or mould.
5   Combine the flavoured gelatine mixture with the seafood and
lettuce mixture. Fold in the whipped cream, adjust the seasoning
and pour the mixture into the prepared dish. Chill in the
refrigerator for several hours.
6   Remove the mousse from the refrigerator 1 hour before you plan
to serve it. Turn it out onto a plate and garnish with very thinly
sliced cucumber. Serve with lemon wedges and buttered brown
bread.

● Soak the thin cucumber slices in iced water for 1 hour; they will
become pliable and you can easily arrange them for the garnish.

 1 hour,
plus chilling

Crab mousse Bellevue

Serves 4
225 g /8 oz white and brown crabmeat, fresh, frozen or canned,
  defrosted if frozen
65 ml /2½ fl oz mayonnaise (see page 49)
45 ml /3 tbls lemon juice
100 g /4 oz cream cheese
1.5 ml /¼ tsp cayenne pepper
salt and freshly ground black pepper
7.5 ml /1½ tsp powdered gelatine
Melba toast, to serve
For the garnish
150 ml /5 fl oz Quick aspic jelly (see recipe)
8 leaves, cut from a cucumber skin
4 pimento diamonds
2 black olives, halved and stoned

1   If using canned or frozen crabmeat, drain it well. In a large
bowl, combine the mayonnaise, lemon juice and cream cheese and
beat with a wooden spoon until the mixture is smooth. Season with
cayenne pepper and salt and freshly ground black pepper to taste.
Add the crabmeat and stir with a fork to mix well.
2   Sprinkle the gelatine over 45 ml /3 tbls cold water in a small
bowl; leave for a few minutes to soften, then place the bowl in a
saucepan of hot water over a very low heat until the gelatine has
dissolved. Do not stir.
3   Add the dissolved gelatine to the crabmeat mixture, stirring well
to blend. Spoon into a 600 ml /1 pt soufflé dish and level the top.
Leave to chill in the refrigerator for 1 hour.
4   To garnish the mousse, the aspic should be almost at setting
point, with the consistency of unbeaten egg white. Pour a little of
the aspic over the mousse and return to the refrigerator for a few
minutes to set.
5   Use the cucumber skin, pimento and olive garnishes to make
flowers which consist of 2 cucumber 'leaves' with a pimento
diamond and half an olive for the centre. Dip each garnish into the
aspic and, using a skewer, arrange the 4 'flowers' near the outer
edge of the mousse. Pour the remaining aspic over the decorations
and chill until set.
6   Remove the mousse from the refrigerator 1 hour before serving.
Serve the mousse with Melba toast.

 1 hour,
plus chilling

Spanish vegetable mousse

Serves 6
450 g /1 lb green beans, topped and tailed
salt
25 g /1 oz butter, plus extra for greasing
30 ml /2 tbls olive oil
2 Spanish onions, thinly sliced
400 g /14 oz canned artichoke hearts, drained, with the liquid reserved
4 eggs
freshly ground black pepper
175 g /6 oz canned pimentos, drained and cut into thin strips, to garnish
a sprig of flat-leaved parsley, to garnish

1 Heat the oven to 200C /400F /gas 6.
2 Cook the green beans in a large pan of rapidly boiling salted water for about 8 minutes, or until very tender. Drain, refresh and drain again. Reserve.
3 Heat the butter and olive oil in a frying-pan. When the foaming subsides, sauté the thinly sliced Spanish onions for 10 minutes or until tender, stirring occasionally with a wooden spoon.
4 Put the beans, the onions and their pan juices and the drained artichoke hearts in a blender with a little artichoke liquid. Blend until smooth.
5 Beat the eggs in a bowl until frothy. Add the beaten eggs to the vegetable purée and blend again. Season with salt and pepper.
6 Butter a 1.1 L /2 pt loaf tin or mould and line the base with greaseproof paper. Butter the greaseproof paper, pour the vegetable mixture into the tin and cover it with greased foil. Place the tin in a baking tin and pour in boiling water to 25 mm /1 in up the sides of the baking tin. Place in the oven for 5 minutes, then reduce the heat to 150C /300F /gas 2 and bake for a further 65–70 minutes, or until the mixture has set – a skewer inserted into the centre should come out clean.
7 Gently run a sharp knife around the edges of the tin and turn the vegetable mousse out onto a heated oblong platter. Discard the greaseproof paper.
8 Garnish with a fine lattice of pimento strips and a sprig of flat-leaved parsley and serve immediately.

1 hour,
then 1¼ hours cooking

Roquefort and egg mousse

Serves 6
oil for greasing
50 g /2 oz Roquefort cheese
500 g /1 lb cottage cheese
90 ml /6 tbls thick cream, whipped
90 ml /6 tbls mayonnaise (see page 49)
30 ml /2 tbls finely snipped fresh chives
2.5 ml /½ tsp Worcestershire sauce
salt
a pinch of cayenne pepper
5 ml /1 tsp powdered gelatine
2 hard-boiled eggs, chopped
For the garnish
lettuce leaves
2 small hard-boiled eggs, thinly sliced
black olives

1 Oil an 850 ml /1½ pt decorative or plain mould. In a large bowl, mash the Roquefort cheese with a fork and gradually beat in the cottage cheese and whipped cream, mixing well.
2 Add the mayonnaise, finely snipped chives, Worcestershire sauce and salt and cayenne pepper to taste.
3 Sprinkle the gelatine over 30 ml /2 tbls cold water in a small bowl. Let it stand for a few minutes to soften. Then place the bowl of gelatine in a small pan of water over a very low heat until the gelatine dissolves. Do not stir.
4 Stir the dissolved gelatine mixture into the cheese mixture, fold in the chopped hard-boiled eggs and pour the mixture into the prepared mould. Chill for at least 4 hours.
5 Remove the mousse from the refrigerator 1 hour before serving. Turn it out onto a serving dish, surround it with lettuce leaves and garnish with slices of hard-boiled egg and black olives.

30 minutes,
plus 4 hours or more chilling

PATES & TERRINES

A classic country terrine, chunky and flavoursome, served from the mould or elegantly sliced, or a smooth pâté of chicken livers or fish, all make delicious and attractive appetizers.

Terrines and pâtés are one of the most successful dishes to make, and popular dishes to serve, as a starter. Many rich and creamy pâtés and brandades – fish pâtés – are quick to prepare and make an ideal appetizer served with hot, buttered toast. A terrine may take more time to prepare, but as most will benefit from a few days maturing, it is still a convenient dish to make for a dinner party.

The words terrine and pâté are now used virtually interchangeably. A pâté will generally be assumed to be a smooth mixture, using ready-cooked ingredients which are not cooked once they have been combined. A brandade refers to a very smooth fish pâté. When making a smooth, uncooked pâté your life will be made so much easier if you have a blender or food processor. It is possible to make many recipes using a mortar and pestle or pressing the necessary ingredients through a sieve, but you may find this hard work.

The name terrine is usually applied to a more textured mixture, made by combining raw ingredients which are then cooked: the name being taken from the dish they are cooked in. Texture is given to a terrine by mincing some of the ingredients while others are left whole or cut into strips. These are then layered in the dish before cooking. Not all terrines are like this, however, and a perfectly smooth effect can be achieved by combining a choux paste with a pâté mixture, as in the recipe for Smooth liver terrine (*see page 108*). Soaked breadcrumbs can be added to make a smoother mixture.

Preparing the mixture
When making a cooked pâté there are several things to watch out for. To avoid a crumbly and uninteresting meat pâté there has to be a high fat content. This is usually added by using fresh pork fat, although fat, unsmoked bacon, or even smoked bacon, may be used if, for example, the basic meat is highly-flavoured game. The fat content can also be supplemented by adding thick cream.

In an uncooked pâté the fat is added in the form of butter or oil and often cream cheese and cream.

Most cooked pâtés are baked for a couple of hours so the uncooked mixture must be very moist – even sloppy – to start with. Lemon juice, brandy, red or white wine or fortified wine can all be included. If the mixture appears to be on the stiff and dry side before baking, don't hesitate – counteract this by adding stock or cream.

By far the trickiest part of making terrines and pâtés is getting the right balance of seasoning. Not many people relish the idea of tasting a pâté mixture raw, and as a result, they tend to season too cautiously. However, there is a simple way round this: when the mixture is ready to be packed into its baking dish, take a spoonful of it, shape it into a patty and sauté in a little butter until cooked through. Or drop it into a pan of simmering water and poach it. When you taste it, make allowance for the fact that the 'tone' of the seasoning will be weaker after cooking and maturing.

The other point worthy of mention in this context is the ingredient *quatre epices* which you will come across in French pâté recipes. The French are able to buy a commercial spice mixture specially blended for seasoning pâtés. Sometimes it comes in the form of *sel epice* – salt seasoned with this special spice blend. If you cannot buy this seasoning salt for pâtés, it is very easy to make a quantity for yourself. Using 15 g /$\frac{1}{2}$ oz of salt, add anything from a pinch up to 1.5–2.5 ml /$\frac{1}{4}$–$\frac{1}{2}$ tsp of each of a variety of herbs and spices such as nutmeg, basil, marjoram, thyme, freshly ground black pepper, bay leaf, ginger, coriander, cayenne pepper and paprika which have been ground or powdered. Mix them together and store in an airtight jar or container for use in pâtés and terrines or to add flavour to stews.

Cooking the pâté
Pâtés and terrines are tradionally baked in deep, glazed earthenware dishes covered with a lid which has a hole in it to allow steam to escape. However, you can easily make do with a loaf tin covered with foil.

One way of ensuring your pâté stays moist during cooking is to line the sides and base of the dish or tin with thin slices of pork fat. The back fat of salt pork is often used as this is firm enough to slice very thinly.

Thinly sliced streaky bacon does the job admirably and looks pretty as well when the pâté is turned out. Use it at room temperature and stretch each slice to paper thinness with the back of a knife. They can then be laid across the terrine or tin and manoeuvred easily so that there are no gaps between the slices.

Most pâtés are baked in a *bain marie*. Cover the terrine with a lid or foil, then stand it in a roasting tin and pour in boiling water to come half or one-third of the way up the side. This is another way (like the lining of fat) to protect the parts of the pâté in closest contact with the heat, and so prevent the pâté turning hard and crumbly. The temperature of the oven is kept quite moderate for the same reason.

To tell whether the pâté is cooked, pierce it through the middle with a skewer: the juices should run perfectly clear, without a trace of blood. If you hold the skewer in the pâté for 10 seconds then put it to your lips, it should feel hot. At the same time, the liquid fat surrounding the pâté should be quite transparent and free of pink or red juices. The pâté itself will have shrunk considerably.

A hot pâté will shrink even more as it cools. To ensure the pâté will cut in neat, firm slices it can be weighted. This

liminates air bubbles and closes up the texture. To weight a pâté, you will need a board or flat dish that fits the top of the pâté as closely as possible, inside the rim. If you are using a loaf tin, another tin the same size is usually the easiest answer.

Remove the roasting tin from the oven, lift out the terrine and pour off the water from the tin. Return the terrine to the tin (in case the juices overflow when you weight it). Lay the board or dish on top of the hot pâté and weight this down with weights from scales, tins of food, etc, until the surface of the pâté is submerged in liquid fat and juices. Leave until cold and set. The pâté will shrink away from the sides, but any spaces will fill with juice that will set to a delicious jelly. The fat should form a seal over the top. Then remove the board or upper dish and refrigerate, leaving the sealing fat undisturbed.

To store pâtés and terrines

Meat and game pâtés improve if they are allowed to mature for a few days. If you intend to store a pâté for longer than 2–3 days, make sure that the top of the dish is completely sealed. Fresh lard is best, although a weighted pâté will have a good surface layer of fat anyway.

If you want to keep the pâté for more than a week, it is best to pour off the meaty juices half-way through the weighting and cooling time. These juices are the first to go off so are best replaced with melted fat. A well-sealed pâté will be safe under mild refrigeration for about 10 days.

An uncooked pâté will not keep for as long as a sealed terrine. However, it is easier

to make smaller quantities of this mixture, using only 225 g /8 oz of the basic ingredient, so calculate as nearly as possible what you will need for the one occasion, and use up any leftovers the next day.

Many people say that it is not worth freezing pâté. A pâté which has been frozen for a long time certainly loses both taste and texture. However, the freezing down and defrosting time can be used to mature the pâté. Do not freeze for more than a month.

Terrine of rabbit and walnuts

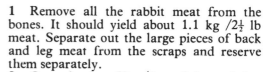 50 minutes, 1 hour marinating, 2 hours, plus chilling

Serves 18
2 kg /4½ lb rabbit, dressed, and liver reserved
225 g /8 oz fresh pork fat
150 g /5 oz raw gammon (not too salty)
60 ml /4 tbls brandy
90 ml /6 tbls Madeira
2.5 ml /½ tsp Seasoning salt for pâtés (see introduction)
salt and freshly ground black pepper
freshly grated nutmeg
a pinch of cayenne pepper
275 g /10 oz pork fillet
60 ml /4 tbls finely chopped fresh parsley
2.5 ml /½ tsp dried thyme
½ garlic clove, crushed
500 g /1 lb salt pork fat, or unsmoked streaky bacon, thinly sliced
90 ml /6 tbls coarsely chopped walnuts

1 Remove all the rabbit meat from the bones. It should yield about 1.1 kg /2½ lb meat. Separate out the large pieces of back and leg meat from the scraps and reserve them separately.

2 Coarsely chop 50 g /2 oz of the pork fat. Sauté it in a frying-pan until the fat runs and coats the base of the pan. Sauté the large pieces of rabbit in the hot fat a few pieces at a time until lightly coloured. Remove the meat from the pan with a slotted spoon.

3 Chop the rabbit liver coarsely. Add it to the fat remaining in the pan and sauté for 3–4 minutes, tossing frequently, until the liver is coloured. Remove from the pan. Reserve the pan juices.

4 Cut the sautéed rabbit meat into finger-thick strips about 4 cm /1½ in long. Cut the gammon and 50 g /2 oz of the pork fat into 15 mm /½ in cubes.

5 In a bowl, combine the rabbit strips, cubed gammon and pork fat. Add the brandy, Madeira, seasoning salt, salt, pepper, freshly grated nutmeg and cayenne pepper to taste. Mix all the ingredients together until well blended, then cover the bowl and leave the contents to marinate for at least 1 hour.

6 Coarsely mince the pork fillet, remaining pork fat, rabbit scraps and the sautéed rabbit liver, together with all the fat and reserved juices from the frying-pan. Put the minced mixture in a bowl and add the parsley, thyme, garlic, salt and freshly ground black pepper to taste. Mix all the ingredients together until well blended.

7 Heat the oven to 190C /375F /gas 5.

8 Line the base and sides of a 2.3 L /4 pt terrine or loaf tin with paper-thin slices of salt pork fat or streaky bacon, reserving enough for the top.

9 Divide the minced mixture into three. Spread the first third in the base of the lined terrine.

10 Divide the marinated mixture in half and arrange one half on top of the minced mixture, laying the rabbit strips neatly in rows lengthways.

11 Spread a second portion of the minced mixture on top. Sprinkle with chopped walnuts, then add another layer of the marinated mixture.

12 Spread the last portion of minced mixture over the top and cover carefully with the reserved slices of salt pork fat or streaky bacon.

13 Cover with a lid or foil. Place the terrine in a roasting tin and pour in boiling water to come halfway up the sides. Bake in the oven for 1¼ hours. To test that the terrine is cooked, insert a skewer into the centre and leave it there for 10 seconds. The juices from the terrine should run perfectly clear and when you remove the skewer it should feel hot to the lips.

14 Remove the terrine from the oven. Drain the water from the roasting tin and stand the terrine in it again. Cover the pâté, inside the rim, with a board or another dish and weight it down. Leave until cold, about 3 hours, then chill until required. Serve the terrine cut into slices.

Terrine of rabbit and walnuts

105

Brandade de saumon

 poaching the salmon,
then 45 minutes, plus chilling

Serves 6
*450 g /1 lb fresh salmon, poached and
   cooled*
75 g /3 oz smoked salmon, chopped
1 small garlic clove, crushed
120 ml /8 tbls thick cream
150 ml /5 fl oz olive oil
juice of ½ lemon
salt and freshly ground black pepper
a pinch of cayenne pepper
quartered lemon slices, to garnish
hot toast and chilled butter, to serve

1 Remove any bones and skin from the
cooked, cold salmon and flake lightly.
2 In a blender or food processor, combine
the flaked salmon, the chopped smoked
salmon and the garlic. Blend lightly.
3 Add half the cream and half the oil to
the blender and blend again until smooth.
Add the remaining oil and cream alternately
until the brandade is creamy and smooth.
4 Turn into a clean bowl, stir in the lemon
juice and season with salt, pepper and
cayenne pepper to taste. Chill until required.
5 Divide the brandade among 6 individual
ramekins, garnish with lemon slices and
serve with toast and butter.

Chicken liver pâté

30 minutes

Serves 6
50 g /2 oz butter
60 ml /4 tbls finely chopped onion
225 g /8 oz chicken livers
2 hard-boiled eggs
175 g /6 oz cream cheese
15–30 ml /1–2 tbls cognac
30 ml /2 tbls finely chopped fresh parsley
salt and freshly ground black pepper
pinch of cayenne pepper
pinch of nutmeg
pinch of allspice
hot toast and chilled butter, to serve

1 Melt 25 g /1 oz butter in a frying-pan
and sauté the onion for about 8 minutes
until transparent. Remove with a slotted
spoon. Melt the remaining butter in the pan
and cook the chicken livers, stirring constantly, over a medium heat for 5–8 minutes
until tender but still pink inside. Drain on
absorbent paper.
2 Purée the sautéed onion, chicken livers
and hard-boiled eggs, a little at a time, in a
blender or a food processor.
3 Beat the cream cheese and cognac
together until light and fluffy.
4 Mix together the chicken liver and
cheese and cognac mixtures. Add the
parsley, salt and pepper, cayenne pepper,
nutmeg and allspice to taste.
5 Serve with hot toast and butter.

Country-style pâté

2½ hours, then cooling
and overnight chilling

Serves 8
350 g /12 oz boneless rabbit, minced
225 g /8 oz lean bacon, minced
250 g /9 oz boneless pork, minced
75 g /3 oz pork fat, minced
2 garlic cloves, finely chopped
1.5 ml /¼ tsp ground allspice
salt and freshly ground black pepper
100 ml /4 fl oz brandy
225 g /8 oz chicken livers
15 g /½ oz butter
175 g /6 oz unsmoked bacon slices
1 bay leaf
75 g /3 oz flour

1 Heat the oven to 180C /350F /gas 4.
2 In a large bowl, combine the minced
rabbit, bacon, pork and pork fat. Stir in the
garlic and allspice and season generously
with salt and black pepper. Moisten with the
brandy and stir again until well mixed.
3 Drain the chicken livers and pat them
dry with absorbent paper.
4 In a frying-pan large enough to take the
livers comfortably in a single layer, heat the

Brandade de saumon

butter. Sauté the livers over a high heat for
1½ minutes, turning them once. Season with
a little salt and pepper. Leave to cool
slightly, then slice thinly lengthways.
5 Line a 1.1 L /2 pt terrine with unsmoked
bacon slices. Spoon half the minced meat
mixture into the terrine, pressing it down
well. Arrange the sliced livers in a layer on
top and press the remaining mixture over
the top and well into the corners. Place the
bay leaf on top and cover with a lid.
6 Mix the flour with 60–75 ml /4–5 tbls
cold water to make a paste. Seal the lid to
the terrine with the paste.
7 Put the sealed terrine in a roasting tin
and pour in hot water to come 25 mm /1 in
up the sides of the terrine. Bake for 1½–1¾
hours, or until the juices run clear when a
skewer is inserted into the centre. After 10
seconds withdraw the skewer and it should
feel warm to the lips.
8 Remove from the oven and take off the
lid. Cover the pâté with foil and press down
with a board or tin inside the rim and weight
down until cold. Leave to mature overnight
in the refrigerator.
9 To serve, unmould the pâté and cut the
required amount into thin slices and arrange
overlapping slices on a platter.

Terrine du chef

This terrine is delicious as it is, but you can also experiment with the ingredients.

20 minutes, marinating, then 2½ hours, plus chilling

Serves 18

900 g /2 lb rabbit or hare
900 g /2 lb boneless pork shoulder
125 ml /4 fl oz brandy
600 ml /1 pt dry white wine
4 chicken livers
30 ml /2 tbls Madeira
large pinch of ground cloves
large pinch of freshly grated nutmeg
large pinch of ground ginger
large pinch of ground cinnamon
salt and freshly ground black pepper
500 g /1 lb salt pork, thinly sliced
2 chicken breasts, skinned and boned
45 ml /3 tbls finely chopped fresh parsley
125 g /4 oz unsmoked bacon, cut into thin
    strips
bay leaves, to garnish
sprigs of thyme, to garnish

1   With a sharp knife, carefully remove all the flesh of the rabbit or hare from the bones.
2   Cut the pork into 25 mm /1 in cubes and place with the rabbit or hare in a deep bowl. Pour the brandy and the dry white wine over the meat.
3   Trim the chicken livers, removing membranes and greenish parts. Quarter them, place in a small bowl and sprinkle with Madeira. Cover both bowls and leave them to marinate in the refrigerator for 24 hours.
4   Remove the meats from their marinades. Cut the better pieces of rabbit into thin strips about 5 cm /2 in long.
5   Put the remaining rabbit and half the pork through a mincer. Put in a bowl, add the spices, the marinade juices and salt and freshly ground black pepper to taste. Add the chicken livers and mix in well with your hands.
6   Heat the oven to 170C /325F /gas 3.
7   Line the base and sides of a 2.3 L /4 pt terrine or loaf tin with thin slices of salt pork, reserving some for the top. Spread half the minced mixture in the lined mould and smooth it off.
8   Cut the chicken breasts into 5 mm /¼ in

strips and roll them in the finely chopped parsley. Arrange them with the rabbit strips on top of the minced mixture.
9   Top with the remaining pork cubes and thin strips of bacon. Top with the remaining minced mixture and cover with the reserved thinly sliced salt pork.
10   Cover with a lid or foil, place in a roasting tin and pour in boiling water to come halfway up the sides of the terrine. Cook in the oven for 1¾ hours. To test whether the terrine is cooked, insert a skewer into the centre and leave it there for 10 seconds, then remove. If it then feels hot to the lips, the terrine is ready.
11   Remove the terrine from the oven. Drain the water from the roasting tin, and stand the terrine in it. Cover the terrine, inside the rim, with a board or another dish and weight it down. Leave until cold, about 3 hours. Then chill the terrine in the refrigerator until required.
12   Serve the terrine sliced and arranged on a serving plate to show off the beautiful layers, garnished with bay leaves and sprigs of thyme.

Terrine du chef

the flour onto a sheet of greaseproof paper
In a heavy-based saucepan bring 150 ml /5 f
oz cold water and the diced butter slowly tc
the boil.
5 As soon as the liquid is boiling briskly
remove the pan from the heat. Quickly pour
in the prepared flour all at once anc
immediately start beating vigorously with a
wooden spoon.
6 Return the pan to a low heat and continue to beat until the paste attaches itself
around the spoon in a smooth ball, leaving
the bottom and sides of the pan clean (about
2 minutes). Remove the pan from the heat.
7 Add the beaten eggs a little at a time
beating vigorously. Then continue to bea
until the paste is glossy.
8 Beat the paste into the sieved pâté
mixture. Test the seasoning by poaching a
small ball of the pâté mixture in a little
boiling water. Add a little more Seasoning
salt, or port, to taste, if wished.
9 Grease a 700 ml /1¼ pt terrine or loaf tin
with butter and pour in the pâté mixture.
Cover with a lid or foil and place in a roasting tin. Pour in boiling water to come halfway up the side. Bake in the oven for 1¼–1½
hours.
10 Remove the terrine from the oven,
drain off the water from the tin and replace
the terrine in it. Weight it well and allow to
get cold, then chill until required.
11 Serve with hot toast and butter.

Spinach pâté

This is an unusual and quick-to-prepare
first course that is ideal to start a light
summer meal.

🍴 30 minutes,
plus 1 hour chilling

Serves 4
25 g /1 oz butter
6 spring onions, finely chopped
30 ml /2 tbls chopped fresh mint leaves
225 g /8 oz young spinach leaves, cooked,
  drained and finely chopped
15 ml /1 tbls thin cream
150 g /5 oz full-fat cream cheese
salt and freshly ground black pepper
pinch of cayenne pepper
15 ml /1 tbls lemon juice
4 thin slices of lemon, to garnish
hot granary rolls or toast fingers, to serve

1 Melt the butter in a pan and sauté the
spring onions over moderate heat for 2–3
minutes, stirring occasionally. Add the
chopped mint and spinach and mix well.
Remove from the heat and leave to cool.
2 When the spinach mixture is cool, stir in
the cream, cream cheese, salt, pepper,
cayenne pepper and lemon juice. Reduce to a
purée by blending in 2 batches.
3 Divide the pâté among 4 individual
ramekin dishes and smooth the tops. Cover
and chill in the refrigerator for at least 1
hour. Garnish each with a slice of lemon and
serve with hot granary rolls or toast fingers.

Smooth liver terrine

Calf's and chicken livers and a choux
paste are used to make a pâté of
incredible smoothness.

🍴🍴 2 hours marinating, then 2½ hours,
plus weighting and chilling

Serves 8
225 g /8 oz calf's liver, sliced
6 chicken livers, quartered
90 ml /6 tbls milk
30 ml /2 tbls port
Seasoning salt for pâtés (see introduction)
500 g /1 lb fresh pork back fat, cubed
15 ml /1 tbls brandy
butter for greasing
hot toast and chilled butter, to serve
For the choux paste mixture
65 g /2½ oz flour
50 g /2 oz butter, diced
2 medium-sized eggs, beaten

1 Soak the sliced calf's liver and quartered
chicken livers for 2 hours in the milk
flavoured with the port and 2.5 ml /½ tsp
Seasoning salt.
2 Drain the livers well and mince with the
pork fat, passing the mixture twice through
the finest blade of your mincer.
3 With the back of a wooden spoon, press
the mixture through a coarse sieve into a
bowl. Then beat in 7.5 ml /1½ tsp Seasoning
salt and the brandy. Heat the oven to 150C /
300F /gas 2.
4 To make the choux paste mixture: sift

Terrine of vegetables

🍴🍴 2½ hours

Serves 6
1.4 kg /3 lb green cabbage
1 large red pepper, core and seeds removed
1 kg /2¼ lb fresh spinach
12 fresh sorrel leaves (optional)
25 g /1 oz butter
300 g /11 oz smoked streaky bacon slices,
  cut across into matchstick slivers
12 shallots, finely chopped
100 g /4 oz finely chopped fresh parsley
30 ml /2 tbls freshly chopped thyme
30 ml /2 tbls freshly chopped marjoram
4 garlic cloves, crushed
6 medium-sized eggs
150 ml /5 fl oz thick cream
75 g /3 oz fresh breadcrumbs
pinch of nutmeg
salt and freshly ground black pepper

1 Remove 8–10 outer cabbage leaves and
blanch them, with the red pepper, in boiling
water for 2 minutes. Drain and reserve.
2 Finely shred the remainder of the
cabbage, discarding the core. Wash, remove
the thick leaf stalks and shred the spinach
and sorrel, if using.
3 Melt the butter in a large saucepan with
a lid over low heat and add the bacon slivers,
stirring thoroughly, then the shallots,
parsley, thyme, marjoram, garlic and
shredded greens. Turn them all together to

ombine evenly with the butter and bacon, over and leave for 8–10 minutes, or until he leaves are tender.

Remove the lid to allow most of the vegetable juice to evaporate. Meanwhile, peel the red pepper and cut it into thin strips engthways. Reserve the strips.

Beat the eggs and cream together, stir hem into the vegetable mixture off the heat and add the breadcrumbs. Add the nutmeg and season to taste with salt and pepper. Heat the oven to 190C /375F /gas 5.

Line an 850 ml /1½ pt loaf tin or rigid aluminium container with the reserved cabbage leaves. Pack in the mixture, laying strips of red pepper lengthways from time to time to give variety of colour. Stand the loaf tin or container in about 25 mm /1 in of water in a roasting tin and then bake the terrine for about 1¼–1½ hours.

7 Unmould, allow any excess juices to drain out and serve cut into thick slices.

Brandade of tuna fish

35 minutes,
plus overnight chilling

Serves 4
4 large potatoes
salt
200 g /7 oz canned tuna fish in oil
For the aïoli sauce
4 garlic cloves, finely chopped
2 medium-sized egg yolks
250 ml /9 fl oz olive oil
freshly ground black pepper
juice 1 lemon
For the garnish
2 × 50 g /2 oz canned anchovy fillets
12 black olives

1 Peel the potatoes and cut into 25 mm /1 in dice. Boil in salted water until cooked but still firm, about 15 minutes.
2 Meanwhile make the aïoli sauce. Crush the garlic to a smooth paste with a little salt, using a pestle and mortar, or pressing it on a plate with a round-bladed knife. In a mortar or bowl, blend in the egg yolks until the mixture is smooth. Add the olive oil, drop by drop at first, as you would for mayonnaise, whisking all the time. Then continue adding the oil in a thin fine trickle, whisking constantly. The aïoli will thicken gradually until it reaches a stiff, firm consistency. Season to taste with salt and pepper. Add the lemon juice.
3 Drain the tuna fish and purée in a blender, adding the aïoli. Transfer the tuna to a bowl. Add the cooked potatoes to the blender and purée. Then add the tuna mixture gradually to the potatoes and blend until it is white and smooth. Turn the brandade back into the bowl, cover with cling film and then chill in the refrigerator overnight.
4 Just before serving, add more lemon juice if you think it is needed and freshly ground black pepper to taste. Mound the mixture in a salad bowl and garnish the top with a lattice of anchovies and black olives.

Danish cheese pâté

1¼ hours, plus
1 hour chilling

Serves 4–6
575 ml /1 pt milk
1 large onion, coarsely chopped
1 large carrot, scraped and coarsely chopped
2 celery stalks, trimmed and chopped
bouquet garni
50 g /2 oz butter
50 g /2 oz flour
60 ml /4 tbls mayonnaise
30 ml /2 tbls lemon juice
3 garlic cloves, crushed
20 black olives, finely chopped
½ bunch watercress, coarsely chopped
350 g /12 oz Danish blue cheese, rind
    removed, and crumbled
2.5 ml /½ tsp ground black pepper
large pinch of cayenne pepper
salt
sprigs of watercress, to garnish
fingers of hot toast, to serve
chilled butter, to serve

1 Pour the milk into a medium-sized saucepan set over a moderately high heat and bring to the boil. Reduce the heat to very low and add the onion, carrot, celery and the bouquet garni. Cover the pan and simmer for 15 minutes.
2 Remove the pan from the heat and leave until the milk has cooled to room temperature. Pour the milk through a fine wire sieve into a large mixing bowl, pressing on the vegetables with the back of a wooden spoon to extract any juices. Discard the vegetables.
3 In a medium-sized saucepan, melt the butter over a moderate heat. Remove the pan from the heat and, using a wooden spoon, stir in the flour to make a smooth paste. Gradually add the milk, stirring constantly. Return pan to heat and cook, stirring constantly, for 2–3 minutes, or until the sauce is thick and smooth. Remove the pan from the heat and set aside to cool to room temperature.
4 When the sauce has cooled, beat in the mayonnaise, lemon juice, garlic, olives and chopped watercress.
5 Put the crumbled cheese in a fine wire sieve over a medium-sized bowl. Using the back of a wooden spoon, rub the cheese through the sieve. Beat the cheese into the cooled sauce until the mixture is smooth. Season with freshly ground black pepper, cayenne pepper and a little salt if necessary.
6 Spoon the mixture into 4 or 6 individual ramekins (75–150 ml /3–5 fl oz each) or a small soufflé dish or earthenware terrine. Smooth the surface with the back of a spoon. Place pâtés in the refrigerator to chill for 1 hour. Garnish with sprigs of watercress and serve with toast and butter.

Brandade of tuna fish

French veal terrine

Serves 10–12

900 g /2 lb lean veal
700 g /1½ lb lean pork
1 Spanish onion, thinly sliced
2 carrots, thinly sliced
2 garlic cloves, sliced
2 shallots, sliced
2 bay leaves
1 sprig of thyme
4 sprigs of parsley

salt and ground black pepper
freshly grated nutmeg
90 ml /6 tbls olive oil
275 ml /10 fl oz dry white wine
225 g /8 oz streaky bacon slices
225 g /8 oz sausage-meat
100 g /4 oz streaky bacon, diced
flour for sealing
fresh vegetables, to garnish

1   Dice the veal and pork and discard any fat or gristle. Combine the meats in an earthenware casserole with the thinly sliced onion and carrots, the garlic cloves, shallots, bay leaves and sprigs of thyme and parsley. Season to taste with salt, freshly ground pepper and nutmeg. Mix well and moisten with the olive oil and dry white wine. Let the meats marinate for 24 hours, tossing them from time to time so that they are well impregnated with the flavours of the marinade.
2   Heat the oven to 170C /325F /gas 3. Line a 1.8 L /3 pt terrine with overlapping streaky bacon slices, reserving about one-third of the slices.
3   Drain the meats, reserving the liquid and discarding the vegetables and herbs. Layer the pork and veal alternately with the sausage-meat and the diced streaky bacon. Strain the marinade juices over the meats and cover with the remaining bacon slices.
4   Cover the terrine. Make a thick paste with a little flour and water and seal the lid well. Place the terrine in a roasting tin and pour in enough hot water to come half-way up the sides of the terrine. Cook in the oven for 4 hours. To test whether the terrine is cooked, insert a skewer in the centre, remove it after 10 seconds and it should feel warm to the lips.
5   Remove the lid and allow the terrine to cool, then place a sheet of greaseproof paper over the cooled terrine and press under weights for 1 day. Leave in the refrigerator for 1 further day.
6   To serve, slice the terrine thickly and lay overlapping slices on a serving plate, garnished with fresh vegetables.

● This terrine is delicious served with a tossed mixed salad and will keep unsliced in the refrigerator for 4–5 days.

 30 minutes, then 24 hours marinating, 30 minutes, 4 hours cooking, then 2 days maturing and chilling

Moulded chicken liver pâté

Serves 8

425 ml /15 fl oz canned chicken
  consommé
2 celery stalks, thinly sliced
1 shallot, finely chopped
2 sprigs of parsley
10 ml /2 tsp powdered gelatine
4 radishes, thinly sliced
500 g /1 lb chicken livers
salt and freshly ground black
  pepper
50 g /2 oz butter

225 g /8 oz cream cheese
60 ml /4 tbls Madeira
60 ml /4 tbls brandy
5 ml /1 tsp Worcestershire
  sauce
60 ml /4 tbls finely chopped
  fresh parsley
hot toast and chilled butter,
  to serve
For the garnish
radish 'accordions' (page 48)
bouquets of watercress

1   In a medium-sized saucepan, combine the chicken consommé, celery, shallot and parsley sprigs. Bring to the boil over a high heat and boil for 5 minutes, or until reduced to 275 ml /10 fl oz. Strain.
2   In a small bowl, sprinkle the gelatine over 30 ml /2 tbls cold water and leave to soften for a few minutes. Place the bowl in a saucepan of simmering water and leave to dissolve. Pour the dissolved gelatine into the reduced consommé and stir well.
3   Pour 150 ml /5 fl oz of the aspic into the bottom of a 1.1 L /2 pt ring mould and leave to set in the refrigerator.
4   Arrange overlapping slices of radish on the set aspic and pour over enough aspic to cover. Leave to set in the refrigerator.
5   Pour in the remaining aspic and chill until set firmly.
6   Meanwhile, drain the chicken livers and pat dry with absorbent paper. Season with salt and freshly ground black pepper. Heat 25 g /1 oz butter in a large frying-pan and sauté the livers in the hot fat for 1½–2 minutes each side. Transfer to a plate.
7   Press the sautéed chicken livers through a sieve into a bowl, using the back of a wooden spoon. Beat in the cream cheese, then blend in the Madeira, brandy, Worcestershire sauce and finely chopped parsley. Season to taste with salt and black pepper.
8   Melt the remaining butter in a small saucepan and stir it into the chicken liver pâté. Spread the pâté carefully over the set aspic and leave to set in the refrigerator for at least 2 hours.
9   When ready to serve, dip the mould into a bowl of hot water for a few seconds and turn onto a serving platter. Garnish, and serve with hot toast and chilled butter.

 making the consommé, 45 minutes and chilling

Index

AIOLI: 49
la bourride provençale 23
brandade of tuna fish 109
Mediterranean fish and soup 25
almond: soup 37
ANCHOVY: quick starters 48
egg appetizer salad with 72
Italian pepper appetizer 87
little Provençal pies 58
potato salad with 86
Provençal dip 60
scrambled eggs provençale 77
Sophie's salad 74
tapenade 61
angostura soup, chilled 26
APPETIZER SALADS:
anchovy and potato 86
artichoke heart, prawn and potato 91
bean and bacon 85
carrot and orange 80
carrot and redcurrant 55
celeriac salad remoulade 82
celery hearts 89
Chinese vegetable salad 82
cooked lentil salad 51
easy salad appetizer 80
egg and anchovy 72
egg and celery in tomato cases 77
grated carrot 51
green bean 50
green pasta and olive 91
herbed salad niçoise 95
Italian tuna and bean 52
Japanese radish and watercress 53
lettuce hearts La Napoule 86
marinated pepper and prawn 62
mussel and celery 62
orange and black olives 55
prawn and cucumber 70
Provençal salt cod 71
raw beetroot 50
raw mushroom and bacon 80
saffron rice 51
tomato and onion appetizer 83
Sophie's salad 74
spicy cooked cucumber 80
tomato 50
tomato with beans and cucumber 54
tuna Waldorf 67
warm courgette and potato 54
APPLE: curried apple soup 29
grilled croustades 76
ARTICHOKE: artichoke heart, prawn and potato salad 91
egg starter with 72
Spanish vegetable mousse 103
ARTICHOKE, JERUSALEM:
soup with lemon 26
ASPARAGUS: leek soup with 28
with walnuts 80
ASPIC: eggs in 79
quick jelly 99
AUBERGINE: creamed salad 84
dip 58
grilled slices 88
soup 27
AVOCADO: Californian 69
cold soup 32
with crab 62
dip (guacamole) 58
mousse 99
pancakes 93
BACON: see also Ham
baked egg with 79
bean salad with 85
Dutch lentil soup 19
raw mushroom salad with 80
barbecue spareribs 93
BARLEY, PEARL: cock-a-leekie 20
old-fashioned lamb broth 19
Polish mushroom soup with 13
batter, beer 85
BEANS, FRENCH AND GREEN:
bean and bacon salad 85
cold curried vegetable soup 15
Italian omelette 75
salad 50
soupe au pistou 16
Spanish vegetable mousse 103
tomato salad with cucumber and 54

bechamel sauce 95
BEEF: see also Oxtail
basic bone stock 11
brown stock 9
consommé 41
Corsican tomato soup 22
light stock 10
BEETROOT:
mixed vegetable borshch 14
raw salad 50
bisque, blender prawn 32
BLUE CHEESE: celery and Stilton soup 29
Danish cheese pâté 109
French onion soup with 12
prawn cocktail with 66
Roquefort and egg mousse 103
savoury mille-feuille 74
Stilton mousse 101
stuffed tomatoes 88
borshch, mixed vegetable 14
la bourride provençale 23
BRANDADE: de saumon 106
of tuna fish 109
brioche, poached eggs en 76
BROCCOLI: cream soup 36
easy salad appetizer 80
broth, old-fashioned lamb 19
BRUSSELS SPROUTS: coleslaw 87
cream soup 35
BUTTER, SAVOURY: green 39
snail 67
CABBAGE: Danish soup 17
garbure 21
CARROT: grated carrot salad 51
orange appetizer salad with 80
potato soup with 28
salad with redcurrant 55
soup with yoghurt 28
cauliflower niçoise 82
caviar: red caviar roll 96
celeriac salad remoulade 82
CELERY: celery hearts appetizer 89
egg salad in tomato cases with 77
mussel salad with 62
Stilton soup with 29
tuna Waldorf salad 67
CHEESE, HARD: see also Blue cheese; Cream and soft cheese
starters 72
Cheddar cheese soup 27
cocktail cheese puffs 59
deep-fried crêpes 78
fritters with ham 72
grilled apple croustades 76
Italian omelette 75
soufflé 74
stuffed courgettes 84
turnip soup 14
chick-peas vinaigrette 92
CHICKEN: see also Liver, chicken
basic stock 11
cock-a-leekie 20
consommé 42
Danish open sandwiches 56
hot mousses 101
Senegalese soup 37
waterzooi 22
Chinese vegetable salad 82
CHOWDER: cod 24
Mediterranean fish 20
smoked haddock 19
cock-a-leekie 20
cocktail cheese puffs 59
COD: see also Roe
chowder 24
mayonnaise 68
Mediterranean fish and soup 25
Provençal salad 71
COLD SOUPS: angostura 26
avocado 32
beef consommé 41
broccoli cream 36
chicken consommé 42
chilled salmon cream 37
consommé creole 43
consommé orientale 43
consommé with vegetable julienne 43
cream of Brussels sprouts 35
curried apple 29
curried pineapple 35
curried vegetable 15
fresh mushroom 34

gazpacho 46
green summer 38
pear vichyssoise Rainbow Room 36
potato and watercress 34
CONSOMMÉ, general 40-1
beef 41
brunoise 43
Celestine 46
chicken 42
creole 43
fish 42
gazpacho 46
with vegetable julienne 43
Madeira 40
mushroom and watercress 44
niçoise 44
à l'orange 40
orientale 43
with pasta 40
saffron seafood 43
sherry 40
soup with eggs, Pavian-style 40
tarragon 45
watercress, with lemon dumplings 45
coquilles St Jacques au gratin 64
CORN (maize; sweetcorn):
cream of tomato soup with 34
sweetcorn crêpes 94
Corsican tomato soup 22
country potato soup 31
country-style pâté 106
COURGETTE: crêpes 94
stuffed 84
warm potato salad with 54
CRAB: quick starters 48
avocado with 62
crab Louis 52
Creole gumbo 25
curried ramekins 68
dressed 70
mousse Bellevue 102
seafood and lettuce mousse 102
stuffed mushrooms 65
CREAM AND SOFT CHEESE:
avocado dip 58
chicken liver pâté 106
cocktail cheese puffs 59
crab mousse Bellevue 102
creamy prawn tart 92
curry chicken liver crescents 60
herb and spinach crêpes 93
herbed cheese dip 60
Italian omelette 75
moulded chicken liver pâté 110
pecan salmon roll 67
red caviar roll 96
Roquefort and egg mousse 103
sardine-stuffed lemons 52
smoked cod's roe dip 58
spinach pâté 108
stuffed tomatoes 88
CREAM SOUPS, general 32
almond 37
blender prawn bisque 32
blender spinach 39
broccoli 36
Brussels sprouts 35
chilled salmon 37
cold avocado 32
curried pineapple 35
fish and saffron 39
fresh mushroom 34
green summer soup 38
pea and cucumber 34
peanut 38
pear vichyssoise Rainbow Room 36
potato and watercress 34
saffron soup with fresh herbs 36
Senegalese 37
tomato 32
tomato and corn 34
crème fraîche 32
Creole crab gumbo 25
CREPES AND PANCAKES:
avocado pancakes 93
consommé Celestine 46
courgette and sweetcorn 94
deep-fried cheese 78
herb and spinach 93
CROUSTADES: grilled apple 76
scrambled egg 97
CROUTONS 14
garlic 46

CUCUMBER: mayonnaise 49
pea soup with 34
prawn salad with 70
spicy cooked salad 80
tomato salad with beans and 54
CURRY: chicken liver crescents 60
cold curried vegetable soup 15
curried apple soup 29
curried crab ramekins 68
curried eggs 72
curried pineapple soup 35
curry cream soup 14
curry dressing 50
easy salad appetizer 80
Senegalese soup 37
Danish cabbage soup 17
Danish cheese pâté 109
Danish open sandwiches 56
devilled whitebait 64
DIPS, general 56
aubergine 58
guacamole 58
Provençale anchovy 60
smoked cod's roe 58
tapenade 61
taramasalata 71
dumplings, lemon 45
Dutch lentil soup 19
EGG: see also Mayonnaise; Mousse
cream soups 32
starters 72
anchovy salad with 72
in aspic 79
baked 72
baked with bacon 79
Californian avocado 69
cooked like tripe 76
croustades of scrambled egg 97
curried 72
eggs mimosa 72
Greek egg and lemon soup 12
Italian omelette 75
Moroccan pepper appetizer with 78
en cocotte with cream and herbs 75
poached en brioche 76
Roquefort mousse with 103
salad with celery in tomato cases 77
sardine appetizer with 62
scrambled 72
scrambled eggs provençal 77
Sophie's salad 74
soup with eggs, Pavian-style 45
FINGER FOOD: general 56
cocktail cheese puffs 59
curry chicken liver crescents 60
Danish open sandwiches 56
little Provençale pies 58
prawn bouchées 56
FISH, see also individual types of fish
basic stock 11
la bourride provençale 23
consommé 42
Mediterranean fish chowder 20
soup with saffron 39
stock 9
French mushroom tartlets 90
French onion soup with blue cheese 12
French veal terrine 110
fritters, ham and cheese 72
garbure 21
GARLIC: aïoli 49
la bourride provençal 23
croûtons 46
snail butter 67
soupe au pistou 16
spaghetti with oil and 91
gazpacho 46
ginger, cold ham mousse with 100
Greek egg and lemon soup 12
green pasta and olive salad 91
green summer soup 38
guacamole 58
HADDOCK:
Mediterranean fish and soup 25
Oriental fish soup 16
saffron rice salad 51
haddock, smoked: chowder 19
HAM: see also Bacon
cold mousse with ginger 100
croustades of scrambled egg 97
fritters with cheese 72
little Provençal pies 58
pasta salad with tomato and 94

111

HARICOT BEANS: garbure 21
soupe au pistou 16
HERBS: *for stock* 8
dressing 50, 74
herbed cheese dip 60
herbed salad niçoise 95
oeufs en cocotte with cream and 75
spinach crêpes with 93
herring: marinated appetizer 69
hollandaise sauce 76
hotch potch 23
Italian omelette 75
Italian pepper appetizer 87
Italian tuna and bean salad 52
Japanese radish and watercress salad 53
Jerusalem artichoke *see* Artichoke, Jerusalem
KNIFE AND FORK SOUPS,
general 18
la bourride provençale 23
cock-a-leekie 20
cod chowder 24
Corsican tomato soup 22
Creole crab gumbo 25
Dutch lentil soup 19
garbure 21
hotch potch 23
Mediterranean fish chowder 20
Mediterranean fish and soup 25
mussel soup 24
old-fashioned lamb broth 19
oxtail soup 21
smoked haddock chowder 19
waterzooi of chicken 22
LAMB: hotch potch 23
old-fashioned broth 19
LEEK: cock-a-leekie 20
soup with asparagus 28
LEMON: dumplings 45
Greek egg and lemon soup 12
Italian pepper appetizer with 87
Jerusalem artichoke soup with 26
sardine-stuffed 52
LENTILS: cooked salad 51
Dutch soup 19
soup with lettuce 31
LETTUCE: hearts La Napoule 86
lentil soup with 31
seafood mousse with 102
liver, calf's: smooth terrine 108
LIVER, CHICKEN: country-style
pâté 106
curry crescents 60
moulded pâté 110
pâté 106
smooth liver terrine 108
macaroni: pasta and kidney beans 97
MAYONNAISE 49
aïoli 49
Californian avocado 69
carrot and orange appetizer salad 80
celeriac salad remoulade 82
cod 68
crab Louis 52
creamed aubergine salad 84
cucumber 49
dressed crab 70
eggs mimosa 72
horseradish 49
mustard 49
prawn and cucumber salad 70
Provençal salad of salt cod 71
quick blender mayonnaise 49
Russian 49
saffron 49
tuna Waldorf salad 67
Mediterranean fish chowder 20
Mediterranean fish and soup 25
minestrone 13
Montpellier appetizer 83
mornay sauce 65
Moroccan egg and pepper appetizer 78
MOUSSES, SAVOURY,
general 98–9
avocado 99
cold ham and ginger 100
cold smoked salmon mousses 100
crab mousse Bellevue 102
hot chicken mousses 101
Roquefort and egg 103
seafood and lettuce 102
Spanish vegetable 103
Stilton 101

MOZZARELLA CHEESE:
fried sandwiches 77
pepper and Mozzarella strip 61
MUSHROOM: beignets 85
à la bordelaise 89
consommé with watercress and 44
crab-stuffed 65
creamed 86
curry cream soup 14
French tartlets 90
fresh soup 34
Montpellier appetizer 83
Polish barley soup with 13
raw salad with bacon 80
MUSSELS: celery salad with 62
Mediterranean fish chowder 20
with snail butter 67
soup 24
stuffed tomato appetizer 86
oeufs en cocotte, cream and herbs 75
OLIVES: *quick starters* 48
green pasta salad with 91
orange appetizer salad with 55
Sophie's salad 74
tapenade 61
omelette, Italian 75
ONIONS: *chopping* 49
French onion soup with blue cheese 12
sliced tomato appetizer with 83
ORANGE:
carrot appetizer salad with 80
consommé à l'orange 40
salad with black olives 55
Oriental fish soup 16
oxtail soup 21
Pasta: *see also individual types of pasta*
consommé with 40
PATES AND TERRINES,
general 104–5
brandade de saumon 106
brandade of tuna fish 109
chicken liver pâté 106
country-style pâté 106
Danish cheese pâté 109
French veal terrine 110
moulded chicken liver pâté 110
sardine-stuffed lemons 52
smooth liver terrine 108
spinach pâté 108
terrine du chef 107
terrine of rabbit and walnuts 105
terrine of vegetables 108
pea and cucumber soup 34
peanut soup 38
pear vichyssoise Rainbow Room 36
pecan salmon roll 67
PEPPERS: appetizer with lemon 87
marinated prawn salad with 62
Moroccan egg appetizer with 78
Mozzarella strip with 61
Sophie's salad 74
pineapple, curried soup 35
pistou, soupe au 16
Polish barley and mushroom soup 13
PORK: barbecue spareribs 93
terrine du chef 107
POTATO: artichoke heart and
prawn salad with 91
bean and bacon salad 85
carrot soup with 28
country soup 31
herbed salad niçoise 95
salad with anchovy 86
smoked haddock chowder 19
soup with watercress 34
warm courgette salad with 54
PRAWNS AND SHRIMPS: artichoke
heart and potato salad with 91
blender bisque 32
blue cheese cocktail with 66
bouchées 56
Californian avocado 69
creamy seafood ramekins 64
creamy tart 92
Creole crab gumbo 25
eggs mimosa 72
marinated pepper salad with 62
potted shrimps 66
salad with cucumber 70
Provençal anchovy dip 60
Provençal salad of salt cod 71
PURÉE SOUPS, *general* 26
aubergine 27

carrot soup with yoghurt 28
celery and Stilton 29
Cheddar cheese 27
chilled Angostura 26
country potato 31
curried apple 29
fresh tomato 30
Jerusalem artichoke and lemon 26
leek and asparagus 28
lentil soup with lettuce 31
potato and carrot 28
red bean 29
watercress 30
QUICHES AND SAVOURY PIES:
creamy prawn tart 92
French mushroom tartlets 90
little Provençal pies 58
quiche provençale 96
RABBIT: country-style pâté 106
terrine du chef 107
terrine with walnuts 105
RADISH: *quick starters* 48
Japanese watercress salad with 53
RED KIDNEY BEANS: pasta and 97
red bean soup 29
redcurrant: carrot salad with 55
RICE: saffron salad 51
ROE: smoked cod's roe dip 58
taramasalata 71
Roquefort and egg mousse 103
SAFFRON: fish soup with 39
mayonnaise 49
rice salad 51
seafood consommé 43
soup with fresh herbs 36
SALAD DRESSING: *see also*
Mayonnaise
basic vinaigrette 50
curry 50
herb 50, 74
mint 50
soy 50, 53
tarragon 50
salads, appetizer, *see* appetizer salads
SALMON: brandade de saumon 106
chilled cream soup 37
pecan salmon roll 67
SALMON, SMOKED:
quick starters 49
brandade de saumon 106
cocktail cheese puffs 59
cold mousses 100
Danish open sandwiches 56
smoked fish rolls 66
SARDINES: *quick starters* 49
egg appetizer with 62
stuffed lemons 52
SAUCES: *see also* Mayonnaise; Salad
dressing
bechamel 95
cheese 84
fish velouté 64
hollandaise 76
mornay 65
pistou 16
remoulade 82
soured cream 93
tomato 75, 85, 101
SCALLOP:
coquilles St Jacques au gratin 64
creamy seafood ramekins 64
SEAFOOD: *see also individual types*
of seafood
starters 48, 62
saffron consommé 43
seafood and lettuce mousse 102
Senegalese soup 37
snail butter 67
SOLE: creamy seafood ramekins 64
fish consommé 42
Sophie's salad 74
soufflé, cheese 74
soupe au pistou 16
soy dressing 50, 53
spaghetti with oil and garlic 91
Spanish vegetable mousse 103
SPINACH: blender soup 39
crêpes with herbs and 93
hot stuffed tomatoes 82
pâté 108
STILTON CHEESE:
celery soup with 29
mousse 101

STOCK, *general* 8–
clarifying 40–
basic bone 1
basic chicken 1
basic fish 1
basic white 1
brown beef 1
light beef 1
STOCK-BASED SOUPS:
cold curried vegetable 1
curry cream 1
Danish cabbage 1
French onion soup with blue cheese 12
Greek egg and lemon 1
minestrone 13
mixed vegetable borshch 14
Oriental fish 16
Polish barley and mushroom 13
soupe au pistou 16
turnip soup 1
unblended tomato 15
vegetable 17
stock cubes 9
sweetcorn *see* corn
TAGLIATELLE: olive salad with 91
pasta salad with ham and tomato 94
tapenade 61
taramasalata 71
TARRAGON: consommé 40
dressing 50
terrines *see* pâtés and terrines
TOMATO: consommé niçoise 44
cream of tomato and corn soup 34
cream of tomato soup 32
egg and celery in tomato cases 77
fresh soup 30
gazpacho 46
hot spinach-stuffed 82
Montpellier appetizer 83
pasta salad with ham and 94
quiche provençale 96
salad 50
salad with beans and cucumber 54
sauce 75, 85, 101
sliced onion appetizer with 83
Sophie's salad 74
stuffed 88
stuffed appetizer 86
unblended soup 15
TROUT, SMOKED: *quick starters* 49
appetizer 53
smoked fish rolls 66
TUNA: *quick starters* 49
brandade 109
chick-peas vinaigrette 92
herbed salad niçoise 95
Italian bean salad with 52
stuffed tomatoes 88
Waldorf salad 67
turnip soup 14
VEAL: chicken consommé 42
French terrine 110
little Provençal pies 58
VEGETABLES: *matchsticks* 49
purée soups 26
slicing 49
starters 48, 80
stock 8
terrine 108
vegetable soup 17
velouté sauce, fish 64
vinaigrette 50
Waldorf salad, tuna 67
WALNUT: asparagus with 80
terrine of rabbit and 105
tuna Waldorf salad 67
WATERCRESS: consommé with 45
dumplings 45
consommé with mushroom and 44
green summer soup 38
Japanese radish salad with 53
potato soup with 34
soup 30
waterzooi of chicken 22
white kidney beans: tuna salad with 52
whitebait, devilled 64
YOGHURT: *cream soups* 32
carrot soup with 28
creamed aubergine salad 84
easy salad appetizer 80
Jerusalem artichoke and lemon
soup 26
smoked cod's roe dip 58

112